Drug Use and Misuse: A Reader

This Reader is one part of an Open University integrated teaching system and the selection is therefore related to other material available to students. It is designed to evoke the critical understanding of students. Opinions expressed in it are not necessarily those of the course team or of the University.

Drug Use and Misuse: A Reader

Edited by

Tom Heller, Marjorie Gott and Carole Jeffery

*Department of Health & Social Welfare, Open University,
Milton Keynes, UK*

*A Wiley Medical Publication
in association with
The Open University*

JOHN WILEY & SONS LTD
Chichester • New York • Brisbane • Toronto • Singapore

British Library Cataloguing in Publication Data
Drug use and misuse: a reader.
  1. Drug abuse
  I. Heller, Tom   II. Gott, Marjorie
  III. Jeffery, Carole
  362.2′93   HV5801

  ISBN 0 471 91684 6

Typeset by MHL Typesetting Ltd, Coventry
Printed by Anchor Brendon Ltd., Tiptree, Colchester

Contents list and author

Section V

Foreword

The use of mood changing substances is not a new phenomenon in Britain, nor in any part of the world. Throughout the whole of recorded history there is evidence of the use of drugs in a wide variety of forms, both for therapeutic purposes and in ways which are ultimately damaging to individuals and societies. From time to time rulers and governments observe the deleterious consequences of drug use. Their typical response is to legislate and to propagandise to reduce consumption. We live in times when official concern is at high levels.

For social, moral or health issues to be treated seriously by governments and the population at large, it now seems necessary for them to be presented through the media in exaggerated and colourful terms. This approach may well be an inevitable corollary of the current patterns of public education and dialogue, but it almost always distorts the evidence and not infrequently results in inappropriate policies and practices. In the case of drugs this has certainly been the case.

It is essential that those who are charged with the responsibility of mobilising society's response to any 'problem' should be in possession of the scientific evidence and be in a position to evaluate it. This Reader and the open learning course with which it is associated starts from such a premise. Both in the study text and in the selection of articles, reports and policy statements, the Course Team has been concerned to provide the student and reader with a carefully considered analysis. Indeed it is the object of the whole Education for Health Project (of which Drug Use and Misuse is one of three courses) that workers of all kinds involved in bettering the health of the community should have an opportunity to clarify their thinking and practice.

The Course Team members have selected material to illustrate points made in the study text and ensured that the resulting volume is not only a close fit with the needs of the course but a volume worthy of a wider readership. In doing so they have added another component to the growing contribution our Department is making to the understanding of social and health care issues. Equally importantly it will provide a firm basis for practical action in the promotion of good health.

Professor Malcolm Johnson
Department of Health and Social Welfare
The Open University

Introduction

Most people use drugs. Luckily the great majority of such use is either beneficial or is at least harmless. 'Drug use' includes a wide range of activities. These encompass the legal use of alcohol and tobacco as well as pre-scribed drugs such as tranquillisers and the use of illegal substances such as cannabis, heroin and cocaine. Sadly, widespread drug use is associated with a huge toll of adverse consequences. These include drug dependence, physical harm (such as heart and liver disease), public order offences and a host of other social problems.

The enormity of drug problems is indicated by a few statistics. Every year over 100,000 people in Britain die prematurely from tobacco-related diseases. Over 200,000 people are convicted of drunkenness and drunken driving and approximately 16,000 people are admitted to hospital for alcohol dependence and alcoholic psychosis. In addition thousands of people are dependent upon prescribed tranquillisers. Apart from these problems related to legal drugs, over 26,000 people are convicted annually of drug misuse offences and hundreds of thousands of young people use illegal drugs. In some cities the sharing of infected injecting equipment by illegal drug users has spread the AIDS virus. Every day the popular press feature stories of drug seizures by customs and police, the tragic deaths of young drug users and the sensational effects of the latest 'designer' drug.

There is a clear link between the general levels of drug use and the extent of drug-related harm. The motives for and causes of drug use are as complex as are the possible strategies to prevent drug problems and to help the misusers. People in many professions — teachers, social workers, health visitors, doctors, nurses, clinical psychologists, the police, the clergy and politicians — are under increasing pressure to react to the problems posed by the use and misuse of legal and illegal drugs. In addition parents and friends are often equally, or even more, perplexed when confronted by the prospect of drug use involving a friend, a lover or a child. It is paradoxical that, although 'drug problems' are widely perceived as having a high priority, there is little formal training in how to cope with these problems for those in the health and social services. This Reader is a major contribution towards facilitating such training. It attempts to provide a 'user friendly' overview of a wide range of drug issues. These are reviewed on the basis of a collection of contributions to the extensive drug literature. So much has been written about drugs that unless one has almost a lifetime to spare it is difficult for most people to become well informed. They simply do not have time to wade through a host of books, magazines and journals. This Reader presents a selective and highly informative guide to the drug field. It combines research findings with practical issues and in so doing presents a fairly comprehensive overview of the background to drug use and misuse and indicates some worthwhile responses to drug problems.

The Reader is divided into five sections. The first of these includes five papers which review the nature and extent of drug use and drug problems and the role of general practitioners in relation to opiate misuse. The second section highlights some of the clinical problems associated with the misuse of illegal and prescribed drugs as well as key topics such as the effects of drug use in pregnancy and the issue of what is meant by the word 'drug'. The third section includes seven papers which discuss specific 'empirical' issues. These include the connection between unemployment and illicit drug use, the processes of becoming a heroin user, alcohol problems in the family, initiation into cannabis use, smoking during pregnancy, women and drug use, and the lifestyle of the heroin user. The fourth section reviews issues related to control policies to curb drug problems. These are discussed in relation to political, economic, social and historical factors, and with specific reference to the United Kingdom. The final, and for many readers, the most 'practical' section, consists of seven papers dealing with different approaches to the management of drug issues and for the provision of help for people with drug-related problems. These cover a wide range of basic issues and methods. The topics reviewed include treatment and change, community initiatives, therapeutic approaches, recognition and treatment of alcohol problems, tranquilliser problems, the prevention of drug problems and health education.

The Open University is to be highly commended for compiling this selective, wide ranging and extremely informative reader. It highlights a considerable number of important topics and will enable those who use it to view drug use and misuse in a balanced and constructive way.

Martin Plant, Ph.D.
Alcohol Research Group
Department of Psychiatry
University of Edinburgh

Overview: The use and misuse of drugs

TOM HELLER

The rapid increase in interest in the subject of drug use and misuse has been accompanied by a wealth of written literature on the subject. In this Reader we have attempted to provide a selection from this literature that will be both stimulating and informative.

Although the major focus of interest in the media and from the Government has been towards drugs that have been made illicit, the literature we have chosen includes discussion on substances that cause equal or greater harm, but are freely available without necessary legal problems for people using them. The use and abuse of tobacco and alcohol is therefore included in the selection of papers for this Reader.

PATTERNS OF ILLICIT DRUG TAKING

There can be no doubt that there has been a recent rapid rise in the amount of illicit drug taking in Britain over the last decade or so. Hartnoll and his colleagues from the Drug Indicators Project have contributed Paper 3 to the Reader that examines the recent trends and patterns in great detail. The paper takes evidence from all the available research and statistical findings, as well as from individuals and agencies around the country. The main features of their conclusions are that the numbers of people regularly using opiates has risen at least tenfold since 1970, and that the illicit drug market has expanded and become more organized. With the expansion has come a change of pattern of use and they state:

It is no longer possible (if it ever was) to describe either drug takers or addicts in terms of simple stereotypes. . . . The use of all drugs is found across a whole range of communities and populations within the British Isles . . . . Hence drug use cannot be characterized as a static phenomenon that is restricted to specific subcultural groupings on the margins of society. It is part of the everyday context in which many ordinary people, especially young people, live and grow.

WHY DO PEOPLE USE DRUGS?

The use and misuse of drugs can not be understood outside the context of people's lives, and the social framework in which they live. When looking at the particular case of heroin, several authors have examined the social context in which the recent growth in use and misuse has occurred. Hartnoll, Daviaud and Power state in Paper 3:

Optimism has been replaced by cynicism, despair and anger, particularly among the young, unemployed working-class and minority groups . . . . Such a sketch of Britain sliding deeper into gloom is neither complete nor 'balanced'. Nor is it a sufficient explanation of problem drug use . . . . But it does provide part of the background against which some groups and individuals start or continue to use a variety of drugs.

Peck and Plant have studied the relationship between unemployment and illegal drug use in great detail and we report their findings in Paper 11. Using both national statistics and the results of a detailed study in the Lothian region they conclude:

There is a clear link between illegal drug use and unemployment. Many possible explanations for this exist, but the most parsimonious conclusion is that high unemployment serves to foster drug use. This conclusion is consistent with a whole body of evidence from many studies conducted in different communities with different sampling techniques, data sources, and methodologies. Such consistency from disparate sources provides compelling support for the validity of this conclusion.

A variety of other studies have looked in great detail at the actual lives of people who chose to take up the use of illegal drugs, and explored the possible reasons why this should apparently be such an attractive option for so many young people. Auld, Dorn and South (Paper 5) argue that:

at both local and neighbourhood levels, the economic and social organization of heroin (and other drug) supply, exchange and consumption is part of a broader response, on the part of the populations affected, to the social problems and entrepreneurial opportunities of the recession, and one which is likely to expand further.

To some extent then it can be argued that taking up illicit drug use is a *positive* response for some people. Certainly the active nature of the lifestyle involved in the drug subculture is vividly portrayed by Preble and Casey in Paper 17:

The street heroin user is an active, busy person, preoccupied with the economic necessities of maintaining his real income — heroin. A research subject expressed the more mundane gratifications of his life this way: 'When I'm on the way home with the heroin safely in my pocket, and I haven't been caught stealing all day, and I didn't get beat, and the cops didn't get me — I feel like a working man coming home; he's worked hard, but he knows he done something, even though I know it's not true.'

We should not be carried away into thinking that this is necessarily a typical experience for people who take, or deal in illicit drugs, but it does serve as a guide to the way in which entry into the drugs 'scene' can be a real alternative source of meaningful existence and individual satisfaction, apart from the particular experience of taking the drugs themselves. Indeed, taking the drugs themselves at first is not necessarily a pleasurable experience, and there is now increasing recognition that the first experience of drug taking might even be quite unpleasant. Often the user has to be fairly determined or persistent to continue with the substance until it may eventually develop into a habit. Pearson, Gilman and McIver (Paper 12) describe from their extensive research that when a person tries heroin for the first time:

Often enough it makes them feel sick, and sometimes this is the end of their heroin using career. But other people persist with heroin, in spite of the nausea, which is hardly surprising in view of the fact that initial encounters with other drugs (including those that are socially sanctioned, alcohol and tobacco) often make people feel ill until they learn how to take the drug properly and how to handle its effects and interpret them as enjoyable.

Becker in his classic study of the process of becoming a marihuana user (Paper 14) details the way in which potential users have to learn the techniques involved in using marihuana and then go on to learn how to perceive and enjoy the effects of its use:

An individual will be able to use marihuana for pleasure only when he goes through a process of learning to conceive of it as an object that can be used in this way. No one becomes a user without (1) learning to smoke the drug in a way that produces real effects; (2) learning to recognize the effects and connect them with drug use (learning in other words, to get high); and (3) learning to enjoy the sensation he perceives.

Women's use of drugs has received particular attention recently, and it is important to examine in some detail the gender differences in the use and misuse of drugs. Graham, in her study of smoking in pregnancy (Paper 15), considers the way in which the issue of smoking in pregnancy is perceived differently by the mass media/medical profession and by a group of expectant mothers themselves:

There is a tendency to view the problem as a function of ignorance, fanned by traditionalism and advertisements, and of irresponsibility . . . however, while in the media, smoking is portrayed as a solitary activity, pursued, apparently, simply for reasons of personal enjoyment, in respondents' accounts, smoking took on an additional significance. The functions of smoking extended beyond the simply pleasurable: smoking became a way of marking out the day into 'work' and 'rest', a method of achieving autonomy from one's domestic role.

The message from this sort of detailed study is that we ignore the social and political context of drug use and misuse at our peril. Gomberg in her study of women and drug use in Paper 16 focuses on the use of legal socially acceptable drugs by women and concludes that:

In the history of men, women and substance usage, there are gender differences in the sanctions for medicinal use and for recreational use of substances, and in attitudes toward drug abuse . . . drug and alcohol abuse among women is a political issue, linked to gender roles, power, ambivalence, and hidden angers and fears.

THE CONTROL OF DRUGS

How might it be possible to control the abuse of drugs in society? What strategies could be used to attempt to stop the rapid growth in numbers of people using illegal substances? The Government has put a lot of energy into developing a five point strategy to tackle drug misuse. We have included an extract of a recent policy statement outlining their strategy (Paper 18):

The Government has drawn up a comprehensive strategy for tackling drug misuse. The objective is to attack the problem by simultaneous action on five main fronts

- reducing supplies from abroad
- making enforcement even more effective
- strengthening deterrence and tightening domestic controls
- developing prevention
- improving treatment and rehabilitation

Some authors have been critical of the balance of effort between the five strands of the Government's strategy, and point to the apparent emphasis on enforcement, rather than on the other measures. Stimson makes this point in Paper 20:

Law enforcement alone is unlikely to be the answer. We need to find the right balance between public expenditure on education, prevention, and treatment — not just on enforcement. Education and information campaigns and 'pump-priming' for local treatment and rehabilitation projects are welcome. But these measures look small by comparison with expenditure on enforcement.

Other authors have pointed to the need to tackle the more general measures of deprivation in society, that they claim will be necessary in order to improve the social conditions under which many vulnerable people are forced to live. In his introductory paper, Addiction: a Challenge to Society, Edwards (Paper 2) firmly throws down the gauntlet:

A flood of relatively cheap illicit heroin is being imported. However, part of the explanation may lie nearer home than in the poppy fields of Afghanistan. What sort of lives have we been offering to young people that they find heroin alluring?

Policy making about the control of drugs does not occur in a vacuum, and often Government policy becomes a delicate balancing act between a variety of competing interests. A case history of the way in which Government policy is formulated is put forward by Dorn in Paper 23. Taking as his example the drinks and alcohol industry he examines the way in which health issues related to the consumption of alcohol have to compete against other interests, for example the tax revenue from drink, and the employment prospects of people working in the drinks industry:

Central government policy-making is made in a broader context than 'alcohol policies alone', . . . any alcohol policy has

to be concerned not simply with drinking and its consequences, but also with Britain's economic interests in terms of wealth creation, employment and exports.

Further problems are created for policy makers when their actions are subjected to the full glare of publicity from the media. Often legislation or other forms of action on the control of drugs is taken in response to intense pressure from the media. One example of the way in which a sudden surge of interest builds up and then dies down is described by Ives in Paper 21. He describes the way in which the 'glue sniffing epidemic' was dealt with by the media and the creation of a moral panic, which makes considered action or objective analysis of the real problems hard to undertake.

DRUGS AND THEIR EFFECTS

The ways in which drugs work and the effects they have on the people who take them are considered by a range of papers in the Reader. The effects of any particular drug are hardly ever totally predictable. The diversity of this response is described in the extract of the paper from ISDD (Paper 7):

Drug effects are strongly influenced by the amount taken, how much has been taken before, what the user wants and expects to happen, the surroundings in which it is taken, and the reactions of other people. All these influences are themselves tied up with social and cultural attitudes to and beliefs about drugs, as well as more general social conditions.

There has been considerable recent debate about what actually is a drug. This debate is outlined in Paper 8 by Cox et al. Many of the major harmful effects that are often ascribed to drugs are actually the effects of impurities or infections associated with the way in which the drug is taken. For example many of the medical problems that intravenous drug users develop are from the multiple use of needles and syringes, rather than from the drugs themselves. The recent concern about the spread of the virus that causes AIDS is discussed in detail in Paper 9 by Brettle. The serious nature of this disease has thrown up a multitude of questions about the way in which the problems of drug use and misuse should be handled. For example if it is the illegal nature of the drugs which leads to their covert use, the sharing of needles and syringes etc. which in its turn leads to the serious side-effects such as AIDS, then one possibility would be either to supply free, clean needles and syringes to intravenous drug users, or even as Brettle questions:

Is it now necessary to alter our attitude towards opiate drug misuse? Is decriminalization and controlled availability of opiate use, similar to the restrictions on alcohol, the way forward?

These sorts of questions are seriously being considered by many of the workers in agencies concerned with helping drug users and the communities from which they come. Preventive efforts are hampered by the legal problems surrounding drug use and the mystique that surrounds the whole issue of drugs. Kay in Paper 29 on ways in which it might be possible to prevent drug problems claims that:

Most people have been led to switch off their common sense and understanding of life and its difficulties when confronted by drug problems. Parents who would take in their stride a teenager coming home drunk on cider, recoil in horror when the same teenager comes home intoxicated on glue or heroin. A major objective of our community education/awareness activities around drugs should be dispelling some of this mystique.

Howe takes up the same theme in arguing for objective, multifaceted solutions to problem drug use in Paper 30:

In the storm of media manipulated panic and moral outrage it is often forgotten that, just as drug misuse throws up a wide range of problems in society, it also necessitates a wide range of responses. No single response will be equally effective at all levels.

INTERVENTIONS AND TREATMENT FOR DRUG USERS

In recent years the emphasis on treatment has shifted from treatment by specialists and hospital-based departments to treatment by generalists and community-based projects. This 'decline of the clinic' is discussed by Stimson in Paper 19:

Clinics appear to be less central than in previous years. This was anticipated in a succinct review of the clinic system which argued that 'To an extent the clinics (not all of them) have become a backwater of our social response to drug abuse

dealing with a problem that no longer reaches the heart of the UK drug scene'.

Strang (Paper 25) argues that the specialist and institutional services should remain as a part of an overall network of services, perhaps becoming more selective in their dealing with the most problematic situations and helping with co-ordination of services and research and evaluation.

Treatment of the individual person with a drug-related problem is the final theme of the articles collected for the Reader. Raistrick and Davidson in Paper 24 make a strong plea for any treatment efforts to be seen against the entire life experience of the person coming for treatment:

Treatment is not an isolated curative insertion into the lives of drug misusers, but rather is part of their whole matrix of experience. . . . This in a way contradicts the more traditional view of treatment as a bridge from illness to cure and administered by external therapists to passive patients.

It is also important not to forget the family dimension in the treatment of drug related problems. Some of the problems of the whole family in which a member has a drug problem are discussed by Orford in Paper 13; in relation to alcohol problems, he recommends:

Much more attention should be paid to the high levels of stress experienced by families with a drinking problem, and also to the role which family members can play in the continuation or successful resolution of such problems. The types of stresses experienced, and the changes of role which occur, are on the whole no different in kind from those experienced by other families in distress, but they are very often of major proportions.

Ritson in Paper 27 considers that primary care workers are in a good position to help in the recognition and treatment of alcohol related disorders. This may well be true for alcohol problems, but there is evidence that general practitioners in particular are not so willing to help with the treatment of opiate misuse. Glanz and Taylor (Paper 6) found that:

Most general practitioners regard opiate misusers as especially difficult to manage and beyond their competence to treat, and most are relatively unwilling to accept them as patients.

For those workers who are willing and able to help people with drug related problems, practical approaches for helping people to withdraw from long-term tranquillizer use are outlined by Hamlin in Paper 28.

Thorley discusses therapeutic approaches to the problem drug-taker in Paper 26 and cautions:

Never forget that almost all drug takers at some time, and often after many years of drug taking still get a tremendous amount of pleasure and reward from their drug habits. This hedonistic element should be recognized and acknowledged from the outset, but a fine line often needs to be drawn between appropriate acknowledgement, and tacit encouragement. Remember all the ways you use drugs (tea, coffee, chocolate, sweets, cigarettes etc.) in order to cope with your week at work! The problem drug taker is after all only someone who has got into difficulties with their drug taking. There but for the grace of God go all of us.

Section I

Addiction: a challenge to society

GRIFFITH EDWARDS

Professor of Addiction Behaviour, Institute of Psychiatry, London University

This introductory paper discusses some of the challenges which the diversity of 'mind-acting substances' forces on society. In particular it focuses on the debate on whether the major responsibility for action lies with the individual or with policy makers and society at large.

Here are two lines of poetry which are part of everyone's schoolroom heritage:

I am the master of my fate,
I am the captain of my soul.

Thus wrote William Ernest Henley, who lived from 1849 to 1903. These lines are relevant to the concerns of this article, because they can help us to understand the thinking of government departments. Here, from a 1976 DHSS document, is a quotation which can be recognised as directly inspired by Henley:

Much of the responsibility for ensuring his own good health lies with the individual. We can all influence others by our own actions. In particular, parents can set their children a good example for healthy living. We can all help to influence the communities in which we live and work as much by our examples as by our efforts.

Who would wish to disagree with these sentiments — with Henley's verse, or with the DHSS prose? And yet that same DHSS document provided data which showed that for men aged 15–64 the standardised mortality ratio was almost twice as high for social class V as for social class I.

We can use mortality statistics (and Henley) to establish the context — to lead up to the argument that addictions are a challenge to society and not just to the individual. I am not arguing that all the ills that afflict mankind are class-related, or stem from the environment. I have used these mortality data only to illustrate

the general proposition that, despite our proud and necessary claim to captaincy of our own souls, much that befalls us will be determined by social and economic forces outside the immediate control of most individuals.

There is, however, no one explanation of social casualty. Alcoholism is rife in many comfortable suburbs as well as in slums, in Moscow as well as New York. What I would, however, firmly argue is that addictions are examples of the very general truth that a wide range of socio-economic influences — influences which are 'a challenge to society' — bear on the individual's capacity to handle his or her inalienable personal responsibility. The central issue is how society is to act in support of the individual, and ensure that people are not overwhelmed by social influences beyond their control. Different substances — cigarettes, alcohol, illicit drugs, medically prescribed drugs — offer variations on this central theme.

Take, first, the case of cigarette smoking. With monotonous consistency, a series of reports has documented the relationship between cigarette smoking and mortality and disease. At a conservative estimate, cigarette smoking is at present contributing to 100,000 premature deaths a year in Britain, as well as much chronic invalidism.

In the context of the evidence, is it responsible for society to allow the advertising of cigarettes to continue (controlled only by voluntary agreement), and in particular to permit sports sponsorship by cigarette manufacturers which drives a coach and horses through the ban on television advertising of cigarettes?

Previously published in *New Society*, 25 October 1984, and reproduced with their permission.

According to Action on Smoking and Health (ASH), in six months of 1980, cigarettes had 190 hours of advertising through sports sponsorship on BBC TV alone. It is disingenuous to claim that this massive advertising assault is likely to be confined in its impact solely to switching of brand loyalty.

Many prestigious and independent organisations concerned with health have advocated the total banning of cigarette advertising. The experiences of three countries — Sweden, Finland and Norway — which have totally prohibited advertising and sponsorship of tobacco, show a fall-off in smoking.

Meanwhile, in our own country, the Chancellor gains £50 million every day from tobacco revenue, which contributes towards the NHS and pays for the next lung cancer operation. The government gives £2 million each year to the Health Education Council, while also providing millions of pounds in grants for setting up cigarette factories. The challenge with which cigarette smoking confronts us is centrally the political priority which is to be accorded by society to health. The National Health Service is a political issue, but that is not equivalent to health itself being given ranking on the political agenda. Only within that perspective is it possible to understand society's farcical and duplicitous response to the most serious remediable health issue which today confronts us.

Cigarettes are an example of a recreational drug which is embedded not only in social custom, but also in the national and international economic fabric. But let me briefly consider the case of another smoked substance. Is it too fanciful to project a future in which the cannabis campaigners have won the day, the tobacco firms have diversified into the marketing of this drug, tennis stars are wearing the logo of Acapulco Gold, and the government is rejoicing in an immense new-found source of revenue?

Those who blithely believe that cannabis is 'the non-drug of the century' will not be worried by such a potential scenario. Ten or more years ago, a sequence of official reports appeared which did much usefully to correct the more wildly alarmist views of cannabis as a drug which led inexorably to crime, heroin and disintegration of personality. More recent reviews of the research evidence on cannabis point to a less reassuring consensus than the appraisal of a decade ago. There is evidence that it is potentially addictive. And there are a clutch of other possible dangers.

There are indications, for example, that THC (the active constituent of cannabis) may not be as free from health risks as was once supposed. Cannabis can cause a short-term psychosis, with a clinical picture similar to that which can be induced by LSD. It is a drug which can impair driving ability and reversibly impair short-term memory.

It is also a general principle of toxicology that, if a drug can cause damage, the risk of damage is likely to be dose-related. At present many 'regular' users of cannabis in this country take only about 5 milligrams of THC a day or less. The practised user in countries where cannabis is rather freely available may consume upwards of 200 milligrams a day. THC can accumulate in body tissues. You may have these chemicals in your body weeks after the last dose.

The challenge which cannabis exemplifies is the need to ensure that any debate is adequately informed, rather than an automatic taking of sides — a matter of being for or against 'permissiveness', with the real facts of a serious matter drowned in the rhetoric.

One 'drug problem' seldom makes the front page — the social significance of the licit medical prescribing of mind-acting drugs. To illustrate this theme, consider the recent story of the benzodiazepines, a group of minor tranquillisers which include such well-known substances as Valium (diazepam) and Librium (chlordiazepoxide).

The story is a matter of recent history, for these drugs were first available in the early 1960s. From the launching, they moved with extraordinary rapidity into the bestseller list. There are benefits that have come from the arrival of the benzodiazepines. They are, so far as we know, generally safe drugs, with few adverse side-effects. In particular, it is difficult to achieve a fatal overdose. They have tended to displace the far more dangerous barbiturates.

Why, then, regard the burgeoning success of the benzodiazepines as constituting a 'problem'?

The reason is that there is now convincing evidence that the benzodiazepines can give rise to 'normal dose' dependence. This means that a patient can become dependent on a prescribed dosage of these drugs, without any escalation in the quantity being taken. When patients try to stop the drug, they will then experience the anxiety and malaise of a withdrawal syndrome, while all too probably mistakenly ascribing those symptoms to the return of the underlying anxiety-state. Prescriptions therefore tend to become repeat prescriptions.

The benzodiazepine story shows us that there is in society a great reservoir of people who are a little bit tense, depressed, bored or frustrated, who will reach readily for a quick chemical answer to their problems. But the real 'diagnosis' cannot exclude the environmental factors. The medical profession, rather than giving society this uncomfortable message, has rather too easily allowed itself at times to be drawn into the role of the 19th century druggist or corner grocer, who purveyed opium pills. The challenge to the doctors is whether they will continue passively to accept this role, or whether they can educate themselves, and share in the education of society, towards the view that health and happiness are not often to be bought in a bottle of pills.

When we turn to drinking problems, we immediately find that here it is the advertising industry that sees in Henley a fount of social wisdom. Here is a quotation from the admen's newspaper *Campaign*:

Of course, I cannot deny that the exposure to alcohol which social drinking provides must occasionally lead to the tragic consequences of anti-social drinking. This begs a fundamental question: do you want to live in the kind of society where you are free to take your own risks and make your own mistakes, or do you want to live in a society where these decisions are taken out of your hands? . . . For my part, I want a society where people do have the freedom to order their own lives.

TRAGIC CONSEQUENCES

A splendid reiteration of Henley's principle. But though this article coyly refers to the *occasional* 'tragic consequences,' it does not care to tell its readers that there are an estimated 700,000 people in this country who

are in trouble with their drinking. Few people today would advocate the introduction of American-style alcohol prohibition. On the other hand, controls aimed at moderating the level of consumption may be a necessary safety measure.

The reason for seeing the overall level of drinking — not just alcoholism — as a cause for legitimate public health concern is the very strong research evidence that the two issues are related. In most circumstances any increase in national *per capita* level of alcohol consumption will be matched by an at least proportionate increase in the level of alcoholism. Between 1950 and 1976, *per capita* alcohol consumption in the United Kingdom almost doubled. No one was arguing during these years that, as a matter of freedom, every citizen needed, on average to consume two drinks where once one would have done.

As a consequence, the country experienced an epidemic of alcoholism, reaching levels of damage which had not been seen since the beginning of the century. If society wants to prevent a further climb in alcohol-related problems, or the situation swinging out of control, it will have to seek means of moderating alcohol consumption. The most readily available control measure is undoubtedly taxation on drink. The use of tax as a regulator in the health interest sets complex questions. But to refuse to consider this possibility is to evade a very tangible challenge. If premature deaths from cigarettes are about 100,000 a year, for the 15 years between 1967 and 1981 the total number of deaths among registered addicts was about 1,500. But it would still be a mistake not to pay due attention to the threat posed by heroin. Let's look briefly at the figures. The table shows the number of heroin addicts and the total number of addicts known to the Home Office for each of the years 1953, 1963, 1973 and 1983:

Addicts notified to Home Office		
	Heroin addicts	Total addicts
1953	60*	290
1963	237	635
1973	847	1496
1983	4787	5866

*approximate
source: Home Office, 1984; Stimson & Oppenheimer, 1982

The true prevalence of addiction may well be several times greater than these figures suggest. Furthermore, although heroin is an important part of the story, other drugs intermingle.

Has something gone wrong with society to have allowed this type of drug use to invade our cities? What are the true roots of this type of problem? Part of the answer undoubtedly lies in the sheer fact of availability. A flood of relatively cheap illicit heroin is being imported. However, part of the explanation may lie nearer home than the poppy fields of Afghanistan. What sort of lives have we been offering to young people that they find heroin alluring?

At this point, the critic will object, 'You can't prove a causal relationship.' And it is true that even if we show co-variance between youth unemployment and heroin addiction, we have not proved a causal link. But we would be unwise to ignore the many lessons that can be learnt from other countries. The heroin problem in the United States may have affected prosperous Scarsdale as well as poverty-stricken Harlem, but America's postwar heroin epidemic was undeniably in

large measure a problem of the slums and the ghettos, of alienation and anomie. If you breed people to frustration, or sheer hopeless passivity, you put our society at risk of heroin or glue or any one of a dozen other chemical manifestations.

The Minister of Health will look bored if he asks us for recommendations how to curtail the drug epidemic, and we come back only with the answer that, if he does not want Brixton to go the way of Harlem, he had better do something about Brixton. But if he gets the social and political job wrong, no amount of committee reports, customs officers, sniffer dogs, life sentences, consultant sessions, or lecturing to schoolchildren, will be able to pick up the broken pieces.

These, then, are some of the challenges which drugs force on society. Drugs matter in their own right. But the problems set by a diversity of mind-acting substances also serve as potent and general reminders that, for an array of other health and social issues, the fashionable Henley principle is not a sufficient basis for policy.

Patterns of drug taking in Britain

RICHARD HARTNOLL, EMMANUELLE DAVIAUD and ROBERT POWER

Drug Indicators Project, Birkbeck College, University of London

This brief account of recent trends in non-medical drug use in Britain is based on evidence taken from all the available research and statistical evidence, as well as on the experiences of individuals and agencies from around the country. The authors are all from the Drug Indicators Project, based at Birkbeck College. The project is concerned with research on patterns of drug misuse that is relevant to policy formulation and service delivery.

Recent trends in problem drug use should be viewed against wider socioeconomic, cultural and political events in Britain. Economic growth, rising living standards and relatively full employment of the 1960s and early 1970s has given way to recession and economic stagnation. Unemployment has risen sharply, more so among the young, the unskilled and minority groups. Many inner-city areas have experienced steady deterioration in housing conditions, transport and other services.

Over the same period, the youth culture(s) of the late 1960s and early 1970s disintegrated, loosening informal constraints which helped define what drug use was acceptable to particular groups and what was not. Optimism has been replaced by cynicism, despair and anger, particularly among the young, unemployed working-class and minority groups. Ageing 'hippies' have few options left.

Such a sketch of Britain sliding deeper into gloom is neither complete nor 'balanced'. Nor is it a sufficient explanation of problem drug use — the rapid expansion of non-medical drug use in the 1960s occurred at a time of boom. But it does provide part of the background against which some groups and individuals start or continue to use a variety of drugs.

CANNABIS

Cannabis is the drug most commonly used for non-medical purposes in Britain. Use increased dramatically during the early 1970s, may have stabilized in the mid-1970s and has since steadily increased. Eight out of ten drug seizures and convictions involve cannabis, usually small amounts.

Since the 1960s cannabis use has diffused across all classes, though it is most common in the under-forties. In line with this development, cannabis use no longer functions as a symbol of affiliation to an 'alternative' culture.

Good quality 'hash' (cannabis resin) retails at around £20 to £28 per quarter ounce; for some regular users this might last less than a week. Due to increased cost, cannabis is now bought in smaller quantities than it was ten years ago, a fact which may imply less heavy use by the majority of users.

COCAINE

During the 1960s, cocaine use was largely restricted to heroin addicts receiving both drugs on prescription. After treatment of heroin addiction was transferred to special drug dependence clinics (in 1968), cocaine became relatively uncommon.

During the mid-1970s, cocaine gained popularity, especially where there was style, champagne and money. Cocaine also became widely used — though usually on an intermittent or occasional recreational basis — by a broad section of the drug-using population from all classes. It is usually sniffed — smoking of freebase is not common.

Cocaine sells for £55 to £70 per gram (typically 30 to 70 per cent pure). A couple of casual users might consume a quarter gram in an evening. Regular users with sufficient resources might use one to two grams a day. Since 1983, prices have fallen while Customs seizures have markedly increased. Coupled with fieldwork observations, these indicate increased supply, though not perhaps as dramatic as some American-inspired reports suggest. It is not used extensively by adolescents and is probably more common in London and the South.

'Crack' has been 'advertised' as if it were a completely new drug. However, cocaine converted to cocaine base for smoking (of which crack is a form) is not new. We were aware of 'freebasing' (smoking) of cocaine in London around 1980–81. Although paraphernalia for both making and smoking freebase were openly on sale in parts of London, the practice remained uncommon.

The main difference with 'crack' is the marketing — cocaine is sold converted to freebase, ready for smoking, and in small quantities, so that each unit appears cheap. However, because quantities are small and the effects short-lived, it is likely that crack works out more expensive than a gram of cocaine hydrochloride. At present there is little convincing evidence that crack is becoming established on the scale claimed in some American cities, though recently there have been intermittent reports, from users, of crack being sold in inner London in £5 bags and £8 phials.

AMPHETAMINES

Amphetamine stimulants, once widely used for both medical and non-medical purposes, are rarely prescribed today. During the early and mid-1970s, illicitly manufactured amphetamine sulphate powder became available and fairly widely used. In the late 1970s, it might appear from enforcement statistics alone that amphetamine use dropped considerably, but it remained available on the street, though at a higher price. Recent statistics suggest a considerable increase, an impression confirmed by fieldwork and a fall in price, indicating large quantities on the illicit market.

Amphetamine powder is usually sniffed; the exceptions are some opiate injectors and that group of multi-drug users who commonly inject opiates, barbiturates and stimulants. Although seemingly more of a working-class drug than most controlled drugs, amphetamine is nevertheless used by various groups throughout society.

Amphetamine is common in some colleges, studios, construction sites, and in the music business. In some of these groups it is used as an aid to maintaining long periods of concentration or physical work, in others purely as a recreational drug. A minority of individuals are compulsive users. After cannabis, amphetamine is the drug most commonly used by adolescents.

Amphetamine sulphate powder 20 to 40 per cent pure retails at around £10 to £12 per gram, similar to the price ten years ago. A compulsive user might get through several grams a day, while a casual user with no substantial tolerance to the drug's effects could take several weeks to consume half a gram.

LSD

Widely used in the late 1960s and early 1970s, LSD became less apparent through the 1970s, though there are indications that use is increasing again. As with other controlled drugs, LSD has lost much of its mystique, and is now used less as a self-conscious instrument of 'mind-expansion' than as simply a 'fun' drug, a trend associated with the dissolution of the 1960s 'counter-culture' movement.

Although used more casually than in the 1960s, LSD is supplied, and therefore probably used, in units of lower average strength. Today a single, usually weak, dose of LSD costs around £2 to £3.

BARBITURATES AND TRANQUILLIZERS

During the early 1970s, barbiturate use by heroin addicts and young multi-drug users aroused particular concern. Changes in prescribing practices have steadily reduced availability, but 'barbs' remain a problem among some heavy multi-drug users. The sources are still physicians, pharmacy thefts and diversion from legitimate prescriptions. There is no evidence of illicit manufacture. In London, barbiturate use is now largely restricted to the more chaotic, multiple-drug use scene in the centre of the city.

Attention has rightly been focused on the issue of long-term prescribing of tranquillizers. However, they are also used as 'street drugs', replacing barbiturates in multiple drug combinations.

SOLVENTS

Glue sniffing gained much publicity a few years ago. Since solvent use is not illegal and is not recorded in any systematic way, it is hard to know its extent. It is likely that there has been an increase since the mid-1970s, both in experimental use (which may involve quite high proportions of adolescents) and in regular use. Although media coverage has waned since 1982/83, it does *not* seem that the extent of use has diminished. One change in some areas is a switch from glue to butane gas — a more dangerous activity.

Solvent use appears to be concentrated in particular areas, such as an estate or a school (this may be partly an artefact of selective reporting), often fading quickly in the manner of other adolescent fads and reappearing elsewhere. A minority of youngsters 'at risk', because of personal, family or social difficulties, become heavily involved in solvent use as a means of coping with their problems, rather than as the more common transient social activity.

HEROIN

Heroin addiction first appeared as a 'problem' in Britain in the 1960s. The number of known addicts increased dramatically, though the absolute numbers were, by current standards, small. Excessive heroin prescribing by a small number of doctors was virtually the exclusive source until 1968, when heroin prescribing for addiction was restricted to licensed doctors, based in special drug dependence clinics or psychiatric units.

The early and mid-1970s witnessed a relatively small growth in heroin addiction. Illicitly imported heroin from South-East Asia became the major source as heroin diverted from legitimate prescription became more scarce. Police activity and a later series of bad harvests appear to have temporarily limited supply, and prices rose steadily until 1977/78.

The major increase in heroin supply in 1979 was partly associated with the influx of Iranian refugees following the fall of the Shah. Since 1981, Pakistan and Afghanistan have become the primary source.

The current price of illicitly imported heroin in London is £80 to £100 per gram (typically 30 to 60 per cent pure) in gram quantities. In larger quantities (e.g. a quarter ounce, approximately 7 grams) the price is lower, perhaps £60 per gram. Relative to inflation, the price has halved since 1978, though since late 1985, it has started to rise again. Prices are higher in other areas, such as Scotland.

Opiate addition treatment clinics have reduced their prescribing of heroin. In 1977, 19 per cent of addicts attending London clinics received some heroin; by 1984, this had dropped to 6 per cent. Over 70 per cent of addicts attending London clinics received oral methadone only in 1984 compared with 29 per cent in 1977. Most of the remainder received ampoules of methadone for injection (21 per cent compared with 52 per cent in 1977).

Since the late 1970s, the incidence and prevalence of heroin use and addiction, as recorded by the Home Office and supported by numerous informal sources, have increased significantly. Illicitly imported heroin has become much more available. Intermittent, recreational use of heroin (usually sniffed or smoked rather than injected) has become more widespread.

Until 1980/81, heroin users and addicts were more likely to be in their mid- to late-twenties or thirties than in the 1960s, when heroin use was predominantly an adolescent/early adult pheomenon. Since then much younger people have become increasingly involved, and the proportion of females among known addicts has increased to 30 per cent.

Increased availability and use has been particularly noticeable outside London, especially in large urban conurbations such as Merseyside, Manchester, Edinburgh and Glasgow. It has also continued to increase in London. In the more depressed parts of some cities, heroin use appears to be developing into a pattern usually associated with the ghetto conditions in some North American cities. The major difference is that heroin use in the UK is still mostly restricted to the white British or Irish population. However, it appears that the situation in some black or other ethnic groups may now be changing, though information is not readily available.

As well as increasing in some working-class urban communities, heroin use has expanded throughout a wide range of social groupings, including the children of the middle and upper classes.

A much smaller proportion of the total addict population is in treatment than fifteen years ago. Then about half the heavy opiate users in Britain were seen and notified by doctors; now the proportion is likely to be a quarter or less. This implies that the total number of people in the UK who used opiates regularly (and were dependent, at least to some degree) at some stage during 1985 was in the order of at least 60 000 and perhaps 80 000. The numbers using regularly at any one time ('point prevalence') would have been lower, at least 30 000 and perhaps 50 000. In London, and some other metropolitan areas, the rate of increase of new heroin users may have levelled off.

FACTORS BEHIND INCREASED HEROIN USE

The recent growth of heroin use in Britain is a consequence of converging domestic and international factors. These include:

- Heroin of high purity and lower cost became increasingly available. Domestic factors meant this increased supply would find a ready market.

- Sniffing cocaine became increasingly popular during the mid-1970s. Sniffing one powder (cocaine or amphetamine sulphate) made sniffing another (heroin) appear a small step.

- Breakdown of many of the subcultural boundaries separating different patterns of drug use in the late 1960s and early 1970s, left a large population of people with experience of drug use who were now

susceptible to using a variety of drugs, including heroin.

- The cost of cannabis rose markedly in the late 1970s, and at times it was in short supply. Simultaneously, the price of heroin fell. Given the loosening of taboos against heroin use (in drug-using circles at least), heroin became more cost-attractive relative to cannabis and, to non-tolerant individuals, perhaps more cost-effective too.

- Many dealers who previously supplied only one or two drugs, notably cannabis and sometimes LSD, have switched to selling a variety of drugs, including heroin. Reasons include the economics of supplying different drugs against the risks involved, collapse of subcultural barriers against drugs such as heroin, and the heavy criminal activity that has become part of the cannabis market.

- Several recent studies suggest that areas where heroin has increased most rapidly are characterized by higher levels of socioeconomic deprivation — unemployment, overcrowding, and so on. Although the causal relationships are not clearly established, there is little doubt that wider socioeconomic factors are a significant element in influencing patterns of drug misuse.

SYNTHETIC OPIATES

Use of synthetic opiates illegally 'diverted' from the legitimate medical market has remained relatively stable. They are used both as drugs of choice and as substitutes for heroin, though heroin's increased availability has diminished their relative importance.

Methadone is prescribed to addicts in treatment at drug clinics, and by physicians outside hospitals under circumstances that may or may not be considered part of a treatment programme. Since stricter prescribing controls imposed in 1984, Diconal use has diminished, but use of codeine and DF 118 appears to have risen.

Despite controversy over the prescribing of synthetic opiates, there can be little doubt that heroin is the major opiate involved in non-medical use.

MULTI-DRUG USE

Multi-drug use has become more widely recognized since the 1960s, though this change may have as much to do with perceptions as with drug using behaviour, which for a long time has often included more than one drug.

THE MAIN FEATURES

Since 1970, the number of people using opiates regularly has risen, probably at least tenfold. Most of the increase has occurred since 1978. The primary drug involved is illicitly imported heroin. This increase may now be slowing down.

The illicit drug market has expanded, especially for cannabis, heroin, amphetamine sulphate and cocaine.

Sums of money involved have increased dramatically. It has also become more organized and attracted the attention of criminal groups who, several years ago, would not have wanted to become involved. This is particularly true of cannabis and amphetamine, and, in the past five years, of heroin and, more recently, cocaine.

Very few addicts now receive heroin on prescription from drug dependence clinics. Methadone is usually prescribed instead. A few years ago, most methadone was prescribed in injectable form; now most clinics prescribe oral methadone only to the majority of new patients or to patients returning into treatment.

Private doctors and GPs have re-emerged as a source of opiates other than heroin. Methadone and DF 118 are the most commonly prescribed (legal restrictions on prescribing to addicts apply only to heroin, dipipanone and cocaine). Similarly, prescriptions are the original source of most barbiturates and of some stimulants such as dexamphetamine, diethylpropion, Ritalin, etc.

Boundaries separating subcultural patterns of drug use became blurred as the 'youth cultures' of the late 1960s

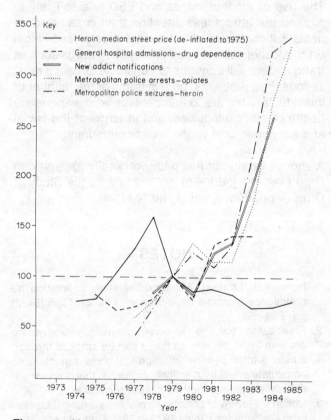

Figure 1 Variations over time in indicators of opioid misuse — London, 1974–85. Relative variations in selected indicators over time respective 1979 figure = 100.

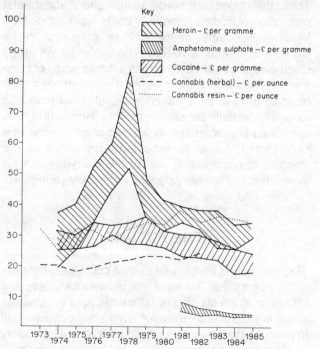

Figure 2 'Real' illicit drug prices — London, 1974–85. Street prices 'de-inflated' to 1975 prices using RPI.

and early 1970s disintegrated. Multi-drug and combination drug use have become more apparent. Dealers are more likely to supply a variety of drugs, although some still supply only cannabis as a matter of principle.

Younger drug users appear to be using cannabis, solvents, amphetamines, pills such as Valium, and alcohol. Apart from alcohol, these are inexpensive and unlikely to lead to convictions for drug offences, though the consequences of use may still be disturbing. In the past five years, a minority have started to use heroin. In areas such as Wirral or Glasgow, this is a substantial minority.

Cannabis ('ganja') is integral to the culture of significant parts of black communities. Among Asian communities drug use is less apparent, though there is some opium and cannabis use. Depending on their degree of integration into British culture, other ethnic communities have assimilated to the general pattern of drug use in Britain. There are recent suggestions of some heroin use among black and Asian communities.

It is no longer possible (if it ever was) to describe either drug takers or addicts in terms of simple stereotypes. Thus, the majority of heroin users, and a substantial proportion of addicts, smoke or sniff heroin rather than inject it. Cocaine users include construction-site workers as well as socialites. The use of all the drugs discussed above is found across a whole range of communities and populations within the British Isles. Patterns of drug use may change rapidly over time and vary substantially between localities. Hence drug use cannot be characterized as a static phenomenon that is restricted to specific subcultural groupings on the margins of society. It is part of the everyday context in which many ordinary people, especially young people, live and grow.

THE FUTURE

The increase in heroin use cannot continue indefinitely. It appears that the rapid rise in new use is levelling off and may be starting to fall as the pool of potential users is exhausted. However, unlike the expected fall in new cases, the total numbers involved will probably

not fall, but will stabilize at around the level which is reached when new people have stopped swelling the total. Long after the 'epidemic' of new use and addiction has subsided, the aftermath will be a much higher level of established addiction than has hitherto been experienced in the United Kingdom. This will continue to make a substantial demand on services for the foreseeable future.

Regarding other drugs, it is likely that cocaine will become somewhat more prominent, though there is little evidence to suggest that its use is approaching the levels reported in the United States. Whether 'crack' will become popular here is not clear. Not all drug fashions cross the Atlantic (ones that have not include phencyclidine and 'designer drugs'). It is likely, however, that the availability and use of cocaine will continue to increase in the immediate future.

The use of amphetamines and LSD is also likely to expand but attract less attention than cocaine. Cannabis will continue to be the most widely used illegal drug. Alcohol, tobacco and prescription drugs such as tranquillizers will continue to constitute Britain's most serious drug problems, both in terms of the number of individuals who are dependent or who experience health or other difficulties, and in terms of the social and economic cost to the wider community.

A shorter version of this paper originally appeared in *Drug Link*, the journal of the Institute for the Study of Drug Dependence, vol. 1, no. 2, 1986.

NOTES

1. Hartnoll R., Lewis R., Mitcheson M. *et al.* 'Estimating the prevalence of opioid dependence', *Lancet*, 1985 (8422) pp. 203–5.
2. Freebasing cocaine involves chemically converting cocaine hydrochloride so that it can be smoked through a pipe, a route of administration that gives a much more immediate effect than sniffing. However, this is an exceptionally expensive method of taking cocaine.
3. Golton I. 'Review of prescribing practices amongst London drug dependence clinics 1977–1984'. Unpublished. Middlesex Polytechnic, 1985.

Paper 4
Is alcoholism a disease?

NICK HEATHER* and IAN ROBERTSON†

* Head of the Addictive Behaviours Research Group, University of Dundee;
† Principal Clinical Psychologist, Astley Ainslie Hospital, Edinburgh

This paper explores the concept of alcoholism as a disease. The authors argue that by putting the blame on individual alcoholics and their 'disease', policy makers and the whole of society are attempting to ignore their collective responsibility.

The idea that alcoholism or problem drinking is a disease has been growing in popularity for the last 20 or 30 years, and would now be regarded as a mark of liberal and enlightened opinion. The irony is that, during this period, among those professionally involved with treating and researching alcohol problems, 'the disease concept of alcoholism' has waned considerably as a credible explanatory and practical tool, and is now often regarded as deeply misleading and unhelpful. The consequence has been the emergence of a huge gap between the popular and the specialist view of the subject and a great deal of confusion. It is high time a serious attempt is made to communicate the new scientific understanding, and the evidence on which it is based, to the non-specialist.

Part of the reason for the confusion is that it is sometimes not made clear what exactly is meant by claiming alcoholism to be a disease. If all that is intended by this is that alcoholics should not be blamed and punished for their behaviour, but should be treated with compassion and care, then this is certainly not an issue. No critic of the disease concept of alcoholism suggests for one moment that we should return to a moralistic and punitive response. The trouble is, of course, that for many members of the general public, this moral attitude is the only alternative to the disease view of which they are aware.

What is essential to get across is that there does now exist an alternative model — one based on the principles of modern psychology and, in particular, on the branch known as *social learning theory* — which makes it possible to deny that alcoholics are 'sick', without at the same time implying that they are 'bad'. We will briefly describe this model later in the article.

But why is the social learning alternative necessary, and what precisely is wrong with the disease view?

The answer is that, quite apart from its general humanitarian content, the disease perspective carries with it a set of specific but erroneous assumptions about the nature of alcohol problems, which have had a profound effect on the way these problems are understood in our society. These assumptions have been strongly influenced by a stereotype of alcoholism propounded by that remarkable fellowship of men and women called Alcoholics Anonymous, and are almost daily reinforced by media representations of the subject, both factual and fictional, and by the pronouncements of celebrities who declare themselves to be 'recovering alcoholics' and affiliates of AA. The efforts of AA in the field have been truly heroic, but it can be argued that its continuing influence on the public understanding of problem drinking is seriously impeding progress.

The main assumptions of the disease perspective, as presented by AA, are that alcoholics possess an inborn, constitutional abnormality which prevents them from ever drinking normally; that this abnormality results in

Previously published in *New Society*, 21 February 1986, and reproduced with their permission.

a 'loss of control' over intake, and an insatiable 'craving' for more which is triggered off by the smallest quantity of alcohol; that these processes are irreversible, so that the only way to arrest the disease is by lifelong and total abstention; and that, if drinking is continued, it leads invariably to further deterioration, insanity and death. Slogans such as 'once an alcoholic, always an alcoholic', and 'one drink, one drunk', embody this disease model. Although originally proposed by a lay fellowship, it has been enormously influential in shaping the medical response to problem drinking.

Such is the popularity of this familiar image of alcoholism that it is commonly thought to be grounded in solid scientific research. Nothing could be further from the truth. Its inadequacies became obvious from the very first introduction of proper scientific methods into the field. Indeed, historical evidence has recently been produced to show that the AA model of alcoholism derives much more from the views of the 19th century temperance campaigners than any body of contemporary scientific support.

In the first place, the evidence shows that the drinking behaviour of 'alcoholics' obeys the same kind of laws and changes in response to the same kind of influences as the drinking of 'non-alcoholics'; it is impossible to draw a hard and fast line between them. Moreover, a great deal of research has shown that the traditional concepts of 'loss of control' and 'craving' are simply unhelpful in the explanation of harmful drinking. At best these concepts are descriptively inaccurate and, at worst, tautologous — they explain nothing whatever.

Though it is true that many individuals with serious drinking difficulties are best advised, on pragmatic grounds, to solve their problem by total abstinence, the evidence clearly shows that drinking problems are not irreversible in principle. Many problem drinkers can return to harm-free patterns of drinking. Finally, longitudinal studies of drinking problems in the natural environment have found no support for the postulation of an inflexible sequence of 'symptoms'. Rather, people move into and out of problem-drinking status much more often than is suggested by the disease view.

Admittedly, debates about what does or does not constitute a disease can become obscure. But aside from the research evidence, there is increasing recognition

among specialists that the disease perspective has many practical drawbacks for the way we respond to alcohol problems. Chief among the disadvantages for treatment is the fact that it has resulted in a restrictive concentration on the upper end of the spectrum of seriousness and dependence, ignoring the huge numbers of individuals in our society who by no means conform to the AA stereotype but who are damaging their lives in some way by their drinking.

Clearly, such individuals are unlikely to accept a treatment goal of lifelong abstinence. If they imagine this to be the only available solution, they are likely to deny having a problem in the first place. The possibility of substituting a goal of controlled or harmfree drinking has meant that problem drinkers can be helped before the maximum damage has occurred. In contrast to this, the evidence shows that AA is still a 'last hope' organisation as far as many problem drinkers are concerned.

The disadvantages of the disease theory for the primary prevention of alcohol problems are perhaps even more striking. The only implication here from the disease standpoint is that, until the elusive 'biochemical abnormality' (on the hunt for which millions of pounds in research funds have fruitlessly been spent) is eventually discovered, all we can do is to provide more and better treatment services. Yet the epidemiological evidence clearly shows that the number of alcohol problems to be found in a particular society is closely related to *per capita* alcohol consumption, and this in turn is related to the availability of alcohol, mainly its retail price.

This has led to the view that alcoholism is an essentially political, rather than medical, problem. Until government acts to reduce the total amount of alcohol we all consume, no improvement in alcoholism statistics can occur. Certainly, from the social learning viewpoint, alcohol problems cannot be reduced to personal characteristics of individual problem drinkers, but must be placed in the entire social and political context which gives rise to them.

In case we risk being misunderstood, we must emphasise that a rejection of the disease concept is in no way to minimise the seriousness of alcohol problems or the tragic consequences they often bring. Nor could anyone possibly dispute that excessive drinking *causes* diseases, or that the medical profession should be centrally involved in treating these diseases and, indeed, in attempting to change harmful drinking patterns. We are concerned here with a shift in perspective, rather than merely a power struggle between medical and non-medical workers.

Significantly, some of the most articulate critics of the disease perspective are themselves medically qualified psychiatrists. Their position is that the disease view — though it has resulted in some improvement in the problem drinker's lot, and in a somewhat more humane attitude from the main body of society — has now outlived its usefulness. It is time to move on to a more rational and empirically based understanding of problem drinking.

This new understanding assumes that problem drinking is a learned habitual behaviour, in the same category as compulsive gambling, some forms of overeating, heroin or tobacco use. Indeed, some of the common features of these phenomena may be observed in a wide range of normal activities carried to excess: compulsive physical exercising, some forms of sexual behaviour, and certain types of compulsive overworking, are just three examples.

The main point is that, when people become dependent on alcohol, the behavioural patterns that develop are not uniquely attributable to the drug, ethyl alcohol. Of course, physical effects *are* important — but these have been highlighted too long at the expense of more crucial social and psychological determinants of the behaviour.

The great advantage of social psychological models of problem drinking is that they have *many* implications for treatment — which disease models do not (apart from the simple necessity of lifelong abstention from alcohol). Social learning theory is an umbrella term for a range of well-established psychological processes, ranging from classic conditioning to self-concept. In this theoretical scheme, conditioning mechanisms are not incompatible with high-level thought processes. Rather, they interact in complex ways. We will outline just a few examples of the application of social learning theory to problem drinking.

In Pavlov's classic experiments, dogs learned to salivate in response to a bell, because the bell was associated with an 'unconditioned stimulus' — the smell of meat powder. Thus, the bell, a previously neutral stimulus, became a conditioned stimulus for salivation. Certain responses in humans can also become classically conditioned.

If you repeatedly drink in a certain environment, or at a certain time of day or with certain people, then these stimuli can become 'cues' for the desire to drink, through a conditioning process. The main difference, in these terms, between problem drinkers and those who drink without problems is that, with problem drinkers, cues for drinking are more numerous and pervasive. There is also evidence that tolerance to alcohol, withdrawal symptoms, and craving for alcohol, are — at least partly — conditioned phenomena. This is of the greatest possible importance for the treatment of problem drinking, because it suggests that these central features of the dependence process are not irreversible and can be extinguished.

A second type of psychological process is known as instrumental learning. Behaviour which is followed by positive consequences will tend to increase, while negative consequences normally lead to a decrease in the behaviour. When applied to problem drinking, this seems at first sight nonsensical, in view of the obvious distress, injury and disruption which follows in its wake. Why do these negative consequences not lead to a decrease in consumption?

The answer lies in a fundamental law of instrumental learning — the reinforcement which follows the behaviour most closely in time will have the greatest effect on it. For problem drinkers, the immediate effect of drinking is often a reduction in the distress produced by withdrawal symptoms — or, at least, a relative decrease in that distress, compared with what is expected if no alcohol is taken. The experience of problems may not occur until hours, days or even years after the behaviour. Psychologically speaking, these consequences have weak effects because they are distant in time.

But drinking is not just a behaviour. It is also a symbol, full of meaning for drinkers and for those around them. Assuming a particular role or self-image can involve the adoption of heavy drinking as a kind of 'membership badge'. You have only to think of such roles as 'hard-bitten journalist', 'biker' or 'tortured poet', to understand that drinking may be as much part of a social uniform as a studded leather jacket or a cravat. At the most obvious level, drinking for men is often a potent badge of manhood. And, increasingly, the drinks industry attempts to construct images of sexuality for female drinking.

This partly explains the epidemiological finding that most people who show some problems due to drinking in their twenties do not appear in the statistics for problem drinking 20 years later. This is because they adopt new social roles and self-images, for which heavy drinking is not an appropriate symbol. Marriage is often associated with such changes. Research shows that this is one of the more commonly cited reasons for stopping heavy drinking.

Society, in fact, has various safety nets, which tend to break up habits of youthful roistering. Obviously, however, some problem drinkers manage to slip through, and more ominous self-images and social roles await them. Heavy drinkers tend to seek each other out. They create subcultures in which excessive drinking, hangovers and complaining spouses become part of a mythology that sustains them in a deviant behaviour pattern, and insulates them from breakdown in other areas of their lives through the bonhomie and inverted values of the pub. This is just one example of how heavy drinking can become enmeshed in an inter-locking set of social roles. But many groups in society create unique 'drinking cultures', where alcohol and its effects are imbued with particular significance.

Another, somewhat different, kind of role is available for the problem drinker, and is dispensed at Alcoholics Anonymous groups and many alcoholism treatment units throughout the country. It incorporates such images as 'I have an incurable disease called alcoholism', and 'I can never drink again'. Often involved is a propensity to confessional-type disclosures and an almost ritual reciting of past misdeeds. This role has been a haven and life-saver for many problem drinkers.

But it has also been unacceptable and even harmful to many others, because of its narrowness, rigidity and exclusiveness, and its tendency to promote self-fulfilling prophecies.

What does this mean in practice? By getting away from the stereotype of the 'alcoholic', action falls into a public health context. From a social learning perspective, the distinction between 'treatment' and 'education' disappears. There could be a spectrum of 'minimal' interventions, aimed at harm-free drinking. This could include self-health manuals; 'alcohol education courses' for groups of homogeneous individuals; or structured information and advice, given by hospital physicians, nurses, general practitioners, company doctors, welfare officers, health visitors, and social workers. The evidence is that minimal interventions can work well.

There will continue, of course, to be many problem drinkers, with more serious difficulties, who need intensive, individual help. But the main message of the new model is that drinking must be understood and treated in the social context in which it has developed and which maintains it — in the problem drinker's everyday world. It is no use whisking problem drinkers off to some residential institution miles away in the country, where they imagine they are completely cured — until they return home and almost immediately relapse in the face of the powerful cues for drinking which have remained unaltered. The days of the specialised alcoholism treatment units, on which much of the British response to problem drinking has been based, are numbered. These are increasingly being replaced by the kind of comprehensive community service heralded by the reports of the DHSS Advisory Committee on Alcoholism in 1978.

Ultimately, what is needed is a radical change in norms about, and attitudes to, drinking — helped by deliberate government policies and intelligent health education campaigns. We should stop trying to ignore alcohol problems by putting the blame for them on individual alcoholics, as in the disease view. Instead, we should make them a matter of collective responsibility in which the whole of society is involved.

Heroin now: bringing it all back home

JOHN AULD*, NICHOLAS DORN† and NIGEL SOUTH‡

* _Senior Lecturer in Sociology, Middlesex Polytechnic_ (deceased);
† _Assistant Director (Research), Institute for the Study of Drug Dependence;_
‡ _Research Officer, Institute for the Study of Drug Dependence_

This paper takes heroin as a case study and examines the ways in which the subculture of drug use and abuse can be understood from the social context of people's lives. It also explores some of the pressures on the producer countries and on the people that live there that tend to make them continue to produce plant drugs.

INTRODUCTION

It is only comparatively recently that the traditional and widely-held image of the heroin user as a victim of some form of pathology or defect of character has begun to be seriously questioned. One of the many consequences of the deep economic recession in this country and the accompanying combination of both a rapid increase in youth unemployment and the development of what some have called a heroin 'epidemic' among young people has been to force the growth of a recognition that heroin use is being indulged in by increasing numbers of young people who are in other respects quite 'normal'.

Interestingly, this shift is to some extent reflected in contemporary political and popular accounts of the drug problem. Although the traditional pathology model is by no means played out, the dominant perspective seems to have become one which attributes the problem to the moral turpitude and cunning of foreigners who scheme to traffic in drugs and pushers who trick youngsters into taking them, resulting in ruined lives of depravity, addiction and crime. In this article we question this perspective, and outline an alternative perspective in which drugs are located within the informal or 'fringe' economy within Britain. We then go

Modified from _Youth & Policy_, no. 9, Summer 1984, and reproduced by permission of the Editor.

on to show how Third World supply of plant drugs to meet demand from the British informal economy is encouraged by the policies of Western financial institutions and to describe the very limited scope for reduction of either supply of or demand for heroin in present political and economic circumstances. We will argue that at both local and neighbourhood levels, the economic and social organisation of heroin (and other drug) supply, exchange and consumption is part of a broader response, on the part of the populations affected, to the social problems and entrepreneurial opportunities of the recession, and one which is likely to expand further (specific anti-drug initiatives not withstanding).

In advancing this argument, we would stress that it is meant to be suggestive and wish to make it clear that the article is largely programmatic. It tries, in other words, to displace some questions and to fore-front others. It is also deliberately provocative, flying in the face of current orthodoxies, both lay and sociological. We have not had an opportunity to make a close study of particular neighbourhoods, social groups therein, their involvements in informal or 'fringe' economies and drug elements thereof, or the motivations in play in these circumstances. All we have attempted is to break through some 'common sense' and often racist assumptions about corruption and addiction, and to suggest that a refocusing upon (a) the appeal of socially active and petty entrepreneurial responses to an unrewarding labour market and (b) the economic position of Third World countries, can help us to understand some aspects of the currently high demand for and supply of drugs.

DEPICTIONS OF THE PROBLEM

Just how many people have ever taken heroin, how many take it repeatedly over any given period of time, and what the balance of consequences is, remain uncertain. At one extreme, one can refer to sources such as a survey carried out on behalf of Radio Merseyside which claimed that up to half of all young adults in certain areas may have tried the drug. Such suggestions became rapidly translated into statements that 50% of children are 'on drugs' or addicted when reported by other media.

These high estimates go hand-in-hand with a re-emphasis upon the pusher as the initiator of drug use.

One story emanating from Cheshire, for example, had pushers creeping about in school playgrounds injecting cartons of milk with heroin, thus causing one-shot addiction and a queue of new customers. One clear element in this total picture is racism: just as was recently the case with stories about suppliers of sniffable solvents, the moral panic over pushers of heroin and other illegal intoxicants carries with it a popular assumption that pushers are foreigners and aliens.

Another element in the construction of 'common sense' conceptions of contemporary drug problems is the new politics of the family and attack on immorality. Since its re-election in June 1983, the present government has wasted little time in making efforts to demonstrate publicly the extent to which it continues to be committed to a policy of arresting and, wherever possible reversing what it perceives as being a progressive and long-term moral decline in British society.

As part of this there has been a direct attempt on the part of government to combat and control what has widely come to be seen as the rapidly growing 'epidemic' of addiction. An announcement about the 'tough measures' introduced for dealing with the problem was made by the Home Secretary. These measures were as follows:

1) STEM the flow of drugs from abroad.
2) CONTROL drugs produced and prescribed in Britain.
3) ENGAGE the police in a nationwide hunt for the chain of 'professional' drug-traffickers.
4) DETER criminals who profit from the misery of drug addiction by introducing stiffer sentences, and laws to confiscate the proceeds of crime.
5) EDUCATE people on the reality of drug abuse, and to provide £6 million to support schemes for the treatment of addicts.

The most important thing to note is that although the sums involved are small when seen in the context of recent increases in levels of experimentation with heroin and other drugs, the DHSS drugs initiative significantly broadens and humanises a conception of drug problems that would otherwise revolve even more tightly around the concepts of 'foreigners', corruption, depravity and criminality. It is within this general perspective that the debate about the numerical size of the problem is currently posed. At the heart of this perspective remains the assumption that all users are addicts, or soon to be addicted.

The DHSS is the government department that has funded street- and estate-level studies of the extent of drug use, and the Department's concern with treatment and patterns of health care delivery incline these studies towards an emphasis upon the addicted/dependent category. The indications from such surveys were that something of the order of 40,000 persons might be dependent on heroin in the early 1980s.

All the indications from the range of agencies in touch with developments at 'street level' are that heroin use, in particular, has undergone a substantial increase in the last few years. However, non-statutory sector staff vary in their readiness to equate heroin use with addiction. It is widely recognized that 'chasing the dragon' by breathing in the smoke from heroin that is heated, or rolling and smoking it with tobacco, are now more common modes of experimentation than injecting. Nevertheless, many staff stress that the drug is addictive regardless of mode and circumstances of administration. There is therefore some ambivalence in the non-statutory field over whether to talk of heroin use, or to reinforce the corruption/depravity image by concentrating on the theme of addiction. Due perhaps to their concern to maintain agency funding and to avoid being discredited, drug workers are generally reluctant to object to the general emphasis upon 'addicts' even though they may not use the term themselves. The result is that the general agreement on recent increases in numbers of even those who merely experiment with heroin becomes articulated within a discourse on corruption and depravity as a moral panic over escalating addiction.

DRUGS AND THE 'FRINGE ECONOMY' IN A RECESSION

In this section we shall attempt to develop an outline of a way of thinking about heroin use that is distinctly different from the orthodox or 'common sense' idea of addiction. We wish to challenge the jingoistic quality of currently dominant thinking expressed in the notion that foreign pushers are corrupting British youth and must be thwarted and in the associated concept of the depraved addict-victim. Certainly there is scope for progressive welfare, youth and community work with users of heroin and other drugs, as the work of many individuals and agencies in the non-statutory sector currently demonstrates. But since it is not possible to articulate those practices within the currently dominant discourses on depravity/addiction, much constructive experience is closed off from public debate.

Central to an understanding of heroin use, we argue, is the general category of *activity*. In quite important respects this perspective runs contrary to that which has dominated mainstream thinking about the lifestyle of heroin users in the past, which portrays it as being one of severe withdrawal, apathy, or so-called 'retreatism': in short, a marked reduction of social activity. This was perhaps a necessary feature of traditional accounts concerning the social origin of heroin use to the extent that the assumed demoralisation and pathology of the person who subsequently became an addict rendered their assumed vulnerability to the pusher more intelligible.

In order to support this contention it is necessary to say something about the nature of the *informal economy* within the context of which we would argue the bulk of heroin use among youth is currently taking place. Recent studies of the informal economy highlight a range of activities that are both economic and social and yet outside the formal boundaries of the wage economy. Small-scale production and provision of a range of services — renovation and repair, odd jobs and cleaning, trading in goods that fell off the back of a lorry, 'cash in hand', fetching and carrying jobs, provision of sexual and other services — these continue and many expand in a recession, as people search for alternative sources of income, and move partially into barter and exchange. This highly entrepreneurial, small-business activity is not simply financially motivated though that is a major consideration. The appeal is also 'political' — making out in the market economy, being independent, enjoying the rewards — and social — having a framework within which to meet and meaningfully interact with other people. It is through the expansion of these aspects of the informal economy that recession and unemployment have been converted into an increase in the demand for a variety of goods and services, including plant-based and synthetic drugs.

Heroin users, for their part, do not come from any specific social class or stratum. Those whose use forms part of the informal economy may originate from a variety of backgrounds, their only common characteristic being some means of recruitment into this informal economy, whether this be by way of family ties, neighbourhood networks and traditions, involvement in criminal activity, or a combination of several or all of these. It is important to recognize that since conventional and quite legitimate modes of employment offer perhaps the widest opportunities for involvement in certain sectors of the informal economy the latter will necessarily include both the employed and unemployed. Consequently, members of both of these categories will be in a position to integrate drug acquisition, sharing, exchange, sale and consumption into the general framework of the informal economy. The key features of all such forms of involvement are (a) the irregularity of acquisition, exchange, sale and/or consumption, and (b) the specific forms of work, social contacts and rewards associated with this irregularity.

As regards irregularity as a characteristic of involvement in the broader informal economy, it is not difficult to appreciate the difference between this and 'regular work' and consumption. Whereas waged work and housework are stretched across fairly continuous blocks of time, with separate but equally continuous blocks of consumption time (for males, at least), involvement in the irregular economy[1] is by definition marked by 'bunching' of intensive work (ripping something off, selling it, etc) and play (splashing out, getting smashed, etc). But what occurs between these relatively short and intensive periods of work and play is not 'doing nothing', but a continuous activity of searching for further opportunities and of surveillance for potential dangers. The active regime of intensive working/searching/surveillance/consumption that characterises the part of the informal economy that we refer to as the irregular economy is the context into which drug acquisition/exchange/use falls.

The implications of this perspective for drug-related advice and welfare work are considerable. Clearly if involvement with heroin can, at least for some users, be understood as an integral part of active involvement in the working life and social life of the irregular economy, then welfare workers and others may need to address the essentially active and entrepreneurial cultures and concerns associated with this economy. Rather than treating users as passive victims, depraved by addiction to the drug, it might be more realistic to address them as people who subscribe to an irregular work ethic in an illicit market, proceeding as best they can with limited social and economic capital.

As the American research literature confirms, users 'are frequently also participants in other criminal behavioural systems (fencing, pimping, prostitution)' and they are also frequently arrested.[1] There is little scope here for dichotomising pushers and victims in any particularly meaningful or helpful way. It may be more useful to recognise the user/small-scale dealer as one and the same person. In a male-dominated market place — the illicit mirrors the licit in many ways — he can be viewed as essentially opportunistic, as someone who may 'come unstuck' every now and then. To render all difficulties as explicable by the label of 'addict' is to misrecognise the person totally. In the case of women, involvement in the informal economy may be overshadowed by the fact that one commodity therein is heterosexual services, and that males routinely work to monopolise other aspects of the economy. Hence women may be obliged to rely either on the support of a particular male or to 'turn tricks'. Heroin use (or other drug use) plus prostitution are quite a different experiential mix from those generally available to men in the informal economy. The subordination of women may here be greater than in the formal or 'regular' economy, with consequences that include an involvement with heroin that corresponds quite closely to the passivity/depression/dependency feelings that are conventionally projected onto male drug users.

THIRD WORLD SUPPLY DETERMINED BY WESTERN COUNTRIES

(a) 'Development', cash-cropping and drug supply

As is widely known, it was — rather ironically — the British themselves who were the first people to engage in large-scale international drug trafficking. By intensive cultivation of opium on the colonial Indian sub-continent, the East India company provided a trading commodity intended not for England, but for exchange with Chinese merchants, whose goods then came to London. The Opium Wars were fought to maintain this trading system. During the twentieth century, and especially since the Second World War, the conditions were established in which the colonial and ex-colonial powers found themselves on the receiving end of this particular trade.

In some Third World countries plant drugs are often the most (or only) profitable cash crop, and it becomes clear that there are heavy inducements all up the chain — from cultivators and those they support, through intermediaries and bribeable officials, to small financiers lacking alternative investment opportunities, export syndicates and even governments. Against these material inducements — which are unintentionally reinforced by the activities of international finance and development agencies — the blandishments and interventions of anti-drug agencies (such as the International Narcotics Control Board and special police and customs agencies of the Western countries) remain relatively ineffectual. The result is that, the deeper that 'developing' countries get into debt, and the tighter the IMF and Western banks turn the political and economic screws, the faster spare agricultural capacity and financial resources re-orientate to the production and export of drugs to those creditor nations in which demand for them exists.

(b) Current trends in the world political economy and the consequences for supply of plant drugs

A large American deficit budget forces up international interest rates and increases the cost of interest payments on Third World debt. These countries then get further and further into debt.

In the context, then, of the relationship that we have discussed between Third World debts, the conditions imposed by international finance capital and by Western governments in return for underwriting these expanding debts, and the consequent stimulation of Third World plant drug cultivation and export to the West, we can hypothesise that the prospects for international drug trafficking in at least the medium term are in the direction of expansion. Thus there seems little likelihood that the demand for these drugs generated as an aspect of Western countries' internal informal economies will be lacking its counterpoint in the realm of supply; and with both demand and supply assured, drug use may be expected to increase.

POLICY AND PRACTICE

We have attempted to establish the basis for a critique of current rhetoric and 'common sense' thinking about heroin and youth in Britain. Far from being a problem that can be understood in terms of a morality play having as its dramatis personae evil outsiders and innocent youth, the latter being led into tragically short lives of depraved pleasures, we have argued that both the demand for and supply of plant drugs today has to be situated within British and international political economies and their associated cultures. It is not, then, a problem that can be remedied simply by the announcement of new law enforcement measures such as an increasingly 'tough' policy towards people breaking the Misuse of Drugs Act in Britain; nor by Show Trials such as those involving the use of the Obscene Publications Act against bookshops selling a relatively insignificant quantity of drugs handbooks; nor by public information and education campaigns about the dangers of addiction advocated in some quarters. There is no system of regulation available to the government other than the criminal law. The use of the law is, however, a double-edged sword, since although it

rebounds to the credit of the government when it appears that the problem is being resolutely contained or overcome, it threatens to bring discredit upon the administration if the problem appears an intransigent one.

Perhaps not surprisingly, it is at the lowest and most humble levels of non-statutory and statutory provision that the most realistic responses to drug-related problems are being made. Staff in non-statutory general advice agencies and drug agencies see heroin users in circumstances in which the market and related bases of such problems as they may present are considerably easier to perceive than they would be from the perspective of psychiatric treatment. Of these problems, it is that of finding one's feet in the housing market that is often most pressing. This is of great significance in the generation of drug-related problems, since many ill-health problems associated with drug and alcohol use emerge most strongly when the person has nowhere to keep warm and dry, to sleep, to wash, to be safe from violence, to be able to regard as 'home'. Associated with problems of keeping warm and dry are those of getting money to eat, whilst adequacy of diet is also an important determinant of health.

All these problems are related to money, and hence to the labour market and its informal adjuncts and alternatives. Progressive advice work and counselling in the drugs field involves responding to these market problems whilst also relating to the drug user's more specific personal and emotional preoccupations. Naturally, the latter is somewhat easier to do than the former in a time of recession and cuts in housing and social security benefits. The general line of our argument, however, has been and remains that a focus upon the market circumstances of drug users — the place of heroin use within the informal economies of the inner cities, small towns and suburbs of Britain in recession — provides the best basis for the further development of practice.

CONCLUSION

Ever since the seminal work of Howard Becker on marijuana use among jazz musicians was first published in the United States in the 1950s,[1] sociologists have come to accept that the consumption of illicit drugs tends to generate and be associated with more or less elaborate subcultural networks composed of persons who perform a variety of tasks necessary for the practice to be sustained relatively unproblematically over time. In order to become a regular user, for example, a person must first of all both learn the technique of using the drug and learn how to enjoy its effects. Success in accomplishing either, Becker argues, will be to little avail if not accompanied by an ability to find a stable source of supply of the drug and, equally, an ability to distinguish sympathetic (if not like-minded) others who can be relied upon not to disclose one's identity to the 'wrong' people, to part with confidential information, or to depart with one's money without supplying the agreed quantity or quality of the drug in return.

In short, the process of becoming — and remaining — a regular drug user necessarily involves a considerable amount of work: not just in the sense of developing and routinely maintaining a daily round of personal contacts in a manner which serves both to keep one on one's toes and to structure the day, but also in the sense of acquiring, passing on and exchanging knowledge ('street wisdom') concerning such things as drug availability, current market prices and the 'right' places to hang around in at certain times of the day or the week.

In all of this, the basic point is that to be a user of heroin is to be someone who is typically more or less tightly enmeshed in a supportive social network whose members are busy keeping one another busy; and that the appeal of being a heroin user is in part a function of this. How much importance should be attached to this source of heroin's appeal, and how much to its physiological and psychological effects, is of course very difficult to determine. Preble and Casey, in their classic article 'Taking Care of Business', appear to have no doubts whatsoever on this score, arguing in relation to their New York City sample that:

The activities these individuals engage in and the relationships they have in the course of their quest for heroin are far more important than the minimal analgesic and euphoric effects of the small amount of heroin available to them. If they can be said to be addicted, it is not so much to heroin as to the entire career of a heroin user.[2]

And, we would add — to the broader career of the socially-active small-time entrepreneur. A small minority of these entrepreneurs may (rather like alcohol suppliers during Prohibition times in the United States of America) rise to become quite successful legitimate businesspersons. Some, on the other hand, will 'come unstuck' and, through a combination of factors such as poverty, general ill-health, accident and bad judgement, a proportion will find themselves in prison, in an Accident & Emergency department, or dead. Not all these casualties can be laid solely at heroin's door: a market economy claims its own victims. For the majority of persons who, through an involvement in the irregular economy, become familiar with heroin as an object of intermittent trade and enjoyment, life will continue much as before.

REFERENCES

1. Reprinted in Becker, H. *Outsiders: Studies in the Sociology of Deviance*, Free Press, 1963, chapters 3 and 4.
2. Preble, E. and Casey, J. 'Taking care of business: the heroin user's life on the streets', *International Journal of Addiction*, vol. 4(1), 1969, pp. 1–24.

Findings of a national survey of the role of general practitioners in the treatment of opiate misuse

ALAN GLANZ and COLIN TAYLOR

Institute of Psychiatry, Addiction Research Unit

This paper reports on a postal survey carried out in 1985 of a 5 per cent sample of GPs in England and Wales to examine the extent of their contact with opiate misusers, and their views on treatment. The results of the survey show that one in five GPs had been in professional contact with an opiate misuser in the four weeks prior to the survey. Detailed results of the survey show that the GPs generally regarded opiate misusers as especially difficult to manage, beyond their competence to treat, and less acceptable as patients than others in need of care.

INTRODUCTION AND METHODS

A major strand in the policy response of government to the unprecedented scale of current drug misuse in the United Kingdom[1] is to strengthen the provision of care under the Health Service by encouraging general practitioners to treat drug misusers. Thus the Department of Health and Social Security has issued *Guidelines of Good Clinical Practice in the Treatment of Drug Misuse* to all doctors and has drawn the attention of family practitioner committees to the need for action on drug misuse.[2,3] For many people, of course, the family doctor is the natural first contact.

Nevertheless, the DHSS has acknowledged that information about the numbers of drug misusers who are treated by general practitioners in England is not available.[4]

A national cross sectional study was planned, with the aim of obtaining descriptive information on (*i*) the scale of contact which general practitioners currently have with opiate drug misusers, (*ii*) how such cases are

handled, and (*iii*) the views that general practitioners hold on issues of policy and practice connected with drug misuse. It was decided that the study should cover only opiate drugs in order to focus on the particular problem that these pose.

An up to date commercial mailing list was used to select a 5% random sample of general practitioners in England and Wales, stratified by regional health authority. Each general practitioner who was selected was sent a questionnaire with a covering letter explaining the background to the study, a list of opiate drugs, and a freepost return envelope. Three follow up sets of questionnaires (with rewritten covering letters) were sent out as reminders to non-respondents. The survey was conducted during the period May to August 1985.

Over the four mailing waves 845 (72%) general practitioners returned usable questionnaires.

RESULTS

Extent of contact with opiate misusers

The general practitioners were asked to report how many different patients they had seen over the past four

Modified from *British Medical Journal*, vol. 293, 16 August 1986, and reproduced by permission of the Editor.

weeks for problems associated with misuse of heroin or other opiate drugs. They could also indicate whether they had never seen such a patient.

For England and Wales as a whole roughly one in five general practitioners came into contact with an opiate drug misuser during a four week period. There is wide variation among regions in the experience of general practitioners in this respect, and it is interesting that of the six 'busiest' regions, in terms of the proportion of general practitioners who reported having contact in the past four weeks, four are provincial (Mersey, East Anglia, North Western, and Wales), whereas the London area (which is partitioned into four regions of North West, North East, South East, and South West Thames) is represented by just two regions (South West Thames and North West Thames).

Profile of opiate misusers and reasons for consulting general practitioners

A total of 329 opiate misusers were seen in a four week period by all responding general practitioners. Of these, 107 (32%) were women. The female to male ratio is roughly the same as that found in a study of intravenous heroin users who attended a Scottish group practice (39% women)[5] and is close to the ratios in Home Office statistics of narcotic addicts who were notified during 1984 (29% women) and of addicts who were recorded as receiving notifiable drugs at the end of 1984 (30% women).[1] Roughly half (52%) of the patients seen were reported by the general practitioners as being under 25 years of age compared with 45% of narcotic addicts who were notified to the Home Office during 1984 and 21% of addicts who were receiving notifiable drugs at the end of 1984.[1]

Roughly a third (35%) of opiate misusers who were seen in a four week period were first time consultors (to that general practitioner) for this problem, with considerable variation between regions in the ratio of 'new' to 'total' misusers seen. What kind of help are these opiate misusers seeking from general practitioners? In the questionnaire general practitioners were asked to allocate first time consultors to categories according to the type of help which, in the general practitioner's view, they were primarily seeking. More than one reason per case was sometimes given, and so the following percentages do not add to 100. Almost two

thirds (61%) were reported to be primarily seeking help concerning withdrawal or rehabilitation, or both. This is almost twice the number reported to be primarily seeking a prescription for opiate drugs (33%), with 23% primarily seeking treatment for medical complications of drug misuse and 20% other kinds of help.

This suggests that, at least in their view, general practitioners are not approached principally as a source of opiate drugs. The apparent substantial demand by opiate misusers for help in coming off their drugs emphasises the important position of the general practitioner as both provider of and gatekeeper for key services in the response to this problem.

Scale of consultation for opiate misuse

For England and Wales as a whole, a minimum of roughly 6600 (more realistically around 9600) individuals will consult general practitioners in a four week period for problems associated with misuse of opiate drugs. Roughly one third of these consultations will be new patients presenting to the general practitioners for this problem. Assuming a steady four week rate, this implies that over a 12 month (13 × four weeks) period general practitioners throughout England and Wales will see a minimum of 30 000 (more realistically around 44 000) new cases of opiate drug misuse.

It is necessary, however, to take into account several qualifying factors. For all the figures there is the inflationary effect of double counting, which results from some individuals presenting at more than one general practice. There is no evidence available upon which to estimate the size of this effect. Also, in the case of the 12 month projection for new cases the summer seasonal rate of consultations (which is obtained in this survey) may not hold for other times of the year.

Prevalence and incidence of person-consultations

Table A gives standardised data for period prevalence ('total' cases) and incidence ('new' cases) of person-consultations in each region, based on the population aged 15–44 years in each region. Press reports about extensive drug misuse on Merseyside may have some foundation (table A).[6,7] Apart from the four Thames

Table A Estimated period prevalence and incidence of person-consultations for opiate drug misuse per 100 000 population aged 15−44 years

Region	Four week prevalence per 100 000 population (aged 15−44)*		One year (13 × 4 week) incidence per 100 000 population (aged 15−44)*	
	(1)	(2)	(1)	(2)
Northern	15.1	20.4	98.3	131.8
Yorks	33.6	44.8	117.7	156.4
Trent	17.0	22.7	51.9	70.0
East Anglia	40.9	50.0	187.7	225.2
North West Thames	60.7	77.7	131.6	167.8
North East Thames	48.6	72.6	236.8	353.5
South East Thames	39.2	52.4	204.1	272.1
South West Thames	42.4	72.3	122.7	208.4
Wessex	8.2	9.4	64.2	72.8
Oxford	16.1	21.5	69.9	93.2
South Western	14.1	20.7	81.5	128.4
West Midlands	16.9	24.8	69.2	101.5
Mersey	57.4	96.2	422.9	709.0
North Western	24.5	37.8	121.5	186.8
Wales	35.6	66.5	220.3	271.0
All regions	30.5	44.5	137.5	204.3

* Office of Population Censuses and Surveys mid-1984 population estimates for local government and health authority areas of England and Wales[8]
(1) Number for all respondents.
(2) Number adjusted for non-respondents (see text).

regions, Wales also has high rates of consultations with general practitioners for opiate misuse. Perhaps most surprising is the high position of East Anglia in the list for consultations for opiate misuse. These consultation rates, however, do not necessarily reflect concomitant levels of prevalence of opiate misuse in the population. The figures for Mersey and Wales should be considered with caution since these regions had the two lowest response rates. East Anglia, on the other hand, had one of the highest response rates.

Given the incidence of 204 'new' consultations per 100 000 population aged 15−44 years for England and Wales (table A), it can be estimated that in the typical general practice with a list of 2000 patients, of whom 1000 are aged 15−44, the general practitioner will have about two new cases of opiate misuse in a year.

DEALING WITH THE OPIATE MISUSER

There is little information available on how general practitioners handle people misusing opiates such as the use made of specialist medical services and social agencies for referral, the likelihood of prescribing opiates, and so on.

The findings presented here concerning their role in the treatment of opiate misuse throw some light on these activities.

Referral and prescribing

Beyond assessing the patient, the findings suggest that the most common response of general practitioners in dealing with opiate misusers is to refer them to specialist hospital drug dependence clinics or to general psychiatric services (table B). Two thirds of the general practitioners made such a referral, including a few who referred the patient to both services.

Although a comparison may be misleading when the raw numbers are so small, there appear to be some wide differences between regional health authorities in the pattern of referrals by general practitioners. These differences are likely to be an effect of the character of local provision of services and policy. The lowest rate of referral to a specialist drug clinic (13%) and the second highest rate of referral to general psychiatric services (47%) are in the South Western Regional Health Authority, where regional policy is: 'Health Service provision (for drug misusers) is based on the general psychiatric service. . . . No special clinics have been established and none is currently planned.[9] Furthermore, just one district in the region is served by a drug treatment centre established under the DHSS Central Funding Initiative.[10] The highest rate of referral to a specialist clinic is in Mersey Regional Health Authority (71%), where the largest financial outlay on a single project under the Central Funding Initiative has been committed to a new outpatient clinic for drug dependency.[10] The region with the highest rate of referral to general psychiatric services is North Western (62%), where the development of 'satellite clinics'

Table B   Proportion of general practitioners who took an action in dealing with the patient whom they most recently attended for opiate misuse

Action	Percentage who took action (n = 384)
(1) Assessment by interview and taking a case history	85
(2) Referral to specialist drug dependence clinic	45
(3) Referral to general psychiatric services	34
(4) Referral to primary health care team	9
(5) Referral to local authority social services	8
(6) Referral to voluntary organisation dealing with drug misuse	11
(7) Prescribing opiate drugs for the short term (<2 weeks)	18
(8) Prescribing opiate drugs for the longer term	17
(9) Screening or arranging for screening of urine for evidence of drugs	6
(10) Notification to the Home Office	33
(11) Other	12

within district psychiatric services has been fostered, aiming at offering easier referral of drug misusers than to the regional specialist unit.[11]

Other potential sources of care appear to be used less often by general practitioners. Few in this sample had referred the opiate misuser to other members of the primary health care team (9%), and referral to local authority social services (8%) or voluntary organisations concerned with drugs (11%) was also done infrequently (table B).

Few of these general practitioners reported that they had undertaken or arranged for screening of urine for drugs (6%). This may reflect difficulties of access to appropriate facilities.[12] On the other hand, a substantial proportion of general practitioners had prescribed opiate drugs, and, as the table shows, this was equally likely to have been for the short term — up to two weeks — as for the longer term. It cannot be determined from these data how much of the prescribing was

part of a withdrawal programme or how much was for maintenance treatment until the patient could be seen by a specialist. Taking into account a small overlap between the general practitioners who prescribed for the short term and those who prescribed over the longer term, the findings suggest that nearly a third (31%) who had had contact with opiate misusers prescribed some form of opiate, and 22% prescribed and did not refer to another agency.

Notification

Notification of certain categories of addicts to the Home Office is a legal obligation for doctors under the Misuse of Drugs (Notification of and Supply to Addicts) Regulations of 1973. It has been suggested that limited awareness of this statutory responsibility results in extensive undernotification.[12] Among this sample of general practitioners one third had notified the Home Office of the opiate misuser who had most recently attended (table B). Since the definition of a case for inclusion in this section of the survey is a person attended for 'problems associated with misuse of heroin or other opiates' it would not necessarily be appropriate to make a notification under the regulations which define an addict in terms of 'an overpowering desire for administration of the drug'.[2]

VIEWS ON TREATMENT

The receptiveness of general practitioners to the policy of promoting a more active role for them in the treatment of drug misusers is uncertain. Evidence pertinent to this question is largely anecdotal. The research findings reported here provide a picture of the pattern of general practitioners' views and thus a firmer basis for assessing the viability of this policy. The questionnaire was designed to elicit the views of general practitioners on a range of issues on policy and treatment connected with opiate misuse. Ten 'position statements' on these issues were presented, and on a five point scale the respondents could register the strength of their agreement or disagreement or indicate uncertainty in respect of each statement.

Table C gives the overall results from this section of the questionnaire. Clearly, general practitioners over-

Table C   General practitioners' views on issues concerning opiate misuse* (figures are numbers and percentages in parentheses)

Position/statement:	Agree or strongly agree	Uncertain	Disagree or strongly disagree	Total respondents	Missing cases (excluded)
(1) The Department of Health is correct in recently requesting health authorities to place the improvement of services for drug misusers in the category of highest priority	721(87)	53(6)	51(6)	825(100)	20
(2) Misusers of heroin/other opiate drugs are likely to present more severe management problems for the general practitioner than any other type of patient	633(76)	111(13)	85(10)	829(100)	16
(3) Even when misusers of heroin/other opiate drugs are not prepared to come off their drugs the general practitioner still has a positive part to play in their treatment	456(55)	207(25)	164(20)	827(100)	18
(4) In my experience, hospital drug dependence clinics provide a responsive service when referrals of heroin/opiate drug misusers are made to them	325(42)	342(44)	114(14)	781(100)	64
(5) The recent DHSS Guidelines of Good Clinical Practice provide me with the basis for a more confident role in the treatment of heroin/other opiate drug misusers	397(49)	326(41)	79(10)	802(100)	44
(6) My capacity to treat heroin/other opiate drugs misusers would be appreciably diminished if the prescribing of all opiate drugs were restricted (as with heroin and cocaine) to specially licensed doctors	281(34)	240(29)	294(36)	815(100)	30
(7) I am prepared to undertake the treatment of heroin/other opiate drug misusers as willingly as any other type of patient in need of care	253(31)	164(20)	400(49)	817(100)	28
(8) Misusers of heroin/other opiate drugs require forms of therapy beyond the competence of the ordinary general practitioner	491(60)	137(17)	190(23)	818(100)	24
(9) I would play a more active part in the treatment of heroin/other opiate misusers if more back up resources were available to me	364(45)	260(32)	190(23)	814(100)	31
(10) Heroin/other opiate drug misuse tends to be a symptom of underlying personality disorder	525(64)	188(23)	109(13)	822(100)	23

* Five point scale has been collapsed into three point scale.

whelmingly support the policy of the Department of Health of granting highest priority to developing services for drug misusers (statement 1)[13], 87% of respondents endorsing this view and 44% strongly agreeing.

To what extent, however, are general practitioners likely to respond to the call for improved services for drug misusers? They appear to be reluctant to accept opiate misusers as patients: less than a third agree that they are prepared to take on opiate misusers as willingly as other types of patients (statement 7). Some possible reasons for this reluctance emerge in the responses to two other statements. Firstly, three quarters of the general practitioners agree that opiate misusers are more difficult to manage than other types of patients; more than a third (37%) strongly agree (statement 2). Also, almost two thirds regard the treatment required by opiate misusers as beyond the competence of general practitioners, with less than a quarter (23%) disagreeing (statement 8). This last finding may be compared with a similar item in a survey on managing alcohol problems in general practice where 44% of general practitioners felt capable of working with drinkers.[14]

This view of the limitations of general practice as the place to treat opiate misuse may reflect what the Royal College of General Practitioners has called 'the special and complex needs of those addicted to hard drugs' and the insufficiency, as it claims, of a general practitioner's training for responding to those needs.[15] Part of the resistance of general practitioners to treating opiate misusers may lie in their understanding of the nature of the problem. Two thirds of the general practitioners endorse the view that opiate misuse is a symptom of underlying personality disorder (statement 10). Perhaps it is in this type of disorder that general practitioners believe lay difficulties in management and treatment.

General practitioners are certainly not entirely averse to treating opiate misusers. Most of the respondents agree that even when opiate misusers are not prepared to come off their drugs there is still a positive role for the general practitioner (statement 3). The *Guidelines of Good Clinical Practice in the Treatment of Drug Misuse* were issued to enhance the confidence of general practitioners in treating these patients.[2] The guidelines may not have been circulated widely or there may not have been time to respond to the recommendations, for nearly one half of the general practitioners (44%) are uncertain on this issue; among the remainder who expressed a view, almost all agree that the guidelines provide the basis for a more confident role (statement 5).

On the grounds that it would discourage general practitioners from treating opiate misusers the government has now rejected a recommendation of the Medical Working Group, who produced the guidelines, to extend the current licensing arrangements for prescribing heroin and Diconal (and cocaine) to all opiate drugs except liquid methadone.[16] From this survey it appears that general practitioners are evenly divided in their judgment of whether or not the effect of such a measure would be to diminish their capacity to treat opiate misusers, a little more than one third agreeing and one third disagreeing with this suggestion (statement 6). Furthermore, there is a significant difference between general practitioners who reported elsewhere in the questionnaire that they had prescribed opiates to the patient whom they had most recently attended for opiate misuse and general practitioners who had not prescribed: 49% of the prescribers agree that extending licensing would diminish their capacity to treat opiate misusers (statement 6) compared with 28% of non-prescribers ($\chi^2 = 17.65$; 2 df; $p < 0.001$).

Also, among the actions that many general practitioners had reported having taken while dealing with the opiate misuser who had most recently consulted was to refer the patient to a specialist drug dependence clinic.[7] How satisfied are general practitioners in general with the response of drug dependence clinics? Almost half of all respondents (44%) were unable to state a view, whereas a similar number (42%) express a positive view (statement 4). Among general practitioners who reported having made such a referral, 59% agree that clinics provide a responsive service and 22% are uncertain, compared with 36% agreeing and 41% uncertain among those who did not make such a referral ($\chi^2 = 21.02$; 2 df; $p < 0.0001$). The findings also indicate that if back up resources were more widely available some general practitioners would be encouraged to take a more active role in the treatment of opiate misusers, 45% of respondents agreeing (statement 9).

This overall picture of general practitioners' views concerning opiate misusers is not particularly comforting for policy makers. There may be grounds for limited optimism in the results showing an association between the pattern of views expressed and how recently the general practitioner had qualified.

Though only a quarter of general practitioners who qualified before 1970 agree that they are prepared to treat opiate misusers as willingly as any other patient in need of care, 40% of the general practitioners who qualified in the 1970s and 1980s agree (χ^2 = 18.44; 2 df; p < 0.001). Newer general practitioners also appear to be more confident of their ability to deal with drug misusers, as 49% of those qualifying in the 1970s and 1980s agree that opiate misusers require treatments that are beyond the competence of ordinary general practitioners, compared with 66% of other general practitioners (χ^2 = 21.27; 2 df; p < 0.0001). Again, the most recently qualified general practitioners take a less unfavourable view in their response to the statement that opiate misusers are likely to present more severe management problems than any other type of patient, with 67% of this group agreeing compared with 81% for the older general practitioners (χ^2 = 19.99; 2 df; p < 0.001). Finally the newer general practitioners would probably play a more active part in the treatment of opiate misusers if more back up resources were available; 54% of general practitioners who qualified in the 1970s or 1980s agree with this statement; while 39% of those who qualified before 1970 agree (χ^2 = 19.27; 2 df; p < 0.001). In numerical terms the variation between the recently qualified general practitioners and the others is not large and does not substantially modify the overall picture.

DISCUSSION

The data show that substantial numbers of opiate misusers are approaching general practitioners in England and Wales for help. A realistic estimate is that 9500 person-consultations for opiate misuse take place in England and Wales in a four week period. Roughly a third of these are cases that are new to that general practitioner, which suggests an annual total of around 40 000 'new' cases.

The picture that emerges, however, is that general practitioners most often responded to these patients by referring them to a specialist drug dependence clinic or to general psychiatric services after having assessed them.

On the other hand, a substantial number of general practitioners prescribe opiate drugs, and the extent to which this is done independently of specialist advice is unknown. Thus the DHSS guidelines might be of considerable value in defining good practice in this respect. Also, given the finding of the rather narrow referral activity, it may be useful to give general practitioners information about the range of services available to deal with drug misusers.

The findings suggest that the policy of promoting the treatment of drug misusers by general practitioners may be difficult to implement: most general practitioners regard opiate misusers as especially difficult to manage and beyond their competence to treat, and most are relatively unwilling to accept them as patients. This must be of concern to those who are interested in improving services for drug misusers. It is therefore not surprising that both the Medical Working Group and the Minister of State at the time with responsibility for policy felt the need to emphasise that general practitioners have a responsibility and 'duty' to provide services to this group of patients.[2,15] The irony of this exhortation will not be lost on those who are aware of the policy implemented about 20 years ago, which specifically aimed at excluding general practitioners from this role.

The government has now rejected the 'carrot' option, suggested by the Social Services Committee, of making additional payment to general practitioners who undertake special training and treat drug misusers.[16] Since general practitioners are independent contractors to the Health Service, working largely outside the planning system, there is little 'stick' that can be deployed to steer general practitioners in line with central strategy.

The level of management of opiate misusers which may legitimately be expected of general practitioners is open to debate. Providing basic medical care for complications associated with drug misuse may be a more acceptable role for the general practitioner than prescribing opiates as maintenance treatment or even limited prescribing to help with withdrawal from drugs. The incentive, however, for general practitioners to undertake a more active role will be found in the establishment of a network of support, which was recommended by both the Advisory Council on the Misuse of Drugs[17] and the Social Services Committee.[15] These recommendations included close liaison with services in hospital and in the community (both statutory and non-statutory) and training opportunities that focus on managing drug misuse or the problems of dependence generally. At the same time the view of drug misusers that general practitioners have might be addressed by a campaign that would challenge certain global assumptions about drug misusers, identify measures that might be taken, and provide information on the range of local and national resources available to the general practitioner in responding to the needs of the drug misuser. Within such a framework the potential benefits of accessibility and early intervention offered by general practitioner services may be realised.

REFERENCES

1. Anonymous, Home Office Statistical Bulletin 23/28. London: Home Office, 1985.
2. Medical Working Group on Drug Dependence, *Guidelines of Good Clinical Practice in the Treatment of Drug Misuse*. London: Department of Health and Social Security, 1984.
3. Department of Health and Social Security. Management of arrangements for family practitioner committees operational requirements and guidelines 1986/87. London: DHSS, February 1986. (Health Circular HC/(FP)23/85.)
4. Department of Health and Social Security. *Prevalence and Service Provision: a Report on Surveys and Plans in English National Health Service Regions*. London: DHSS, 1985.
5. Robertson, J.R. Drug users in contact with general practice. *British Medical Journal*, 1985; **290**: 34–5.
6. Brown, P. Business as usual in smack city. *Observer*, 1985, Aug. 4.
7. Davenport, P. Liverpool, a city in disarray: police and public determined to stamp out drugs traffic. *The Times*, 1985, Aug. 13.
8. Office of Population Censuses and Surveys. *Monitor*, London: OPCS, June 1985 (PPI 85/2).
9. Department of Health and Social Security. *Prevalence and Service Provision: a Report on Surveys and Plans in English National Health Service Regions*. London: DHSS, 1985.
10. Home Office. *Tackling Drug Misuse: a Summary of the Government's Strategy*. London: Home Office, 1985.
11. Strang, J.S. and Creed, F.H. Treatment of drug dependence — the role of the satellite clinic. *Health Trends*, 1985; **7**: 17–8.
12. Advisory Council on the Misuse of Drugs. Department of Health and Social Security. *Treatment and Rehabilitation*. London: HMSO, 1982.
13. Department of Health and Social Security. *Health Service Development. Services for Drug Misusers*. London: DHSS, June 1984 (Health Circular HC(84)).
14. Anderson, P. Managing alcohol problems in general practice. *British Medical Journal*, 1985; **290**: 1873–5.
15. Social Services Committee. *Misuse of Drugs, with Special Reference to the Treatment and Rehabilitation of Misusers of Hard Drugs*. Fourth report. London: HMSO, 1985.
16. Department of Health and Social Security and other departments. *Misuse of Drugs. Government Response to the 4th Report of the Social Services Committee Session 1984–85*. London: HMSO, 1985.
17. Department of Health and Social Security, Advisory Council on the Misuse of Drugs. *Treatment and Rehabilitation*. London: HMSO, 1982.

Section II

Drug abuse briefing

ISDD LIBRARY and INFORMATION SERVICE

> This short paper is an extract from the introduction to the Drug Abuse Briefing produced by the ISDD Library and Information Service. It explains in simple language the meaning of some 'drug terms', and discusses notions of drug taking and risk taking. The full document, from which this extract is taken, goes into more detail about these issues for a whole range of individual substances.

The use of drugs (including alcohol, tobacco and coffee) for non-medical purposes is a little understood aspect of human behaviour. The most extensive and solid scientific work on drugs is about their chemical compositions and effects on laboratory animals. We also know something about the characteristics of people who use large amounts or get into some kind of trouble with drugs (because they are the ones most likely to come to the attention of doctors, drug agencies, police etc. and are therefore most accessible to researchers).

But information derived from these areas of research doesn't necessarily help much in understanding the 'everyday' use and misuse of drugs, nor how social and psychological processes influence the outcome of drugtaking behaviour, and can only be a very rough guide to whether the consequences will be beneficial or harmful in any individual case.

Drug effects are strongly influenced by the amount taken, how much has been taken before, what the user wants and expects to happen, the surroundings in which it is taken, and the reactions of other people. All these influences are themselves tied up with social and cultural attitudes to and beliefs about drugs, as well as more general social conditions. Even the same person will react differently at different times. So it is usually misleading to make simple cause-and-effect statements

The full version of this paper is available from: Institute for the Study of Drug Dependence, 1–4, Hatton Place, Hatton Garden, London EC1N 8ND. Reproduced by permission of ISDD.

about drugs, such as 'drug X always causes condition Y'.

DRUG TERMS

The terms 'tolerance', 'withdrawal', 'dependence' and 'addiction' are often used to describe the consequences of drug use — especially the non-medical use of drugs — but without much accuracy or consistency.

Tolerance refers to the way the body usually adapts to the repeated presence of a drug, meaning that it takes higher doses to maintain the same effect.

Withdrawal effects are also common, and can be thought of as the body's reaction to the sudden absence of a drug to which it has adapted. The effects can be abolished by taking more of the drug, but generally fade after 2 or 3 weeks. They can vary from headaches after stopping drinking coffee, to convulsions and possibly death after stopping barbiturates. Many people will have experienced withdrawal effects without resulting in any, or any lasting, desire to continue taking the drug.

Dependence describes a compulsion to continue taking a drug as a result of its repeated administration. In so far as this is to avoid the physical discomfort of withdrawal, we speak of *physical dependence*; in so far as the compulsion has a psychological basis — the need for stimulation or pleasure, need for a chemical 'crutch', desire to obliterate reality, etc — then it's referred to as *psychological dependence*. Psychological dependence is recognised as the most widespread and most important.

Addiction implies that a drug dependency has developed which has serious detrimental effects on the individual and on society. As such it is intimately tied up with society's reaction to that dependency, so medical experts now generally avoid the term as carrying too many non-medical connotations.

Detrimental consequences may also be experienced by drug users who are not dependent. Hence the term '*problem drug use*' has been coined to refer to drug use resulting in social, psychological, physical or legal problems associated with dependence, intoxication, or regular excessive consumption.

Drug 'abuse' or *drug 'misuse'* are terms that are hard to pin down. Essentially they indicate the observer's belief that the drugtaking in question is a harmful (abuse) and/or a socially unacceptable way of using that substance (misuse — hence 'Misuse of Drugs Act'). Since authorised medical use of drugs is almost by definition acceptable and not harmful, both terms overlap with the less subjective term, *non-medical use*.

As might be expected, the term '*recreational*' drug use denotes the use of drugs for pleasure or leisure purposes. Although sometimes used as a synonym for non-medical use, recreational use is distinct from dependent use on the one hand and 'functional' use (use of drugs to aid performance at non-leisure activities, such as stimulant use amongst some groups of workers) on the other.

DRUGTAKING AND RISKTAKING

The vast majority of people who use drugs come to no harm, and many will feel they have benefited (and may well have done so) from the relaxation, diversion or temporarily improved social, intellectual or physical performance that can be afforded by some drugs. But there are very serious risks, and a large part of this publication is about these and how they arise. Some of the most important points to be made about the risks of drugtaking apply to all or most of the drugs in this briefing. To an extent these represent rules of thumb about what not to do with drugs in general, though each drug

has its own array of potential risks. It should not be assumed that the extent to which a drug is legally restricted is much of a guide to how harmful it can be.

Overdoing it

The adage about moderation applies to drugs, in two different ways. First, taking too much at one go risks an experience that gets out of control and causes distress, or even fatal overdose. Obviously the more is taken, the greater the risk of accidents due to intoxication, including choking on vomit whilst unconscious.

Secondly, anyone taking a psychoactive (affecting the mind) drug frequently, in high doses, and for a long time, is likely to distort their perception of and response to their environment such that normal functioning and normal development are impaired. Social relationships may narrow down to a small group of people with similar habits, and finding or keeping work and housing may be difficult. As tolerance/dependence develop, the problems of financing drug purchases can add to the deterioration of diet, housing, and lifestyle, and may result in revenue-raising crimes. Normal desires for say food and sex, and reactions to discomfort and pain, may be dulled by the drug, and the resultant self-neglect can damage health. Indirect damage — arising from the lifestyle associated with heavy, and especially, illegal drug use, rather than a direct effect of the drug on the body — is often the most significant, but can sometimes be minimised even if drug use continues. Obviously heavy use is most likely if someone becomes dependent on the drug, when they will find it hard to stop, despite their health being affected.

Wrong time, wrong place

Even in moderate doses most of the drugs in this briefing (except the stimulants) impair motor control, reaction time, and the ability to maintain attention, effects which can last several hours. No matter how the person *feels*, they are not as capable as before, and such activities as driving, operating machinery and crossing roads, become more hazardous to themselves and to others. They will also be less effective at their job.

Even stimulants may impair delicate skills and the learning of new skills, and in high doses will impair performance on tasks they previously enhanced.

Also many drugs amplify mood such that if someone is feeling — or is in a situation that makes them feel — depressed, anxious or aggressive, they could make things a lot worse. Even drugs (like alcohol and tranquillisers) we think of as calming people down, can also release aggressive impulses because they weaken the grip of social and personal inhibitions.

Individual differences

Statements about drug effects are often statements about what might happen in extreme cases, or alternatively about what usually happens with most people. But not everyone is 'usual'. For instance, some people develop a toxic reaction to a single cup of coffee, and the normally insignificant elevation of heart-rate caused by cannabis can be painful for people suffering from angina pectoris. Glaucoma patients on the other hand may find cannabis beneficial, but three strong cups of coffee will aggravate the condition. Individuals with pre-existing psychotic tendencies may be 'pushed over the brink' by their experiences under the influence of powerful hallucinogens like LSD.

Also the extent to which a drug affects the body tends to vary with body-weight, so in general less heavy people will get greater effects and consequently greater dangers for the same drug dose than will heavier people. Sex differences in response to psychoactive drugs are poorly researched, but, for instance, it is known that women alcoholics are more susceptible to liver disease than men, due to physiological differences. Individual differences in the degree of response to the same amount of a drug mean that dose levels for a given effect quoted in this publication can only be generalisations.

These are just a few examples. But in general it can't be guaranteed that the effects a drug has on an individual will match those cited in briefings like this, especially if that person is particularly vulnerable due to illness or due to their psychological make-up.

Adulteration and mistaken identity

Drugs offered on the illicit market are not always what they're claimed to be, and if illicitly manufactured they are likely to contain any one of a range of impurities or adulterants. Also the buyer can rarely be sure how

strong the substance is. And even if they did know, they wouldn't necessarily know how much to take.

These factors add greatly to the unpredictability of the effects of, and damage from, the use of drugs obtained without the safeguards of medical supervision or the quality control imposed on licit manufacturers.

Doubling up

People who attempt suicide using large amounts of benzodiazepine tranquillisers almost invariably wake up unharmed. But the same dose on top of a large dose of alcohol could easily prove fatal. This example illustrates the point that effects of drugs which individually depress body functions (alcohol, solvents, sedatives, hypnotics, opiates, tranquillisers) will add up if they are taken together, so that much lower doses of each will be fatally depressant than would normally be the case. Since drugs remain effective for varying periods, often many hours, the two substances don't even have to be taken at the same time.

Doubling up on depressant drugs is probably the most dangerous, but complex interactions can occur between other drugs. Doctors and experienced drugtakers make use of these to 'fine-tune' drug effects, but for most people loading one drug on top of another multiplies the risk of a harmful outcome.

Pregnancy

There are several ways in which drugs might damage the foetus. Firstly heavy use may affect the mother's health either directly or through self-neglect and poor nutrition.

Secondly, drugs may directly affect the foetus through the mother's bloodstream. Very rarely they cause malformations; this risk is at its greatest in the first third of pregnancy.

More significantly, some of the drugs listed in this publication affect the foetus in the same way as they affect adults, and the baby's immature body is less able to cope. Thus drugs like alcohol, opioids, sedatives and tranquillisers, which depress the adult's respiration and other body functions, will also depress these functions in the foetus and in the neonate.

There is also the possibility that babies born to mothers dependent on opioids, sedatives, tranquillisers or alcohol, will need medial care to avoid withdrawal symptoms.

These risks are by no means the same for all drugs, and are best established for drugs with depressant effects. But in general, heavy drug use in pregnancy is associated — probably for a variety of reasons — with premature birth and low birth-weight, and an increased risk of losing the baby around the time of birth. On the other hand, the evidence on the effects of moderate drug use during pregnancy is generally inconclusive, and many heavy drug users give birth to perfectly healthy babies. But this is an under-researched area, and doctors generally advise pregnant women not to take drugs if it can be avoided.

Injection

Injection of drugs is much less widespread than other ways of using them, and also the most hazardous. Drugs that are injected are mainly of three kinds: opioids, sedatives (especially barbiturates), and stimulants (amphetamines and cocaine). These may well be mixed to combine their different effects.

When injected into a vein, all the drug enters the blood stream and some is carried directly to the brain, producing a noticeable effect within seconds. For these reasons the onset of the drug's effects (the 'rush') is quicker and more striking after injection. In general, the short-term effects of injected drugs are along the lines of those taken by mouth, but more intense. Opioids, for instance, produce a sensation of warmth and relief from physical and mental discomfort, but when injected these effects can be magnified into a short-lived burst of intensely pleasurable sensations. Drugs can also be injected under the skin or into muscles, when the effect is more delayed and less intense than with intravenous injection.

The major dangers of injecting are overdose; infection from non-sterile injection methods (including hepatitis and other diseases transmitted by more than one injector sharing the same needle); abscesses and gangrene caused by missing the vein when injecting; and damage from using crushed-up tablets and other dosage forms not meant to be injected.

Dependence is more likely when a drug is injected than when taken in other ways. This is partly due to the fact that high doses are common, partly due to the gratification and immediacy of the 'rush', and partly connected with the meaning of the injection ritual to the user; for a few people the injection may become as important as the effect of the drug, and if no drugs are available almost anything will be injected. Nevertheless, dependence is not inevitable and will take time to develop.

_____ *Paper 8* _____
Understanding drug use

T.C. COC, M.R. JACOBS, A.E. LEBLANC and J.A. MARSHMAN

This paper outlines many of the dimensions of drug use. In particular it discusses the definition of the concept 'drug' and the sources, identification, analysis and classification of psychoactive drugs.

A variety of chemical, pharmacological, and behavioral factors influence the nature and outcome of psychoactive drug use. The impact of drug dependence and drug toxicity on the individual user, on specific drug-using populations, and on society can be adequately understood only if we examine the many dimensions of the drug-use situation: the actual drug involved, its pharmacological effects, the hazards of particular patterns of use, and the characteristics and risks of the method of administration. Moreover, since many situations involve more than one drug, it is important to consider the interactions among drugs both within the same drug class and across different classes, for some of these interactions are potentially dangerous.

Our knowledge of these fundamental issues has developed through research in that branch of science known as pharmacology. The application of knowledge derived from this study permits an effective response by a broad spectrum of medical and nonmedical professionals, paraprofessionals, and others in practical situations involving drug users. Basic pharmacology explores the nature and effects of the drug substances as they impact on the human physiological system. However, perhaps the most fundamental and persistent question which basic pharmacology must address and to which the answer is continually evolving is 'What is a drug?'

From *Drugs and Drug Abuse*, Addiction Research Foundation, Toronto, 1983.

DEFINITION OF THE CONCEPT 'DRUG'

The ancient Greeks called drugs *pharmakon*, a word which meant both poison and medicine. Similarly, *pharmakeuein* was either the practice of witchcraft or the use of medicine depending on the context. These simplistic concepts, reflective of a certain ambivalence, represented the attempt of Greek society to come to terms with the powerful effect of drugs on the mind and body of the individual.

Even in more recent times, society has had great difficulty in arriving at one satisfactory definition of the word 'drug'. For many people, a drug is simply whatever the doctor prescribes to treat their disease or discomfort. Such a definition, however inoffensive, does nothing to alleviate the confusion that arises whenever a precise answer to this question becomes important to us.

The question 'What is a drug?' is complicated by the fact that various substances not usually considered as drugs may function as drugs under certain circumstances — for example, foods and beverages, or solvents and aerosols. For instance, most people think of alcohol merely as a beverage which with normal use could easily be interchangeable with other beverages. Yet many people often prefer alcohol over other beverages because it gives rise to a feeling of relaxation and helps to remove inhibitions in close social interactions, effects resulting from its activity as a central nervous system (CNS) depressant. When people drink it for these reasons, it becomes reasonable to view it as a drug. Less commonly, alcohol can be termed a drug when it is prescribed for its high energy content in the intravenous feeding of patients with special medical problems. Other food substances such as glucose, salt, and vitamins can be termed drugs when they are used respectively in the treatments of diabetes, shock, and malnutrition. Regular, heavy use of caffeine-containing beverages and of tobacco supports the view that these substances are commonly used as drugs to produce certain psychological effects related to central nervous system stimulation.

The gases in aerosol cans and the solvents found in household and industrial cleaners (e.g., petroleum distillates, acetone, and trichloroethane) can be reasonably considered as drugs when they are inhaled, whether accidentally or deliberately. If they are carelessly handled, spilled in an enclosed space, or taken intentionally for their mood-altering effects, in sufficiently large quantities they affect the functioning of the brain in much the same way as the sedative/hypnotic and anesthetic drugs.

On the basis of the above examples, it is evident that the human intent behind use may serve as a criterion in determining whether and under what circumstances substances should be called drugs. It follows from this viewpoint that, in the case of both pharmaceutical preparations and naturally occurring substances, a substance is a drug whenever its use is intended primarily to bring about change in some existing process or state, be it psychological, physiological, or biochemical. The intended modification can be directed toward changes in medical, behavioral, or perceptual states and for either therapeutic or nonmedical purposes. In the case of foods, beverages, and industrial chemicals, a substance can be considered a drug when its use is diverted toward bringing about these types of changes.

It is evident from these definitions that a vast number of substances from a wide variety of sources may be considered to be drugs. However, throughout the discussions which follow, we shall, with a few exceptions, consider only those drugs which have, either as primary or secondary characteristics, mood-altering properties.

SOURCES OF PSYCHOACTIVE DRUGS

Psychoactive drugs can be divided into three major types, according to source: naturally occurring, semisynthetic, and synthetic.

1. Certain plants and animal tissues contain psychoactive drugs; in some cases the crude material is used as the drug preparation, while in other cases the drug substances are extracted and purified. These drugs are described below as *naturally occurring*.
2. Chemical manipulations of psychoactive substances which have been extracted from natural materials may result in drugs with somewhat different properties. These drugs are called *semisynthetics*.
3. Psychoactive agents neither found in nature nor derived from natural psychoactive agents are known as *synthetics*; they are created entirely by laboratory manipulation of two or more relatively simple chemicals which in themselves are usually psychoactively inert.

Naturally occurring psychoactive substances

Plants are important sources of mood-modifying drugs. Both primitive and modern societies have relied heavily on plant resources for both medical and nonmedical drugs. In China, for example, the CNS stimulant ephedrine has been extracted from a local plant, *mahuang* (*Ephedra equisetina*), and used in traditional medicine for thousands of years. Ephedrine has also been widely used in Western medicine since its introduction at the turn of the century; the ephedrine used initially was isolated from plant material, but that used nowadays is synthesized in a chemical laboratory. The stimulant cocaine, contained in the leaves of the *Erythroxylon coca* shrub, has been in both medical and nonmedical use in Peru for hundreds of years. It is both a local anesthetic and a stimulant. The active alkaloid, cocaine, is easily extracted from the plant by chewing or pressing the leaves. Opium and its chief alkaloid, morphine, have long been in use as analgesics and euphoriants in medical and nonmedical circles. It is a relatively simple matter to extract these drugs from the resin in the unripe seed pods of the opium poppy, *Papaver somniferum*.

Most of the natural psychoactive drugs have been in use for centuries. It is worth noting that folk medicine discovered and took advantage of the drug effects without knowledge of their chemical nature and without the advantages of the sophisticated analytical techniques and international searches now utilized in pharmaceutical and pharmacological investigations.

Semisynthetic psychoactive drugs

Chemists often use a substance derived from a natural source as a starting material for the chemical synthesis of some other drug substance. Heroin (diacetylmorphine), for example, is prepared in the laboratory from the natural product, morphine, in chemical combination with another substance, acetic anhydride or acetyl chloride. Similarly, LSD (lysergic acid diethylamide) is derived from certain ergot alkaloids — naturally occurring substances in certain *Claviceps* fungi which grow on grains. The naturally occurring ergot alkaloids are used to control postpartum hemorrhage and restore normal uterine tone and to treat migraine headaches. LSD is an example of a semisynthetic derivative with pharmacological actions which transcend those of the substances from which it is derived.

Synthetic psychoactive drugs

Synthetic drugs are prepared entirely from relatively simple chemical substances in a laboratory; they do not depend on plant or animal substances as a starting material. Many of the drugs prepared in this way do not occur in any natural state and have been designed in such a way as to have some particular pharmacological property or combination of properties which cannot be obtained in naturally occurring drugs. Methadone is a synthetic compound which was developed initially in Germany during World War II, when the opium poppy resin needed to produce morphine was difficult to obtain. Dextromethorphan is an example of an entirely synthetic cough suppressant; while structurally related to the opium alkaloids, it is designed to combat cough effectively without the risk of dependence — a disadvantage of most cough suppressants derived from opium.

Within any pharmacological drug class, there may be examples of drugs obtained from each of these three types of source. For example, opium and morphine are naturally occurring analgesic psychoactive drugs. Heroin, derived from morphine through chemical modification, is a semisynthetic drug with similar properties. Methadone and meperidine, again with similar properties, are totally synthetic. Although these substances are not identical, they can be used interchangeably for the relief of certain types of pain and are all sought by abusers principally for their euphoriant effects.

LEGAL (ETHICAL) AND ILLEGAL MANUFACTURE OF PSYCHOACTIVE DRUGS

The term 'pharmaceutical industry' is commonly used to designate the group of legally sanctioned industrial/commercial enterprises which prepare and market drugs. Some companies carry out only the processes which result in preparation of large amounts of active drug substances; these they sell in bulk to other companies which prepare individual dosage units (tablets, capsules, vials of solution, syrups, suppositories, etc.) The company which prepares the dosage units may itself market them to hospitals, pharmacies, and medical, dental, and veterinary practitioners, or it may wholesale them to other companies involved in distribution. Many large pharmaceutical companies carry out all manufacturing functions as well as marketing and distribution.

Similar kinds of functions are carried out in the illicit drug industry. Some individuals or groups specialize in large-scale production of the drug substances, leaving others to prepare the dosage forms.

In Canada, the legal and ethical manufacture of drugs takes place in laboratories or factories which must comply with government standards. The drugs are formulated into stable preparations of known strength and purity so that dosages can be prescribed with accuracy and confidence and can be relied on by the user. In addition, the products are carefully labelled with instructions for storage and appropriate use, in many cases with an expiry date. Most are intended for use by those following a medically supervised program. Many may be obtained only with a prescription. Over-the-counter drugs, prepared under the same strict control, are intended for safe self-medication of minor ailments.

Illegal manufacture of psychoactive drugs takes place in clandestine laboratories where very often little attention may be given to matters of purity, safety, or reliability. In some cases the production methods used are crude and outdated and the skills of the producer quite limited. Indeed, anyone with a rudimentary knowledge of chemistry can manufacture drugs, provided the clients' standards of acceptability are not very high. However, it must be acknowledged that in certain large and well-organized illicit enterprises, both the equipment and the chemical skills are very sophisticated. But overall, with the products of illicit laboratories, buyers are uncertain what drug they are getting, in what strength, or with what it has been adulterated.

Illegal manufacture is directed ultimately toward the dealers ('pushers') who sell the drugs on the street. However, a secondary market for some drugs comprises a very small number of dishonest pharmacists or wholesalers who buy counterfeit drugs that are considerably cheaper than the regular pharmaceuticals and pass them off to customers as the legitimate product.

It is important to note that not all drugs available on the street are manufactured illicitly. Many legitimate pharmaceutical products are diverted to the illicit market in the course of distribution, stolen, or obtained on forged prescriptions.

IDENTIFICATION AND ANALYSIS OF DRUGS

Visual identification of drug preparations

Generally speaking, legally produced drugs can be identified much more easily than illegal drugs, for illegal drugs are usually unlabeled and devoid of the identifying marks which are being used increasingly for the legal products. Occasionally, however, illicit producers do attempt to identify their products for the street market: for example, 'Raggedy Ann' was a dosage form of LSD on blotting paper bearing the drawing of a doll. Illicit producers may also counterfeit the size, colour, shape, and markings of the dosage form for a particular legal product, using discarded punch-and-die sets or using the original capsules emptied and refilled or adulterated. In most cases, it is impossible to identify

visually a drug substance that is encountered outside of legitimate channels.

The problem of reliability in illegal drugs

On the illegal drug market, reliability is a serious problem for the buyer, because neither buyer nor pusher can be certain of the identity, purity, or potency of the drug being sold.

Purity is most likely to be a serious problem when the drug is in liquid form intended for injection. Unsanitary material and insoluble diluents are a major source of drug-related infections and associated tissue damage among those who inject drugs. Even with drugs taken orally, however, it is possible to become extremely ill from impurities mixed in with the desired drug.

In addition, even when the desired drug is sold to the user with no misrepresentation and without impurities, there remains the question of potency or dose level. The ideal drug preparation from the user's viewpoint is one potent enough to give the desired effect but not so potent that it constitutes an overdose. If the dose is at the appropriate level, little damage is likely to be sustained. With drugs which create physical dependence, such as heroin, if the potency of the dose is far below the accustomed level, the user may go into a withdrawal state. Conversely, if the potency is far above the accustomed level, the user can die from overdose. Heroin in street samples shows a wide variation in potency. Discrete doses may contain as little as 3% or as much as 90% heroin. Yet drug users often may not be aware of this: and even when they are, few are capable of checking a drug's potency.

Users' ignorance about the identity, purity, and potency of street drugs leads to greater and more frequent health-related problems than can be attributed to the pharmacological actions and effects of the drugs themselves. Overdose, life-threatening drug interactions, infections, and tissue damage are everyday results of users' not being able to depend on the reliability of the drugs available to them.

Laboratory identification and analysis of drug products

Law enforcement activities concerned with monitoring the distribution of illicit drugs have resulted in the development of the science of 'pillistics'. The punch-and-die sets employed in the production of tablets produce characteristic marks on the tablets that can be used to identify them in much the same way that rifling marks on bullets can be used to identify weapons.

However, the most satisfactory approach to identifying drugs with real certainty is a detailed, modern laboratory characterization of the actual drug substances. This approach is useful:

- whenever medical, community, or legal professionals or others concerned with drug abusers or drug-abuse situations need to know what drug substance has invaded their communities and has affected or may affect their clients;

- whenever it is necessary to determine what drug is involved in a case of drug poisoning so that proper therapeutic procedures can be instituted;

- whenever it is necessary to determine what substances were in a victim's body at time of death in order to assess what role these substances may have played in the death itself;

- whenever law enforcement agencies require a definitive characterization of a drug product so that they can monitor its distribution and criminal use.

Qualitative analysis involves identification of the drug substances present in the dosage form or body fluid presented for analysis and, in some cases, the nature of contaminants. The identification process often begins with establishing the class of drugs to which the sample belongs (e.g., narcotic analgesics) and only then focuses on the specific drug (e.g., heroin, as opposed to codeine or morphine). The process of qualitative analysis becomes more difficult if one has no idea of the nature of the substance to be analyzed. The systematic but laborious procedures available are often too time-consuming to be helpful especially in medical emergencies. Often a physician who needs an analysis for an immediate therapeutic decision is kept waiting because there is no local analytical laboratory which maintains an extensive collection of reference drug samples for purposes of comparison. In that situation the physician will engage in symptomatic treatment (maintaining breathing, monitoring body temperature,

etc.) until recovery or until further information is available. In the absence of a satisfactory laboratory analysis, the physician may be able to obtain some useful information about the identity and quantity of the drug ingested by asking the patient or friends of the patient (although such information is subject to the limitations noted above) and by examining drug materials found in the patient's possession.

Qualitative analysis is further complicated by the fact that many drug preparations contain more than one drug: in such cases the component drugs of the sample must usually be separated before they can be identified. A further complication relates to the greater potency of some of the newer synthetic and semi-synthetic compounds. As potency increases, the amount of drug present per unit dose decreases. Thus there may be only a minute amount of material available to analyze.

A wide range of analytical technologies are employed in this process. They range from classical color and crystal tests (which tend to be of low specificity and sensitivity), through paper, thin-layer, and gas-liquid chromatographic methods, spectrofluorometry, and infrared and ultraviolet spectrophotometry, to X-ray diffraction and mass spectrometry (the last often coupled to a gas-chromatograph/computer system).

While qualitative data establish only the identity of the drug or drugs present in the sample (and in some cases impurities and/or adjuvants), quantitative analysis establishes how much is present. Thus, quantitative analysis is often as important a tool as qualitative analysis. It permits assessment of the quantity of the drug present in the system at a specific time, and can therefore shed some light on the role of the drug in the event under investigation. In medical emergencies, given knowledge of the concentration of drug in plasma and of the usual plasma half-life of that drug, the physician can estimate the size of the original dose and the time it will take for the patient's drug level to be reduced to an inconsequential level.

Techniques which are widely used for quantitative analysis of drugs include several which are also used in qualitative analysis, notably ultraviolet spectrophotometry, colorimetry, and gas-liquid chromatography (the last often coupled to a mass-spectrometer/computer system). In addition, many classical colorimetric methods of quantitation continue to be used to some extent. Although thin-layer or paper chromatography is used primarily for separation and identification of drugs, new methods are being employed which involve the scanning of these chromatograms by various detectors which permit quantitation of the materials present.

DIFFERENT WAYS DRUGS CAN BE CLASSIFIED: METHODS/CATEGORIES OF DRUG CLASSIFICATION

As the number of drugs available to us increases along with ever greater detailed knowledge of their effects, it has become desirable to classify them in various ways, partly as a means of simplification when referring to them in special contexts and partly as a means of delineating and emphasizing the relationships between the properties of different drugs.

Each classification yields important information with respect to the source, function, or effect of a given drug. The different classifications reflect the distinctive needs of different scientific or social contexts. There are seven basic drug classifications.

1. Classification by origin

Drugs derived from natural sources such as plants are often classified by source or origin. The term 'opiate' is an example of classification by origin, the source of all true opiates being the latex of the opium poppy, *Papaver somniferum*. Yet, as this classification reflects only the source, it may include many compounds with diverse actions.

Opium, the dried latex from the poppy, contains a number of alkaloids, including morphine, its most potent analgesic constituent; papaverine, a smooth-muscle relaxant; and codeine, an effective antitussive (cough-suppressant) agent with essentially lower analgesic potency than morphine. All these drugs are referred to as opiates, with the term reflecting their common natural source. Frequently the source name is applied not only to these drugs but also to semi-synthetic compounds such as heroin and to entirely synthetic compounds such as methadone or

meperidine. However, some purists insist that the synthetic drugs, which are not actually obtained from opium but only mimic the effects of opium alkaloids, should be termed 'opioids', or opiate-like drugs, and should not be referred to as opiates.

2. Classification by action prototype

This type of classification is generally used to compare a newly discovered or developed drug to an older drug, usually on the basis of similarity of overt effects as assessed by drug screening procedures. There are a number of standard drugs, such as atropine and amphetamine, against which the actions of other drugs can be compared. For example, tetrahydrocannabinol (THC), the major active principle of marijuana, is often described as having an atropine-like effect because, like atropine, it can speed up the heart and dry the mouth. In classification by prototype, marijuana or THC could therefore be listed under atropine-like drugs. Classification by prototype is generally an early designation which is discarded as soon as more specific information about the drug is known.

3. Classification by therapeutic use

Although classification of a drug by its therapeutic use is convenient for medical personnel, it often does not reflect accurately the nature of the nonmedical use and abuse of the drug. For example, amphetamine, a major drug of abuse, is often classified clinically as an anorexiant (appetite suppressant); yet its abuse is primarily based on its psychoactive stimulant effects. Similarly, morphine is commonly classified as a narcotic analgesic (pain killer); yet its considerable abuse arises from its effect as a euphoriant. Moreover, many drugs have more than one therapeutic use and must therefore be included in several therapeutic classes. Thus, preparations derived from opium are sometimes included in the class of antidiarrheal agents because of their efficacy in stopping diarrhea, or in the class of antitussive agents because of their efficacy in cough suppression.

Frequently, the therapeutic or medical use of a drug is dependent on an effect which is quite undesirable from the point of view of the nonmedical user. For example, while chronic users take narcotic analgesics in order to achieve euphoria, at the same time they frequently experience great discomfort from the constipating effect — the same effect for which the drugs are often prescribed in the treatment of moderate to severe diarrhea.

4. Classification by site of drug action

Classification by site of action is of limited usefulness, for any one drug may have an effect on several different areas in the body. Cocaine, for example, has both CNS-stimulant effects and local-anesthetic properties; therefore, to categorize it as a CNS stimulant tells only one part of the story. In addition, several drugs chemically very different from each other and with markedly differing mechanisms of action and/or net effects may affect the same tissue. For example, the classification 'CNS stimulant' is very general and covers such widely disparate drugs as cocaine, amphetamine, and strychnine.

5. Classification by chemical structure

Many purely synthetic compounds with no alternative natural source are classified by the chemical structure of the parent synthetic compound. The barbiturates are a good example of this type of classification: all drugs belonging to this group are named after the parent compound, barbituric acid, because they all share a common core structure. Pharmacological activity may vary both quantitatively and qualitatively within such a grouping, however. Barbituric acid, for example, unlike the barbiturates that derive from it, does not have sedative/hypnotic properties.

6. Classification by mechanism of action

This classification, which is based on an analysis of how the drug produces its effects, is the ideal method of classification, although it is the least used. The problem is that for most drugs we do not understand the mechanism of their action, although a major emphasis of current pharmacological research is the investigation of this area. One drug normally classified by mechanism of action is tranylcypromine (Parnate). From the mechanism perspective, this drug is classified as a monoamine oxidase (MAO) inhibitor — that is, a substance that renders the MAO system in the body less active. The MAO system works in the following way. Certain amines which occur as normal body constituents, as well as some which occur in everyday foods, must normally be destroyed by the MAO system. The amines in wine and aged cheese, for example, if not destroyed, can produce a severe and sometimes fatal hypertensive crisis. To classify tranylcypromine by its mechanism of action, therefore, is to underline to the physician some of the properties and risks associated with the drug and the need to instruct the patient carefully in the foods to be avoided.

This method of classification defines a profile of various drug activities some of which may be useful and others of which may be quite undesirable.

7. Classification by street name of drug

Nonmedical use of drugs has also given us a term of classification which emerges from the drug subculture and especially from the street drug market. The slang names coined in these environments reflect a variety of associations, as in the numerous names for marijuana — pot, weed, Mary Jane, etc. Sometimes, however, these names do indicate pharmacological effects. 'Speed', for example, is a reasonable description of the effect on the central nervous system of the stimulant drug methamphetamine. By a similar logic, sedative hypnotic drugs are referred to as 'downers'.

Multiple classification

Heroin is an example of a drug which can be classified in several ways, in accordance with the above headings. Under classification by origin, heroin is an opiate. Under chemical structure, it is of the morphine type. Under therapeutic use, it is a narcotic analgesic as well as an antidiarrheal agent. Under site of action, it can be classified as both a CNS depressant and a gastrointestinal drug. Under mechanism of action, however, there is no clear-cut classification, because the mechanism of action of heroin and other narcotic analgesics is not yet fully understood. Each classification reveals an important piece of information about the drug's impact. Even some street names suggest information about the drug's effect. For example, 'smack' describes the sudden extremely intense physical sensation that heroin produces almost immediately after intravenous injection. Therefore, to understand fully the nature of the drug and its effects, it is useful to be familiar with all of the methods of classification.

The infective complications of drug misuse

Ray P. Brettle

Consultant in Infectious Diseases and Senior Lecturer, Department of Medicine,
Edinburgh University, City Hospital, Edinburgh

This paper focuses mainly on AIDS and the ways in which it is connected with drug users and misusers. It discusses the spread of the virus, the management of the infection itself and the outlook for the future.

The infections associated with drug misuse usually occur as a consequence of the method by which the drug is administered. For instance the use of animal excreta as fertilizer in the cultivation of marijuana has resulted in its contamination by Salmonella with subsequent outbreaks of gastroenteritis. In the main, however, the infections associated with drug misuse centre around the use of non-sterile equipment such as needles, syringes, spoons, cups, etc. in the preparation and administration of drugs by injection. The use of non-sterile equipment and solutions allows bacteria such as the Staphylococcus, which is the cause of skin boils, direct entry into the user's blood stream, skin or muscles. These organisms may then produce life threatening bacterial infections.

The sharing of equipment such as needles or syringes between users allows the spread of a number of blood-borne viruses. Two practices favour this spread, firstly washing the heroin out of the syringe by repeatedly drawing back and injecting the user's own blood. This results in heavy contamination of the equipment with blood which can then be passed on to the next user. Secondly the practice of washing the equipment in a communal glass or bowl of water which rapidly becomes contaminated with blood.

The most well known blood-borne virus associated with needle drug abuse is Hepatitis B virus which results in hepatitis, i.e. inflammation of the liver. The virus probably only produces an identifiable illness in about 10 per cent of those infected but individuals may be infectious for a period of weeks, months, or years and the sharing of equipment during this time is an ideal method of spread. The illness may be mild or produce death rapidly. A small number of individuals go on to develop chronic hepatitis which may lead on to cirrhosis or a scarred liver and to a premature death.

More recently another blood-borne virus, the AIDS virus or the Human Immunodeficiency Virus has been spreading through drug misusers via similar practices.

AIDS

AIDS or the Acquired Immunodeficiency Syndrome is a remarkable disease not only for its effect on patients but also for its dramatic effect on society. Since its first description there has been considerable lay and medical publicity about AIDS, much of it inaccurate. The headline from a *Reader's Digest* article 'AIDS — The Plague of Fear' succinctly summarizes the problem. This fear persists despite the reassuring evidence which has been widely publicized that it is not a highly contagious condition.

The original description of AIDS or the Acquired Immune Deficiency Syndrome appeared in 1981 and described patients from New York and California with an unusual skin tumour or an unusual form of pneumonia. These conditions were suggestive of susceptibility to infection, i.e. immunodeficiency. The connection between the two groups was that they were all young male homosexuals with a mean age of 32 years. The first nine cases of AIDS amongst drug abusers were diagnosed retrospectively in 1980 and four of these were also homosexuals. By the end of 1986 there were more than 30 000 cases of AIDS known in the world, 29 000 of them in the USA, more than 3000 in Europe and nearly 600 in the UK. The number of cases associated with drug abuse in the USA increased from 29 in 1981, to 148 in 1982, 324 in 1983 and over 4500 by the end of 1986.

Between 1983 and 1984 the virus of AIDS was isolated and characterized. There have been a profusion of names used for this virus but recently Human Immunodeficiency Virus or HIV has been adopted.

The isolation of the virus has allowed the development of a variety of tests to detect those that have been exposed to the virus without developing AIDS. The virus is transmitted in three ways; by sexual intercourse, by exposure to contaminated blood and from mothers to their newborn children. The groups most at risk in the USA have been homosexuals (70 per cent of cases), drug abusers (17 per cent), recipients of blood products (5 per cent), children of AIDS cases, heterosexual intercourse and unknown causes (8 per cent).

AIDS AND THE UNITED KINGDOM

To date, unlike the USA 90 per cent of the patients with AIDS notified in the United Kingdom have involved homosexuality or bisexuality and only 1 per cent of such reports have implicated Intravenous Drug Misuse or IDM alone as a high risk activity. Only 2.5 per cent of the AIDS cases have been diagnosed in Scotland. In England and Wales IDM represents only 2 per cent of reports of those infected with HIV and this contrasts markedly with the position in Scotland in which over 60 per cent of those infected with HIV have implicated IDM. Sixty per cent of those reports have come from Edinburgh.

AIDS AND DRUG MISUSE

The first indications that Edinburgh had a particular problem came with the finding that over 40 per cent of haemophiliacs had acquired the virus between 1983 and 1984 after being treated solely with locally produced blood products. In 1985 and 1986 surveys found that between 38 and 52 per cent of Edinburgh and 39 per cent of Dundee drug misusers had been infected with HIV.

The average age of drug abusers in Edinburgh is 25 years, 24 years for those found to be infected and 28 years for those not infected. The average age for starting intravenous drug abuse is around 19 years, 17 for those infected and 21 years for those not infected. One-third of drug misusers are female and at any one time only about one-third are currently still misusing drugs.

By comparison only 4.5 per cent of drug misusers in Glasgow and 10 per cent in England and Wales are infected with HIV. This geographical variation of infection amongst misusers has also been noted in Europe and the USA, for instance the overall incidence of IDM associated AIDS is 17 per cent but it is 72 per cent in New York and only 2 per cent in California.

In order to attempt to understand some of the reasons for these differences it is important to appreciate that drug misuse in Scotland in general and in Edinburgh in particular is different from England. Intravenous drug misuse with heroin appears to predominate in Edinburgh, and important differences in the habit of sharing of needles seems to exist.

Comparisons of self-reported habits between Edinburgh and Glasgow or Edinburgh and South London reveal considerably more sharing of needles and syringes in Edinburgh. For instance, the sharing of equipment occurred 46 times per month in Edinburgh compared with only 15 times per month in Glasgow. In addition sharing occurred with twice as many individuals, 14 versus 7 per month. Forty per cent of Edinburgh's drug misusers shared daily whilst only 30 per cent of South London misusers had shared in the last three months. There is supportive medical evidence of this intense sharing of equipment in Edinburgh misusers from the high rate of markers for previous Hepatitis B infections currently between 60–80 per cent as well as a definite increase in the rate of skin sepsis and heart infections (endocarditis) in 1983–4.

Historically, drug misusers report that needles and syringes have been legally unavailable within Edinburgh since around 1981 to 1982 when a surgical supplies shop ceased trading and pharmacists were generally unwilling to supply misusers. There appears to have been an attempt to control IDM by limiting the supply of equipment. Misusers also report that equipment was commonly removed from them by the police during searches and then destroyed. Possession of equipment contaminated with heroin may be used as evidence of illicit use and misusers might then give evidence against a supplier. This resulted in suppliers (pushers) forcing misusers to use drugs on site so that on leaving the premises they were free of any incriminating evidence. Unfortunately, because of the limited supply of equipment considerable sharing occurred; possibly only one or two sets of equipment for all the pusher's clients which could number 20 to 40 per day. There were also large gatherings of misusers, anything from five to twenty, in the style of American 'shooting galleries' where one set of equipment was passed around.

With this background it is perhaps not entirely surprising, therefore, that when in 1983 HIV was introduced into Edinburgh it spread rapidly as a consequence of the habit of equipment sharing.

CONSEQUENCES OF THE HIV EPIDEMIC

The consequences for Edinburgh in particular as well as the rest of the UK of this epidemic are considerable.

(a) The most immediate consequence of the AIDS epidemic was the threat to the blood bank. The Government's response when antibody testing became available was to introduce screening of all donated blood in October 1985. The necessity to screen individuals extends into other areas such as organ donation, bone banks, semen banks, etc. In the South-East of Scotland the positivity rate amongst voluntary bood donors is 1/13 000 and this compares with 1/40 000 in the West of Scotland and 1/50 000 for the UK as a whole.

(b) With the screening of blood donations came the necessity to discourage individuals in high risk groups from donating blood, since such individuals may be infectious but not be detected by the HIV tests. It was, therefore, necessary to provide voluntary confidential screening and counselling at alternative testing cen-

tres to prevent the Blood Transfusion Services being used as a testing facility.

(c) In January 1986 in response to the AIDS problem, the Pharmaceutical Society in Scotland recommended to its members that needles and syringes should be sold to drug misusers.

(d) Now that a body of infected individuals has been established spread to other individuals will occur:

(1) The rapid rise of HIV infection seen between 1983−5 in Edinburgh IDMs will continue over the next two years if nothing is done and HIV positivity rates will approach those of Hepatitis B which are currently 60−80 per cent. Over 700 HIV infected individuals have been identified in Scotland and over 500 in Edinburgh. Estimates of the size of the drug abuse community in Edinburgh are poor but it is thought that there are probably at least from 2000 to 2500. The three surveys from Edinburgh on HIV infection in drug misusers would suggest a level of 50 per cent infection and there are therefore probably already 1000 infected individuals in Edinburgh.

(2) Unlike IDM itself or Hepatitis B, *all* HIV individuals are infected for life; therefore, the size of the infected group continues to grow. Estimates of new misusers entering the community are scarce and the best that can be made is an expansion of around 10 per cent per year.

(3) Geographical spread to other misusers in other cities is occurring. Forty-four of 191 Edinburgh based misusers had shared needles in 48 other cities and 52 per cent of these were positive for the HIV antibody.

(4) Because the majority of drug misusers in Edinburgh seem to be heterosexual we are faced with the fact that heterosexual spread will occur, but at what rate?

The number of AIDS cases involving heterosexual contact is currently small, only 1 per cent of men and 16 per cent of women in the USA. The data from the sexual partners of well but HIV infected haemophiliacs suggests that 6−10 per cent of the partners are affected at present. The experience in Edinburgh suggests that about 15 per cent of regular sexual contacts of current or ex-drug misusers have acquired the virus and since the virus arrived in Edinburgh in 1983 this suggests a transfer rate of around 5 per cent per year.

Whilst the general heterosexual population cannot, at present, be considered at great risk, unchecked this may not remain so for long. HIV may become a general STD and it appears as if this is beginning to occur in the USA. The US military introduced HIV screening of recruits in October 1985 and the prevalence was found to be 1.6/1000. Perhaps of more importance was the fact that the male/female ratio was 3/1 whereas in AIDS patients at present, it is around 13/1. This suggests either that HIV is already a heterosexual disease or drug abuse is more prevalent than hitherto suspected.

(5) Spread of the virus to newborn children occurs and this is occurring in Edinburgh because one-third of the affected population are female. The data on transmission to children is also scant. There is evidence that the virus can infect the child before and during birth as well as after birth via breast milk. The rate of infection is less well documented but is estimated at around 50 per cent. Definite infection cannot be ascertained for up to 12 months because of the problem of passive transfer of maternal antibodies and exposure to blood at birth.

(6) The remaining method of spread out of high risk groups is horizontally to non-sexual and non-drug abusing individuals. Whilst the risks are small they are certainly not perceived as so by the medical and general public. A household survey of contacts of AIDS patients revealed no non-sexual spread whereas, by comparison in hepatitis B, spread to family members is around 37 per cent. Similarly, the risks for Health Care Workers involved in the direct care of AIDS patients is only 1 per cent compared with 30 per cent for hepatitis. The commonest mode of transmission to Health Care Workers is by needle stick injury.

MANAGEMENT OF HIV INFECTION

Effective therapy is not yet available for AIDS or asymp-
tomatic HIV infection and therefore, as a consequence of available information the current management of HIV is based on (1) the prevention of spread and (2) the prevention of progression to AIDS once infected with HIV. Many of the measures such as prevention of pregnancy and barrier contraception are effective for both aims and are particularly important for a heterosexual population.

The three most important methods of transmitting the virus are via sexual intercourse, blood spread via contaminated needles etc. and to newborn children from infected mothers. Measures which have been suggested to reduce transmission are

- a reduction in the number of sexual partners
- avoidance of anal intercourse for homosexuals and heterosexuals
- use of barrier contraceptives especially condoms or sheaths combined with spermicides
- avoidance of needle and syringe sharing
- avoidance of pregnancy with the increased chance of infecting the child

Obviously the less sexual partners the less individuals are at risk. Anal intercourse is a particularly effective method of transferring the virus between individuals and transfer of virus during intercourse is hindered by barrier contraceptives and the use of spermicides which have been shown to kill the virus. Pregnancy in an infected female is an effective method of infecting the child and where possible infected females should avoid pregnancy. The majority of these measures are not contentious except perhaps in the methods of informing the population.

A more major problem in dealing with some of these patients is how to cope with their addiction. Perhaps the most contentious issue is how to reduce needle sharing amongst drug abusers without condoning illegal acts.

Abstinence has, until now, been the major goal of dealing with misusers but with the appearance of HIV these goals need to be adjusted to one of 'risk or harm reduction'. Conversion from homosexuality to heterosexuality is not proposed as a means of dealing with HIV and in a similar way a message based on abstinence is currently unrealistic. The *eventual* goal is still one of abstinence but initially it is important to start with a more realistic goal identified for each patient. Depending upon the individual, this may encompass substitution therapy on a long- or short-term basis in order to avoid needle drug abuse, or the provision of needles and syringes to reduce sharing.

Education is important not only with regard to the dangers of sharing but also concerning the need for cleanliness and sterility in the use of equipment. However, exhorting abusers to use clean equipment is pointless unless they are available and this is not the case in some parts of the UK. Equally the widespread availability of equipment is not the only measure necessary since this is the situation in Italy and sharing is still common. Education and availability must go hand in hand. Because of the concern about the dangers for the general public of large numbers of infected needles, exchange systems have been used in Amsterdam and Edinburgh to not only provide equipment safely but also to increase the access to misusers for further education efforts.

Once infected there are a number of measures which are suggested as ways of reducing progression to AIDS. Many of them are not totally proven but seem prudent at the moment:

- avoidance of anal intercourse for heterosexuals and homosexuals
- avoidance of recurrent infections such as venereal disease.

In a heterosexual population other measures may be more important such as:

- the avoidance of pregnancy and
- the use of barrier contraceptives to reduce any further infection with HIV and to reduce the largely theoretical possibility that normal semen increases females' susceptibility to infections.
- the avoidance of needle drug abuse in order to reduce the possibility of further infection with HIV from sharing, to reduce the increased susceptibility to infection from drug abuse and to reduce the exposure to recurrent bacterial infections from drug abuse.

One-third of the patients with HIV in Edinburgh are female and the prevention of pregnancy is important on the grounds of progression to AIDS in the mother as well as the prevention of transmission to the child.

In the USA only 25 per cent of HIV infected mothers were well 2.5 years after delivery. However, these mothers were selected by the fact that they had already produced one child with AIDS and this data may not apply exactly to Edinburgh. Despite what seemed to be adequate counselling unwanted pregnancies have occurred and as with other IDM problems it is necessary to do more than just offer the advice such as 'avoid pregnancy' or 'use barrier contraceptives'.

The use of barrier contraceptives may reduce progression by preventing further exposure to the virus or other sexually transmitted diseases. The latter have been shown in homosexuals to hasten the onset of AIDS in infected individuals. There is some evidence that normal male semen increases the susceptibility to infection for normal females and this is another reason for infected women to use barrier contraceptives.

As with the prevention of spread, tackling drug abuse is very important in preventing progression to AIDS once infected. There is evidence from New York that continued injecting drug abuse hastens the onset of AIDS in those infected. Thus the major therapeutic endeavour in those already infected is in fact to reduce needle drug abuse, if necessary by prescribing substitute oral drugs rather than providing clean equipment.

With the arrival of AIDS, coordination in tackling the drug problem is a priority for society. For instance any mismatch between the regions in drug policy may reduce the price of heroin or increase needles and this may encourage the movement of infected individuals around the country further spreading the virus. Similarly the rising price of heroin, often used as a parameter of the effectiveness of the Customs and Excise service may force users to switch from the safe practice of smoking or sniffing heroin to injecting. Similarly a sudden increase in needles in areas where injecting is uncommon could again alter local practices. It is important therefore that before decisions are made the local situation should be evaluated.

THE FUTURE

Many individuals think this is a problem that will go away in time because the patients are all going to die.

This assumes total control of spread, something we have only once managed with an infection, i.e. smallpox. There are two reasons why this problem will remain with us for the rest of our working lives.

(1) Although the mean incubation period for AIDS is four years the current maximum recorded is fourteen years which means that the patients currently infected will not all present with AIDS until the year 2000.

(2) A large number of infected individuals are now present in the community. Even if 10 per cent die each year and spread is not prevented then a steady state will be achieved because it will only require 10 per cent spread per year for all methods, i.e. old misusers new misusers, heterosexual, homosexual and vertical spread.

The problems facing society with regard to AIDS are many and varied but IDM introduces a number of specific problems that society must consider. IDM must now be viewed in the light of the fact that AIDS is now the number one cause of death amongst drug misusers in New York and overshadows the problems of overdose, Hepatitis B and endocarditis. Some of the problems that must be considered are:

(1) How to educate individuals into 'safe drug misuse' without encouraging or increasing IDM.

(2) Is an increase in the availability of needles and syringes which is designed to curtail the spread of HIV possible without an increase in IDM?

(3) Is it now necessary to alter our attitudes towards opiate drug misuse? Is decriminalization and controlled availability of opiate use, similar to the restrictions on alcohol, the way forward?

(4) Is the use of substitution therapy a viable method of eliminating heroin related prostitution?

(5) Will a non-caring attitude by society towards HIV infected individuals provoke the use of 'their infectivity' as the ultimate weapon against such a society?

REFERENCES AND FURTHER READING

Acheson, E.D. (1986) AIDS: A Challenge for the Public Health. *Lancet*, 22 March vol. 1, pp. 662–7.

AIDS: Medical Briefing (April 1985) The Terrence Higgins Trust. BM AIDS, London WC1N 3XX.

Curran, J.W., Morgan, M., Hardy, A.M., Jaffe, H.W., Darrow, W.W. and Dowdele, W.R. (1985) The epidemiology of Aids. *Science*, 229:1352–7.

Drucker, E. (1986) AIDS and addiction in New York City. *Am. J. Drug Alcohol Abuse*, **12**(1&2), 165–81.

Farthing, C. (1986) The HIV antibody test — how to use it and what it means. *Maternal and Child Health*, pp. 354–9.

HIV Infection in Scotland (1986) *Report of the Scottish Committee on HIV Infection and Intravenous Drug Misuse*. Scottish Home and Health Department. September.

Jeralis, D.C., Friedman, S.R. and Hopkins, W. (1985) Risk reduction for the Acquired Immunodeficiency Syndrome among intravenous drug users. *Annals of Internal Medicine*, vol. 103, no. 5, pp. 755–9.

Miller, D. (1986) How to counsel patients about HIV disease. *Maternal and Child Health*, October, pp. 322–30.

Miller, D., Weber, J. and Green, J. (eds) (1986) *The Management of Aids Patients*. Macmillan Press. London.

Benzodiazepine withdrawal

HEATHER ASHTON

Honorary Consultant in Clinical Pharmacology, Newcastle Health Authority, and Senior Lecturer in Psychopharmacology, University of Newcastle Upon Tyne

This paper discusses the problems involved in withdrawal from benzodiazepines (minor tranquillizers). It describes the outcome of 50 patients who completed a course of supervised withdrawal, often after many years of use.

INTRODUCTION

Dependence upon prescribed benzodiazepines is now recognized as a major clinical problem,[1-4] involving perhaps half a million patients in Britain.[5-8] There is growing agreement with the view that 'most patients currently taking benzodiazepines should stop them'.[8] However, little information is available on the outcome of withdrawal, and no large-scale, long-term results have been published.

The reported outcome of benzodiazepine withdrawal in patients referred to psychiatric clinics appears discouraging. Higgitt, Lader and Fonagy,[8] from a review of the literature and personal experience of 60 patients over seven years, concluded that only one-third of patients are free of problems after withdrawal. Of the remaining two-thirds, about 50 per cent need antidepressants and many return to benzodiazepine use. These results may not be representative of the whole population concerned. It seems likely that the majority manage to stop benzodiazepines on their own, or with help from their general practitioners and/or tranquillizer support groups.[9] However, there have been no investigations on how this group has fared.

Yet is it clearly important to know the outcome of benzodiazepine withdrawal. Is it worth spending time and trouble on benzodiazepine withdrawal if most patients relapse back on to benzodiazepines, develop

Reproduced by permission of the Editor, *British Journal of Addiction*, June 1987.

psychiatric problems, or need treatment with other more expensive and more toxic drugs?

In view of the dearth of information, it is relevant to report the intermediate term outcome of a third population of benzodiazepine-dependent patients who were referred to a Clinical Pharmacology Unit. This report is not intended as a controlled study of withdrawal symptoms or methods; indeed, these questions are largely irrelevant to the issue of outcome, since in practice patients withdraw in a variety of ways and suffer a range of transient or prolonged withdrawal symptoms.[1,3,4,5,10] Instead, it records the clinical outcome in 50 consecutive patients who attempted benzodiazepine withdrawal and were followed up for from ten months to 3.5 years and examines some variables which might be expected to influence outcome.

PATIENTS

There were 40 females and 10 males, aged 20-72 years (mean age 45.92 years). The patients had been taking prescribed benzodiazepines for 1-22 years (mean duration 9.76 years). Benzodiazepine dosages at the start of withdrawal varied from 4 mg diazepam daily to 5 mg lorazepam plus 30 mg diazepam daily (approximately equivalent to 80 mg diazepam daily).[11] The patients themselves all wished to stop taking benzodiazepines, to which they attributed adverse effects. None abused alcohol or other drugs. All except one were successful in withdrawing completely. Three patients relapsed after withdrawal. One patient committed suicide and two died of unrelated causes following withdrawal. The remaining 43 patients have been off benzodiazepines for over three years (10 patients), two to three years (7 patients), one to two years (20 patients) and 10–12 months (6 patients).

HISTORY AND SYMPTOMS ON PRESENTATION

All the patients had symptoms on presentation. These symptoms were the reason for referral and included the full range of psychological and somatic symptoms described previously in relation to chronic benzodiazepine use and withdrawal.[3,4] Most had made previous attempts at dosage reduction or complete withdrawal and had found that this exacerbated their symptoms.

Several features of interest confirm and extend the findings of a previous report.[3] Ten of the present series of patients, while on chronic benzodiazepine medication, had taken drug overdoses requiring hospital admission (sometimes on several occasions); only two of these had a definite history of depressive illness before they were prescribed benzodiazepines, although several had been prescribed antidepressant and other psychotropic drugs while on benzodiazepines. Ten had incapacitating agoraphobia which first developed after several years on benzodiazepines. Nine patients had undergone extensive gastroenterological investigations for gastrointestinal symptoms which had ultimately been attributed to 'irritable bowel', diverticulitis or hiatus hernia. Three had been referred for neurological investigations and had been told that they had multiple sclerosis (not subsequently confirmed). Although most patients complained of paraesthesiae in the extremities associated with panic attacks, two women aged 64 and 63 had constant severe burning pain in the hands and feet which regressed slowly after benzodiazepine withdrawal. It was also of interest that triazolam taken chronically in doses of only 0.25 mg nightly provoked typical symptoms (including aggressiveness, hallucinations, poor memory and concentration, paraesthesiae, panic attacks and headaches) in one patient. In this case these symptoms subsided almost immediately on stopping the triazolam.

DRUG WITHDRAWAL

Management of withdrawal was individually tailored for each patient. The duration of the withdrawal period ranged from one week in a patient taking triazolam (0.25 mg nocte) to 15 months in a patient taking a combination of lorazepam 5 mg and ketazolam 30 mg daily. The general procedure was to change all patients taking other benzodiazepines to an approximately equivalent dose of diazepam[11] and then to reduce diazepam dosage gradually. One patient found it impossible after three attempts, to change from lorazepam (1.5 mg daily) to diazepam. 'Equivalent' doses of diazepam,[8,11] whether introduced slowly or rapidly, paradoxically induced a state of acute anxiety and panic combined with extreme drowsiness. This patient was finally withdrawn directly from lorazepam by 0.125 mg decrements.

Various drugs were used temporarily in individual patients for symptomatic control, as described previously.[3,8] These included proranolol, non-benzodiazepine hypnotics, tricyclic antidepressants, clonidine, and analgesics. These drugs helped to control certain individual symptoms but were not successful in alleviating the withdrawal syndrome as a whole. Many patients (19, 38 per cent) took no additional drugs during the course of withdrawal.

Apart from pharmacological advice, the mainstay of management was the provision of frequent consultations and repeated encouragement. About 60 per cent of the patients also attended a tranquillizer support group.

CLINICAL COURSE

In general, the period of benzodiazepine dosage reduction caused only slight exacerbation of symptoms already present before withdrawal.

After withdrawal, the clinical course was protracted; symptoms persisted for over a year in some patients, though diminishing in intensity. Depression was common during this period. One patient committed suicide; three were diagnosed by psychiatrists as having major depressive disorders, and 17 were prescribed antidepressant drugs (usually for not more than 3–6 months). However, the depression lifted in most patients within a year and none have taken drug overdoses since withdrawal.

Gastrointestinal complaints were also frequent but declined gradually in most patients including those who had had 'irritable bowel' for years. Similarly, agoraphobic symptoms abated dramatically within a year of withdrawal, even in patients who had previously been housebound, and none were incapacitated by agoraphobia at the time of follow-up.

OUTCOME

As an interim evaluation of the results of benzodiazepine withdrawal, the outcome was assessed at an arbitrary time in the first 50 patients attending the clinic. Outcome was graded into categories using the following criteria: Excellent (minimal symptoms, leading a normal life, in full-time employment where applicable, taking no regular medication); Good (some symptoms but able to lead a normal life and/or cope with a full-time job without regular medication); Moderate (better, but symptoms which interfere with life or require other drugs, such as beta-blockers or antidepressants, still present); Poor (off benzodiazepines but not improved, polysymptomatic and/or needing other psychotropic medication); Failed (relapsed or unable to withdraw benzodiazepines).

The results are shown in Table 1. The outcome was graded as excellent in 24 patients (48 per cent), good in 11 (22 per cent), moderate in 8 (16 per cent), poor in 3 (6 per cent) and failed in 4 (8 per cent). Thus, 70 per cent of this group did excellently or well after withdrawal and a further 16 per cent were moderately improved. All these patients claimed to feel better after withdrawal than when they were taking benzodiazepines and were glad they had withdrawn. One patient failed to achieve complete withdrawal and three relapsed on to regular benzodiazepine usage, one after a year and two after a month of abstinence. Five other patients temporarily took benzodiazepines one to three months after withdrawal, but all were successful at a second attempt and achieved final outcomes rated as excellent (1), good (3), and moderate (1).

RELATIONSHIPS BETWEEN OUTCOME AND OTHER VARIABLES

In the 46 patients who were successful in withdrawal, younger age was highly significantly associated with a favourable outcome. The mean age of the 35 patients whose outcome was judged good or excellent was 43.4 years (SD 11.1) while the mean age of the eleven with a moderate or poor outcome was 58.0 years (SD 13.0) ($df = 44$, $t = 3.65$, $p < 0.001$, two-tailed t-test). Nevertheless, the four patients who failed withdrawal or relapsed were all in the younger age group (mean age

Table 1   Outcome after benzodiazepine withdrawal

Grading		Definition	Number of patients
Excellent	Fully recovered	Minimal symptoms, leading normal life, full-time job, no regular medication. (May still be 'highly strung'.)	24(48%)
Good	Much better	Some symptoms but able to lead normal life, full-time job.	11(22%)
Moderate	Better	Coping but symptoms which interfere with life or require other drugs (e.g. beta-blockers, antidepressants) still present.	8(16%)
Poor	No better	Off benzodiazepines but still polysymptomatic and/or needing other psychotropic medication (e.g. antidepressants, sedative/hypnotics).	3(6%)
Failed	Relapsed, unable to withdraw	Started benzodiazepines again after withdrawal, unable to withdraw, multiple symptoms still present.	4(8%)

34.5 years), while two patients aged 64 achieved a good outcome and one aged 69, rated as excellent, was able to continue a full-time career as a distinguished author.

Somewhat surprisingly, outcome of withdrawal did not appear to be related to the duration or age of onset of benzodiazepine usage, dosage at the time of withdrawal, type of benzodiazepine, rate of withdrawal, severity of symptoms, marital status, or sex. No clear relationship was found between outcome and psychological factors. The four patients rated as failed and two of the three rated as poor had histories of psychiatric disorder but this was also true of nearly 30 per cent of patients who achieved a good or excellent outcome. Since most of the patients had been on benzodiazepines for long periods, it was difficult to obtain a reliable estimate of pre-benzodiazepine personality. The failures had all been labelled 'inadequate personality' during the course of benzodiazepine use, but so had several of the patients who achieved an excellent result.

DISCUSSION

A clear result of the present study is that a substantial majority (70 per cent) of these patients were doing well 10 months to 3.5 years after benzodiazepine withdrawal and the rate of relapse and of failure to withdraw was low (8 per cent). The more favourable outcome compared with that of Higgitt, Lader and Fonagy,[8] who found that only a third of patients were free of problems after withdrawal, may have been due to patient selection. Patients with psychiatric problems are presumably referred mainly to psychiatric departments, and most of the available data has been obtained from such patients. Patients referred to clinical pharmacology departments may have a better prognosis because they have fewer underlying psychiatric problems. (It is worth noting, however, that some patients in the present series were referred by psychiatrists.)

Secondly, the study shows that long-term benzodiazepine use is associated with a considerable morbidity. While on benzodiazepines, ten of the 50 patients had taken drug overdoses requiring hospital admission, sometimes on several occasions. Ten patients had become agoraphobic, for which several had received (unsuccessful) behavioural and other therapy. Twelve

had undergone extensive investigations in gastroenterology or neurology departments and treatment had been ineffective. None of these symptoms or behaviours were the original indication for starting on benzodiazepines but developed during chronic use. It is arguable whether the patients would have developed the symptoms over time in the absence of benzodiazepines, but the fact that they were not present before benzodiazepine use, were not amenable to treatment during benzodiazepine use, yet largely disappeared when the drugs were stopped, suggests that benzodiazepines may actually cause or aggravate a variety of psychological and psychosomatic problems.

It was difficult to quantify psychological factors leading to the initiation and continuation of benzodiazepine use. As shown in Table 1, the original indication for benzodiazepines was usually, though not exclusively, anxiety or depression. Nevertheless all patients had a variety of anxiety/depressive symptoms on presentation, and these had been gradually increasing over the years despite continuous benzodiazepine use. In the large majority of patients, these symptoms greatly improved after withdrawal. Although many patients, even those whose outcome was classed as excellent after 2–3 years, still have occasional anxiety symptoms, especially during periods of stress, they appear now to have learned to cope with stress better than when on chronic benzodiazepine medication. A large-scale, long-term comparison of anxious patients who were or were not prescribed benzodiazepines would be needed to clarify this issue. The study of Catalan and Gath[12] suggested that benzodiazepines were no more effective than brief counselling for patients with minor affective disorders seen in general practice and followed for over seven months.

It seems likely that the mechanisms for the worsening of symptoms during chronic benzodiazepine use include the development of tolerance to the anxiolytic effects, so that withdrawal symptoms emerge even in the continued presence of the drugs, and the onset of long-term adverse effects. These effects and mechanisms have been discussed elsewhere.[3,4]

Finally, the results show that it is worthwhile withdrawing benzodiazepines in motivated patients such as those in the present study. Depression may be a problem after withdrawal as previously noted[3,12] and as evidenced by one suicide and three cases of major depression in this group. Antidepressant drugs may be indicated temporarily in such cases. In general, the outcome appears to be better in younger patients, but age is no absolute bar to success. For the future, prevention of benzodiazepine dependence is clearly a preferable strategy and may be achieved by more thoughtful prescribing of benzodiazepines and by reserving them for short-term use.[13]

REFERENCES

1. Petursson, H. and Lader, M. (1981) Withdrawal from long-term benzodiazepine treatment, *British Medical Journal*, **283**, 643–5.
2. Owen, R.T. and Tyrer, P. (1983) Benzodiazepine dependence: a review of the evidence, *Drugs*, **25**, 385–98.
3. Ashton, H. (1984) Benzodiazepine withdrawal: an unfinished story, *British Medical Journal*, **288**, 1135–40.
4. Ashton, H. (1986) Adverse effects of prolonged benzodiazepine use, *Adverse Drug Reaction Bulletin*, **118**, 440–3.
5. Tyrer, P., Owen, R. and Dawling, S. (1983) Gradual withdrawal of diazepam after long-term therapy, *Lancet*, i, 1402–6.
6. Hallstrom, C. and Lader, M.H. (1982) The incidence of benzodiazepine dependence in long-term users, *Journal of Psychiatric Treatment and Evaluation*, **4**, 293–6.
7. Balter, M.B., Manheimer, D.I., Melinger, G.D. and Uhlenhuth, E.H. (1984) A cross-national comparison of antianxiety/sedative drug use, *Current Medical Research Opinion*, **8** (Suppl. 4), 5–20.
8. Higgitt, A.C., Lader, M.H. and Fonagy, P. (1985) Clinical management of benzodiazepine dependence, *British Medical Journal*, **291**, 688–90.
9. Trickett, S. (1986) *Coming off Tranquillisers*. Thorson's Northampton.
10. Busto, U., Sellers, E.M., Naranjo, C.A., Cappell, H., Sanchez-Craig, M. and Sykora, K. (1986) Withdrawal reaction after long-term therapeutic use of benzodiazepines, *The New England Journal of Medicine*, **315**, 854–9.
11. Drug Newsletter (1985) *Benzodiazepine dependence and withdrawal — an update*, **31**, 125–8.
12. Catalan, J. and Gath, D.H. (1985) Benzodiazepines in general practice: time for decision, *British Medical Journal*, **290**, 1374–6.
13. Lader, M. and Higgitt, A.C. (1986) Management of benzodiazepine dependence — update, 1986, *British Journal of Addiction*, **81**, 7–10.

Section III

Paper 11
Unemployment and illegal drug use

DAVID F. PECK* and MARTIN A. PLANT†

Senior Lecturer;
† Senior Research Fellow, Alcohol Research Group, Department of Psychiatry, University of Edinburgh

This paper explores the relationship between unemployment and illegal drug use. Using both national statistics and the results of a detailed study in the Lothian region it shows a clear link between the two.

INTRODUCTION

From 1979/80 to 1983 a study was undertaken of the self reported alcohol, tobacco, and illicit drug use of a cohort of 1036 young people in the Lothian region. The subjects of this study were aged 15 to 16 at the beginning of the study and were followed up three to four years later. The study indicated that, though subjects who were unemployed during 1983 did not smoke or drink more heavily than other respondents, they had significantly more experience of illegal drugs such as cannabis, lysergic acid diethylamide (LSD), and opiates.

In this study we therefore investigated the relation between unemployment and illegal drug use in more detail by examining the inter-relation between duration of unemployment and the use of illegal drugs, alcohol, and tobacco. In a separate analysis national trends in unemployment were related to two indices of illegal drug use based on official statistics.

SUBJECTS AND METHODS

In 1979/80 baseline data were collected through a standardised questionnaire completed by 1036 respon-

From *British Medical Journal*, Volume 293, 11 October 1986, pp. 929–931. Reproduced by permission of the Editor.

dents, aged 15 to 16, in the Lothian region in groups of sizes ranging from 20 to 200 during school hours and under supervision by the researchers. During 1983 members of the entire study group were sought for follow up interviews. Fieldwork was undertaken by 28 trained interviewers, and data were elicited with a standardised schedule that took from 30 minutes to one hour to complete. Both the initial questionnaire and the follow up interview collected information on biographical details such as social class background, alcohol use, and tobacco and illegal drug use. The follow up interview also elicited information about educational qualifications, incomes, job histories, and unemployment. Additional details of the methodology used in the study have been given elsewhere.[1-3]

RESULTS
Prospective study in the Lothian region

Data collection Baseline data were collected from 1036 respondents in 1979/80. During 1983, 957 (92%) were reinterviewed. At both times specific items on the questionnaire were sometimes left unanswered. In 1979/80 the average number of people not answering a question about drugs was 36 (3.5%), whereas the corresponding number for 1983 (largely owing to interviewers failing to record negative answers) was 43 (4.5%). We analyse here the data collected during 1983 and compare them with those obtained during 1979/80. The 1983 data related to 929 of the 957 people who

Table 1 Duration of unemployment experienced by respondents who were unemployed when reinterviewed during 1983

Duration of unemployment (months)	No. of respondents	
	Men	Women
<1	2	1
1–3	10	8
4–6	9	8
7–12	26	13
13–24	13	17
>24	3	5
Total	63	52

were reinterviewed and from whom complete data were elicited about relevant drug use and employment. These 929 people constituted 89.7% of the original study group of 1036. The comparison of 1979/80 and 1983 data (see table 2) relates to 811 people who provided full responses during both collections of data to questions on drugs and also on their employment state during 1983. These 811 people constituted 78.3% of the original study group or 84.7% of those reinterviewed in 1983.

Unemployment and biographical traits When reinterviewed during 1983, 12% of the original study group were either unemployed or taking part in the Youth Opportunities Programme. This was equivalent to 19.2% of those who were economically active (excluding housewives and students). The modal dura-

tion of unemployment experienced by those who were unemployed at the time of reinterview was seven to 12 months for men and 13 to 24 months for women (table 1). In addition, 136 (36.7%) of the 370 men and 157 (35.4%) of the 444 women who were currently employed reported having been unemployed at some time since leaving school. During July 1983 unemployment in the Lothian region, 12.1%, was the same as the average unemployment in Britain as a whole.[4] The unemployment among young people in the United Kingdom, however, is higher than that among the overall labour force. In July 1983, 23.4% of men and 16.9% of women aged 20 to 24 were unemployed. The corresponding figures for those aged 18 to 19 were 28.7% and 21.6%, respectively.[5] Thus the study group showed a rather lower level of unemployment than that prevailing among their peers in the United Kingdom as a whole. The study group also differed from the overall population of comparable young people in the Lothian region; fewer respondents were married, and slightly more were from high socioeconomic backgrounds.

Illicit drug abuse and unemployment At the ages of 19 and 20 unemployed men were significantly more likely than other men to report having used drugs. Women, however, did not differ significantly in this respect. The significant difference among men is striking because those who were unemployed had not differed significantly from the other men when data were first collected in 1979/80. Table 2 shows these results. Men who were unemployed when reinterviewed in 1983 were also significantly more likely than other men to

Table 2   Prevalence of admitted illicit drug use among unemployed respondents 1979/80 to 1983

	No. (%) of men using illicit drugs			No. (%) of women using illicit drugs		
Year	Unemployed (n = 49)	Others (n = 331)	Significance	Unemployed (n = 34)	Others (n = 397)	Significance
1979/80	12(24.5)	53(16.0)	$\chi^2 = 2.16$ df = 1 NS	6(17.6)	49(12.3)	$\chi^2 = 0.39$ df = 1 NS
1983	26(53.1)	113(34.1)	$\chi^2 = 5.80$ df = 1 $p < 0.02$	12(35.2)	82(20.7)	$\chi^2 = 3.12$ df = 1 NS

report having used drugs such as LSD, heroin, and cocaine, which are classified under category A of the Misuse of Drugs Act 1971 (χ^2 = 12.62, df = 1, p<0.001). Unemployed women did not differ from other women in this respect (χ^2 = 0.16, df = 1, NS). The duration of unemployment for respondents who were currently unemployed was weakly but positively associated with the number of illicit drugs ever used (η = +0.27, p<0.001) and with the number of drugs used that are classified under category A of the Misuse of Drugs Act 1971 (η = +0.16, p<0.05). To further clarify the apparent relation between duration of unemployment and illicit drug use an additional analysis by partial correlation was conducted. Partial correlation produces a coefficient that describes the relation between two variables while adjusting for the effects of one or more additional variables.[6]

In this analysis the possible confounding variables were respondents' social class background and educational qualifications. Social class was defined from the socioeconomic state of the head of each respondent's household, determined from the standard classification of the Registrar General. There was still a significant but weak association between the number of illicit drugs ever used and duration of unemployment (r = 0.25, p<0.001).

Psychoactive drug use and incomes Prices and incomes have been suggested as important determinants of the use of psychoactive substances.[3,7,8] Moreover, it has been suggested that some young people in the United Kingdom do choose between legal and illegal drugs partly on the basis of their respective costs (P Rørstad, personal communication). Thorley has further suggested that there may be a 'hydraulic' relation between different drugs, whereby drug B is substituted for drug A if the price of drug A is increased or its availability is curtailed (A Thorley, personal communication). The relation between the disposable incomes and patterns of psychoactive drug use of the study group were examined. This showed that, as expected, incomes were weakly but positively correlated with the consumption of both alcohol (r = 0.11, p<0.001) and tobacco (r = 0.10, p<0.01). In contrast, high disposable income was not significantly associated with illegal drug use (r = 0.03, NS). This analysis was repeated for only unemployed respondents. Among these subjects neither alcohol nor tobacco use were

significantly related to disposable income. Illicit drug use was, however, significantly and negatively associated with income (r = 0.16, p<0.05) but only to a modest degree.

National patterns

The results of the first study were obtained from a relatively small group in one part of the United Kingdom. To examine general patterns of association, if any, between unemployment and illegal drug use some national data were compared. This comparison was based on annually published figures for the years 1970 to 1984 and relates to men and women in the United Kingdom as a whole. The data examined were as follows:

(a) Average annual unemployment. From 1970 to 1984 this increased from 2.6% to 13.1%.[9]
(b) Cautions and convictions for offences concerning drug misuse. The data from 1970 to 1972 related only to convictions. These increased from 9160 in 1970 to 25 022 in 1984[10] (Home Office, personal communication).
(c) Narcotic drug addicts reported to be receiving notifiable drugs during treatment for their dependence at 31 December each year. These increased from 1426 in 1970 to 5869 in 1984[10] (Home Office, personal communication).

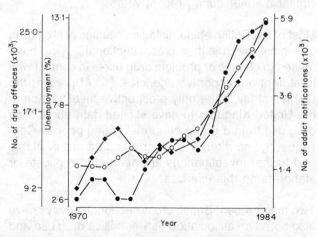

Figure 1 National unemployment, addict notifications, and drug offences, 1970 to 1984. ● = Unemployment. ○ = Addict notifications. ◆ = Drug offences.

Figure 1 shows the pattern of these three variables and indicates a close association between unemployment and these two indicators of illegal drug use. The Pearson correlation coefficients for unemployment and drug cautions or convictions and addict notifications were 0.92 and 0.96, respectively. Both correlations were significant ($p < 0.001$). Whenever changes in two variables are measured simultaneously over time the correlation between them may be spuriously high. To measure these associations while controlling for the possible confounding effect of time partial correlations were calculated. This analysis confirmed that unemployment was significantly and positively correlated with drug misuse (drug cautions or convictions: $r = 0.63$, $p < 0.01$; addict notifications: $r = 0.77$, $p < 0.001$).

DISCUSSION

The two sets of data described above produced compatible results. Both indicate that illegal drug use is associated with unemployment. In contrast, the Lothian study indicated that alcohol and tobacco use are not positively linked with unemployment,[3] a conclusion that is also supported by national data. Cigarette sales in the United Kingdom declined substantially between 1970 and 1984, and per caput alcohol consumption has also fallen since 1979[11,12] (Tobacco Research Council, personal communication). As shown in the figure unemployment and the two selected indices of illegal drug use have increased sharply and in a strikingly similar manner during recent years.

Most of the British epidemiological studies of illicit drug use have been either cross sectional[13-15] or have related to chronic or problem drug users in contact with treatment or supportive agencies.[16-18] At present the Lothian study is the only prospective investigation in the United Kingdom to have elicited data about illicit drug use from a group of normal young people. Consequently, no directly comparable data are available and further investigations are needed to replicate or elaborate on this exercise.

Two major recent British cross sectional surveys have also noted an association between illicit drug use and unemployment. The first of these, the British Crime Survey, was conducted in 1981. This showed that self reported cannabis use among unemployed respondents in Britain as a whole (but not in Scotland) was significantly higher than that among other respondents.[19]

The second survey was carried out by Research International during 1985 to assess the impact of a publicity campaign on drugs commissioned by the Central Office of Information and the Department of Health and Social Security. This study indicated, through cluster analysis, that the subgroup of respondents at the highest risk of exposure to drugs was characterised by, among other factors, above average unemployment.[20] Additional evidence was collected during 1985 by a survey of 212 young people attending youth clubs and centres in the London borough of Tower Hamlets. This indicated that self reported drug experience was far higher among those who were 'compulsorily' unemployed than among other respondents (C Evans, unpublished findings).

Several British authors have noted a connection between illicit drug use and unemployment. Young stated that becoming a drug user was especially attractive to young people with little stake in the workaday world.[21] Plant noted that more contact with illicit drugs was particularly common among people of low status or who were unemployed.[18] Wells and Stacey also concluded that regular users of cannabis were especially likely to be unemployed or to indulge in frequent job changing.[22] Recent studies in the Wirral, the north of England, and Glasgow have indicated that the use of illicit drugs is, at least in part, a symptom of urban deprivation and unemployment.[23-25]

Several American studies have reached similar conclusions. Clayton and Voss, referring to Manhattan, concluded that among whites the highest proportion of self reported heroin use was evident among the unemployed.[26] Newmeyer and Johnson, referring to San Francisco, concluded: 'Heroin use is perhaps related to unemployment. Thus the drastic rise in Bay Area unemployment during the late Johnston and early Nixon years provoked a rise in the use of heroin. The slow easing off of unemployment in 1971 and 1972 paralleled a drop in the number of new addicts.'[27]

Kandel, reviewing the use of marijuana, or cannabis, by a sample of 1325 young adults, noted that regular users of this drug were more likely than others to have left full time education and to experience frequent job changes.[28] Avico et al, when screening Italian men being considered for drafting into the army, noted that opiate use was significantly more common among those who were unemployed than among other men.[29]

Several authors have echoed Young's comments about the value of illicit drug use to those who lack conventional occupational status. Catton and Shain have advanced the following view of heroin use:

The sense of belonging to a group, the feeling of purpose and accomplishment and the sense of prestige are all important needs which this life appears to fulfil for the user. In the conventional world these needs are much harder to satisfy for the under-educated individual who has difficulty maintaining even a menial job. The life-style seems to be so important that some individuals feign addiction.[30]

This view has been elaborated on by Sackman et al, who have suggested that drug use is a form of work, having similar social and psychological value to the protagonists as do legal forms of employment.[31]

Both sets of data discussed here are limited. The Lothian study related to a medium sized study group in only one area during a short period of time. In addition, the national data presented in the figure provide an imperfect measure of illegal drug use in the general population. They do, however, provide a useful indication of the trends of drug related problems. Many other indicators, such as drug related admissions to hospital and deaths, could also usefully be examined. A further complication is the alteration in the official definition of unemployment during recent years. Had the definition current in 1970 remained in force the increase in recent unemployment depicted in the figure would have been even steeper.

In spite of these qualifications the evidence reviewed above supports the conclusion that there is an association between illicit drug use and unemployment. Association does not necessarily impute a causal relation. Sometimes the adoption of certain patterns of drug use may render some people unemployable.[19,32] Sometimes unemployment may serve as a risk factor that increases the attractions of drug use and of the associated lifestyles. It would be naive to contend that unemployment is the only cause of illicit drug use. People use and abuse drugs for a perplexing and

sometimes conflicting variety of reasons, and several reviews have noted the complex aetiology of psychoactive drug use.[33-35]

There is a clear link between illegal drug use and unemployment. Many possible explanations for this exist, but the most parsimonious conclusion is that high unemployment serves to foster drug use. This conclusion is consistent with a whole body of evidence from many studies conducted in different communities with different sampling techniques, data sources, and methodologies. Such consistency from disparate sources provides compelling support for the validity of this conclusion.

As indicated by Smith a considerable body of evidence connects unemployment with morbidity and mortality.[36-38] Even so, it is often difficult to disentangle the influence of unemployment from that of a host of other social and economic factors that operate simultaneously and may also have an impact on health. Several authors have noted that illegal drug use, like alcohol and tobacco consumption, is influenced by economic factors.[39,40] It is notable that illegal drug use in the United Kingdom has been increasing at a time when both tobacco and, more recently, alcohol consumption have been decreasing. The relation between illegal drug use and legal drugs is unclear. One possible reason for increased illegal drug use is that the price of illegal drugs compared with that of alcohol and tobacco has declined. This may have enhanced the relative appeal of illegal drugs, especially to those on low incomes.

We recommend that in future policies to curb the use of alcohol and tobacco should be formulated on the basis of an awareness that illegal drugs may sometimes be used as substitutes for legal ones. The link found in this study suggests that illegal drug use may continue to proliferate in step with unemployment. Illegal drug use, once established, may prove to be a persistent legacy even if unemployment declines.

REFERENCES

1. Plant M.A., Peck, D.F., Stuart R. Self-reported drinking habits and alcohol-related consequences amongst a cohort of Scottish teenagers. Br J Addict 1982;77:75–90.
2. Plant M.A., Peck D.F., Stuart R. The correlates of serious

alcohol-related consequences and illicit drug use amongst a cohort of Scottish teenagers. *Br J Addict* 1984;79:197–200.

3. Plant M.A., Peck D.F., Samuel E. *Alcohol, drugs and school-leavers*. London: Tavistock, 1985.

4. Manpower Services Commission. *Labour market quarterly report (Scotland)*. Edinburgh: Manpower Services Commission, 1984.

5. Peters M., ed. *Department of Employment Gazette* 1983;94:S37.

6. SPSS Inc. *SPSSX user's guide*. 2nd ed. New York: McGraw Hill, 1986:649.

7. Plant M.A. *Drugs in perspective*. London: Hodder and Stoughton, 1981.

8. Grant M., Plant M.A., Williams A., eds. *Economics and alcohol*. London: Croom Helm, 1982.

9. Peters M., ed. *Department of Employment Gazette*. March 1975–February 1986.

10. Home Office. *Statistics of the misuse of drugs in the UK, 1984*. London: Home Office, 1985.

11. Lee P.N., ed. *Statistics of smoking in the United Kingdom*. 7th ed. London: Tobacco Research Council, 1976.

12. Produktschap Voor Gedistilleerde Dranken. *Hoeveel alcoholhoudende dranken worden er in de wereld gedronken?* Thurman C., adapter. London: Brewers' Society, 1986.

13. Hindmarch I. Patterns of drug use in a provincial university. *Br J Addict* 1970;64:395–402.

14. Plant M.A. *Drugtakers in an English town*. London: Tavistock, 1975.

15. Williams A. The Thatcher generation. *New Society* 1986;Feb 21:312–5.

16. Ghodse A.H. Drug dependent individuals dealt with by London casualty departments. *Br J Psychiatry* 1977;131:273–80.

17. Stimson G.V., Oppenheimer A. *Heroin addiction*. London: Tavistock, 1982.

18. Robertson J.R. Drug users in contact with general practice. *Br Med J* 1985;290:31–2.

19. Mott H.J. Self-reported cannabis use in Great Britain in 1981. *Br J Addict* 1985;80:37–43.

20. Research International. *Heroin misuse campaign evaluation*. London: Research Bureau Ltd, 1986:appendix I.

21. Young J. *The drugtakers*. London: Paladin, 1971.

22. Wells B., Stacey B. A further comparison of cannabis (marijuana) users and non-users. *Br J Addict* 1976;71:161–5.

23. Parker H., Bakx K., Newcombe R. *Drug use in Wirral: the first report of the Wirral misuse of drugs project*. Liverpool: University of Liverpool, 1986.

24. Pearson G., Gilman M., McIver S. *Young people and heroin*. London: Health Education Council, 1986.

25. Haw S.C. *Drug problems in greater Glasgow*. London: Chameleon Press, 1985.

26. Clayton R.R., Voss H.L. *Young men and drugs in Manhatton: a causal analysis*. Rockville, Maryland: National Institute on Drug Abuse, 1981. (NIDA Research Monograph No 39).

27. Newmeyer J.A., Johnson G.R., The heroin epidemic in San Francisco: estimates of incidence and prevalence. *Int J Addict* 1976;11:417–8.

28. Kandel D.B. Marijuana users in young adulthood. *Arch Gen Psychiatry* 1984;41:200–9.

29. Avico V., Pocchiari F., Zuccaro P., Donato L., Mariani F. Prevalence of opiate use among young men in Italy, 1980 and 1982. *Bull Narc* 1983;xxxv:63–71.

30. Catton K., Shain M. Heroin users in the community: a review of the drug use and life-styles of addicts and users not in treatment. *Addictive Diseases* 1976;2:421–40.

31. Sackman B.S., Sackman M.M., de Angelis G.G. Heroin addiction as an occupation: traditional addicts and heroin addicted polydrug users. *Int J Addict* 1978;13:427–41.

32. Blumberg H.H. British users of opiate-type drugs: a follow-up study. *Br J Addict* 1976;71:65–77.

33. Fazey C. *The aetiology of psychoactive substance use*. Paris: UNESCO, 1977.

34. Plant M.A. What aetiologies? In: Edwards G., Busch C., eds. *Drug problems in Britain*. London: Academic Press, 1981:245–80.

35. Peck D.F. Some determining factors. In: Plant M.A., ed. *Drinking and problem drinking*. London: Junction/Fourth Estate, 1982:65–83.

36. Smith R. 'He never got over losing his job': death on the dole. *Br Med J* 1985;291:1492–5.

37. Smith R. 'I couldn't stand it any more': suicide and unemployment. *Br Med J* 1985;291:1563–6.

38. Smith R. 'I'm not right': the physical health of the unemployed. *Br Med J* 1985;291:1626–9.

39. Bernard G. An economic analysis of the illicit drug market. *Int J Addict* 1983;18:681–700.

40. Lewis R., Hartnoll R., Bryer S., Daviaud E., Mitcheson M. Scoring smack: the illicit heroin market in London. *Br J Addict* 1985;80:281–90.

Paper 12

Becoming a heroin user and heroin using careers

GEOFFREY PEARSON*, MARK GILMAN† and SHIRLEY MCIVER‡

* Professor of Social Work, Faculty of Social Science, Middlesex Polytechnic;
† Prevention Development Officer, North West Regional Drug Training Unit, Prestwich Hospital, Manchester;
‡ Research Worker, University of York

This paper describes the ways in which people become heroin users, the stages and statuses of their involvement, and the concept of a 'career' in relation to their use of heroin. It is based on extensive fieldwork in the North of England during 1985.

Why do people use heroin, and how are they first introduced to it? Can people control heroin use, so that it remains merely an occasional recreational pastime, or is addiction an inevitable outcome of experimentation? Why do people take such risks with their health when the dangers of heroin are so widely known, or are many people still ignorant of its addictive properties? Is the drug in fact as enslaving as popular stereotypes insist, and are the horrors of withdrawal so engulfing as in the common notion of 'cold turkey'? Why is it that so many ex-addicts seem to say that 'coming off' is easy, but that 'staying off' is the most difficult part of abstinence?

DIFFERENT STATUSES OF INVOLVEMENT WITH HEROIN

There is no such thing as a 'typical' heroin user, nor a typical heroin user's career. Nevertheless, it is useful to think in terms of a simple four-phase model to describe the different levels of involvement with the drug through which a heroin user's career will pass.

Extract from: _Young People and Heroin Use in the North of England_. A Report to the Health Education Council 1986, published by the Gower Publishing Group.
© Geoffrey Pearson, Professor of Social Work, Middlesex Polytechnic.

1. The Non-User
2. The Initial Offer and Experimentation
3(a). Occasional Use on a Recreational Basis
3(b). The 'Grey Area' of Transitional Use
4. Addictive Use

So, the non-user having been offered the drug will either accept it or reject the offer. If the offer is accepted and the person tries it on an 'experimental' basis, they might either discontinue their experimentation quite quickly because they do not enjoy the experience, or they might embark on a more prolonged period of experimentation. At this point they might begin a pattern of recreational use on a very occasional basis, and continue this pattern over a long period of time without becoming addicted. Or they might begin to use the drug more frequently and enter upon what we have called the 'grey area' of transitional use where it is not clear, either to themselves or others, whether or not they are becoming addicted — a phase of heroin use open to widespread misinterpretation in terms of the person's status of involvement with the drug, which is why we choose to call it the 'grey area'. And finally, if this pattern of transitional use continues for any length of time the heroin user will suffer an imperceptible drift into addiction.

Each of these phases can be thought of as different _statuses_ of heroin involvement, and the passage between these different statuses as _transition points_. For health education purposes, these different statuses imply different *audiences*, with differing educational and informational needs. The transition points will also be crucial target areas for health education. Finally, each status will imply different possible *exit-routes* towards abstinence.

In moving from one status to another, conscious choices will sometimes make themselves apparent to the individual. But equally, a person can move imperceptibly from one status to another without any conscious decision-making. This is especially the case in the patterns of transitional use which take a person from the status of occasional user to compulsive user and addiction. At this fateful transition point it is not uncommon for a heroin addict to say that they were taken by surprise when they first experienced withdrawal symptoms, sometimes to the extent that they did not identify what these symptoms were.

There is nothing inevitable about the passage from one status to another in the career of a heroin user. Some people do slide rapidly into habitual use and addiction, following the pattern of progressive decline and escalating drug consumption which characterises the dominant stereotypical image of the heroin addict. But other people can, and do, arrest their involvement at different points in this hierarchy of statuses. So that some people discontinue their heroin use after a brief flirtation with the drug, whereas others maintain stable patterns of occasional use over long periods of time (cf. Zinberg, 1984). But because the hidden figure of experimental or recreational use is unknown, it is not possible to say what proportion of heroin users follow the pattern of progressive decline into addiction which is commonly (but wrongly) assumed to be the inevitable consequence of heroin use.

Exit-routes also vary considerably. Different motivations trigger them, different methods are used in order to come off heroin, and different timescales are involved. Some people try to make a clean break with heroin, while others try to withdraw themselves slowly by gradually reducing their intake. Some try to do it with professional assistance, whereas others do it on their own. And a crucial distinction must be made between 'coming off', which for many heroin users is relatively effortless, as against 'staying off' which has been repeatedly described to us as much more difficult.

This simple model could undoubtedly be refined, and it will be overlaid with important considerations such as whether a person smokes heroin or injects it. For example, an exit-route for someone who injects might first involve moving onto smoking heroin for a time and overcoming 'needle fixation' before attempting to come off the drug completely. Nevertheless, this simple model will serve usefully as a framework for our subsequent discussion which will focus on crucial points of transition: the circumstances of the initial offer; experimentation and the perceived benefits of heroin use at this stage; the 'grey area' of transitional use into addiction; and finally exit-routes and the process of 'coming off' and 'staying off' heroin.

However, first it is important to recognize that even habitual heroin use is compatible with a wide range of lifestyles and patterns of use (cf. Stimson, 1973; Stimson & Oppenheimer, 1982). Before moving onto a consideration of different statuses of involvement, it will be useful to exemplify what some of these different patterns of habitual use amount to, on the basis of experiences that we have gathered together in our research.

Kevin started smoking heroin four years ago in a circle of friends and at its peak his habit amounted to 1 gramme of heroin daily. He supported his habit by shoplifting, for which he was caught more than once. It was when he was facing a further Court appearance, which seemed likely to result in a custodial sentence, that he discovered the motivation to enter a treatment programme.

Joe had a pattern of heroin use, stretching back for nearly ten years, which involved episodic binges during which he would consume the drug hungrily. When he felt that his habit was spiralling out of control, he would register for a methadone-reduction programme whereupon he would remain abstinent for as long as 18 months before starting his next binge.

Julie maintained her heroin habit, and that of her boyfriend, for nearly two years by prostitution. At one time they were consuming $1\frac{1}{2}$ grammes daily, costing something like £600 per week, which she said she could earn easily by a couple of hours work per night.

When Harry first tried heroin he had several thousand

pounds in the bank, consisting largely of redundancy money from when he had been made unemployed. He quickly developed a heavy habit of more than a gramme smoked daily and was always generous with his friends who also smoked heroin, so that he blew all his money in a matter of months. When his debts began to increase he stopped using heroin and he now receives methadone.

Carol first tried heroin with a girlfriend, and says that she did not know what it was at the time. She became heavily involved with a circle of heroin users for 12 months, but she now receives methadone while still buying a £5 bag of heroin every other week and enjoying 'a little toot'.

THE INITIAL OFFER AND EXPERIMENTATION

Very little is known in any detailed way about early patterns of heroin use. The beginning user is elusive, and not only because the practice is illegal and therefore kept well hidden. A person who tries heroin will sometimes quickly discontinue use, either because they find that they are unable to maintain a supply of the drug, or because it makes them feel ill and they have no desire to continue, and there is no reason why people such as this should come to the notice of public authorities or researchers. Only those who sustain their heroin use over time are likely to come to public notice, and then because of their involvement in crime, ill health, or domestic difficulties. There is no reason to suppose that the early experiences of those people who do come to public notice should correspond to the experiences of those who do not. So that what follows might only be a partial reconstruction of early experiences with heroin.

Nevertheless, a number of certain features of the circumstances of the initial offer can be briefly summarised.

1. The initial offer will always be made in the context of a friendship network.
2. The stereotype of the 'pusher' and the 'free sample', so beloved of the news media, is false and unhelpful for health education purposes.
3. There is no guarantee whatsoever that the known

dangers of heroin will deter people from accepting the initial offer. Indeed, an emphasis on the dangers of heroin might sometimes even enhance the sense of risk and excitement to be enjoyed from the drug and increase the likelihood that the initial offer will be accepted.
4. Nor is there any guarantee that because a person has refused an offer of heroin in the past, they will not accept in the future.

The first time that a person is introduced to heroin it will be by a friend, and not by a so-called 'pusher'. This point is so important that it cannot be emphasised too strongly. Indeed, this makes it more likely that the offer will be accepted, because the context of friendship (or kinship) will make the drug seem that much safer than if it had been offered by a stranger. It is indeed a sobering fact that if the stereotype of the 'pusher' and the 'free sample' to lure people into addiction were true, then its possibilities for epidemic growth within a friendship network would be considerably reduced.

When asked how they first got into heroin, our informants offered different versions of the same story:

'I was just gave some, for nothing like, by a mate. And the feeling is different, I liked the feeling . . . and after that I started buying my own bags, £5 bags and that, I just got into it that way' (Colin, 23 years, Manchester)

'It's like everything else, the heroin came round and . . . I was curious so I tried it and I liked it. . . . There was a few of us, we were all good mates and that like, we all tried it and eventually everyone just got hooked' (Eddie, 21 years, Merseyside)

THE EARLY EXPERIENCE

What does it feel like when a person first tries heroin? Often enough it makes them feel sick, and sometimes this is the end of their heroin using career. But other people persist with heroin, in spite of the nausea, which is hardly surprising in view of the fact that initial encounters with other drugs (including those that are socially sanctioned, alcohol and tobacco) often make people feel ill until they learn how to take the drug properly and how to handle its effects and interpret them as enjoyable. The first surreptitious 'drag' or 'swallow' on a cigarette, with its attendant effects of dizziness or nausea; the 'never again' feeling which accompanies the first hang-over, or the sickness from excessive drinking: these experiences lay a sound foundation upon which people will persist with drugs which are not immediately experienced as pleasurable, having learned that these are inhibitions which must be overcome if an intoxicant is to be enjoyed. And in this respect there is no reason why heroin should be different from other drugs.

If the likelihood that heroin will make someone feel ill cannot be relied upon to deter them from continuing use, then what are the pleasurable effects? Often in the accounts of ex-addicts we hear only of the painful and enslaving absorption into the drug: 'the monkey on your back'. But a major reason why people use, and continue to use heroin, is that they enjoy it. This is sometimes a difficult thing for health education to admit to, but it is true nevertheless.

Precisely what is the nature of this enjoyment? Here we enter into an area of difficulty, because drug users do not employ a very complex vocabulary by which to describe and label the internal states experienced when under the influence of a drug. So that words such as 'stoned', 'buzz', 'high' and 'wrecked' not only sum up the limits of this restricted voabulary, but are also employed to describe the effects of a variety of substances (cannabis, amphetamines, opiates) which are otherwise totally dissimilar.

A typical description of the initial effects of heroin, then, will often be set in a characteristic vagueness:

'First, when I was on it, like, I donnow . . . it made me feel dead pleasant, I donnow . . . as if I never had a care in the world, d'you know what I mean? It wasn't like a "high". . . . It was just like . . . you haven't got a care, y'know, it was just different' (Paul, 24 years, Merseyside)

Sometimes heroin's effects were described, in straightforward and immediate terms, as simply pleasurable:

'It was just the *nicest* drug going. You feel just *great*! Just . . . phoo . . . blows your mind, like, you start nodding and . . .' (Eddie, 21 years, Merseyside)

Some people described heroin's effects as peaceful and relaxing:

'With smoking, it comes on you gradually and you just feel dead relaxed and dead tired, and what have you . . .' (Mick, 23 years, Manchester)

Whereas other people described the initial effects as a feeling of great personal power with an immediate impact:

'As soon as you chase it, it just hits you straight away and you just feel like the boss, like . . .' (Jack, 22 years, Merseyside)

And there were those who liked the helpless feeling of being 'wrecked' and 'gouching', which is a common British expression for the North American term 'nodding off', and which comes through in this Liverpudlian's version of drug argot as 'grouching':

'So what's so special about heroin?'
'The way you take it. I loved it, like . . . And the hit's brilliant. . . . You just sit there and just . . . like helpless. You must look bad and all that, because I've seen me mates and thought they did, like. And, I'm just sitting there grouching, it's brilliant' (John, 19 years, Merseyside)

If the active elements of heroin's effects were open to a wide variety of forms of description and interpretation, these people were nevertheless in agreement that they liked the drug's effects. Another common feature in many of the accounts that we were given was the drug's capacity to take away a person's worries:

'I'd just finished with my girl . . . and I suppose I was on a bit of a downer myself like, a bit depressed and all that. And as I say I took some heroin, and all my worries that I had just seemed to float away. . . . When I had heroin, I didn't have a problem, I didn't have any worries' (Paul, 24 years, Merseyside)

In many of the accounts that we were given an ambivalence surrounded descriptions of the drug's pleasures, which is hardly surprising since many of the people whom we talked to were trying to stay off heroin. Indeed, sometimes it was not easy to get people to talk about the enjoyable aspects of heroin use at all, in that they preferred to dwell upon the damage which heroin had caused in their lives. At one extreme, in an interview with a self-help group of ex-users the group-leader vetoed any discussion of the pleasures of heroin at all. The group's philosophy involved a total renunciation of drug experiences, which is common to organisations such as Alcoholics Anonymous, and even to think about the pleasures of heroin was defined as a sign that a group member might relapse.

The early experiences of heroin use, from the accounts that we have been given, suffer from a wide variation. For some people the drug is an instant 'buzz' or 'hit'. For others it is a matter of relaxation. For some it brings an enhanced sense of personal power. For others it means being 'wiped out' and 'wrecked'. But with different shades of emphasis, one common feature was the ambivalence felt towards the drug, while another was that heroin 'took your worries away' and made people feel 'at ease' with themselves and in their minds. Indeed, if anything it was this cushioning effect from external pressures which caused people to form an initial attachment to the drug and which then led them onto a regular pattern of consumption which eventually resulted in addiction.

On occasion, this feeling of release from external pressures and worries was so all-consuming in a person's recollections of their early heroin use that the positive drug-effects (in the sense of a 'buzz' or a 'hit') were almost entirely absent from their account. And this seemed to be particularly so where someone's construction of the subjective meaning of their drug-use was closely tied to their experiences of social deprivation. In other words, where heroin appeared to 'solve' a person's difficulties with housing, unemployment or low income.

THE QUESTION OF OCCASIONAL NON-ADDICTIVE USE

If there is very little research on early patterns of heroin use, except as reconstructed from the experiences of addicts and ex-addicts, then the occasional user who only takes heroin on a recreational basis is even more elusive. Indeed, there are authoritative traditions within the addictions field which question whether heroin use is even possible without eventually becoming addicted. Nevertheless, a substantial body of research evidence on non-compulsive opiate use has been collected by Zinberg and his colleagues in the USA, where occasional heroin use on a recreational basis is known within the drug culture as 'chipping'. This has established beyond doubt that stable patterns of non-

addictive heroin use can be sustained if certain rules are adhered to (cf. Zinberg, 1984). Zinberg's work, which contains a useful summary of research in this little explored area, has also attempted to identify what these rules, rituals and routines amount to. Briefly, the necessary underlying supports which can sustain a non-compulsive pattern of opiate use include the following: access to a knowledgeable network of controlled drug users who can offer advice to the novice; strict adherence to rules on the frequency of use, so that the drug is only used on certain occasions such as at weekends and at no other time, and never on consecutive days; the existence of other valued commitments in a person's life such as employment, family life and recreational pursuits which conflict with opiate use; and a circle of friendship which includes non-users as well as users.

In Britain a smaller study by Blackwell (1984) identified similar features within the lifestyles of controlled opiate users, while also pointing to the way in which people sometimes move between different statuses of involvement with heroin.

TRANSITIONAL USE: MISTAKEN IDENTITIES IN THE 'GREY AREA'

Addiction does not follow on instantly from experimentation with heroin, and although the rate at which a person becomes addicted probably varies between individuals it will have been necessary to use the drug regularly on a daily basis for some time before the actual development of a 'habit'.

The transition into compulsive, addicted use is clearly an important change of status in the career of a heroin user, and it will often be characterised by an imperceptible drift — a 'grey area' where a person's growing involvement with heroin is unclear and open to misinterpretation. We can identify two kinds of such misinterpretation within this transition, each of them with its own attendant dangers. The first is where a person believes themselves to be addicted when in fact they are not. The second is when a person does not believe that they are addicted, when in fact they are.

The first case of mistaken identity is probably more common than is usually recognised. In one locality a drug squad officer reported to us that he had often noticed that people who had been arrested on drug charges did not exhibit any withdrawal symptoms when they were held in custody on remand, even though they believed themselves to be heroin addicts. His explanation of this phenomenon was that people who claimed to be heroin addicts when they were not were 'showing off' in front of their friends, and one thing which certainly has to be reckoned with is that in some localities being a 'smack-head' is assuming something of a heroic status. However, this is not necessarily a conscious choice, and we can identify a number of subtle, interacting influences which play a part in these misrepresentations of self within the 'grey area' of transitional heroin use.

Perhaps the most important is that in the absence of a well informed drug culture a person might be a victim of the mythology of heroin's 'instantly' addictive powers, and therefore pursue and consume the drug in fear of withdrawal before an actual physical dependence has been established. In a situation such as this a person's mistaken belief that they are addicted will quickly become a 'self-fulfilling prophecy', and a number of ex-users whom we talked to described in their own terms how these mistaken identities might arise and then lead eventually to addiction.

'I think people get the wrong ideas, you know, people who've just started on it . . . and they've smoked it for a month or two months, and then they haven't got it one day. Well, alright, you know, they might feel a bit rough. But they start, y'know, they've got it in their heads that they're going through withdrawal symptoms. So they're out to get more to make them feel that bit better because they were feeling rough . . . and before you know it, they *are* hooked on it' (Paul, 24 years, Merseyside)

'When you get hooked on it you get, sort of, psychologically hooked at first. Do you know what I mean? You're saying, "I *need* this . . . I need it", like . . . and you don't. But you buy it again, and then one day you just wake up and you're fucked' (Eddie, 21 years, Merseyside)

An alternative set of reasons why a person might embark upon a regular pattern of heroin use even before they become addicted, is that it gives them some meaning in life, either in the shape of an identity ('I'm an addict') or as status within the peer group.

Auld *et al.* (1985) have also described how an assumed addict-identity can give people not only local status, but also other forms of social-psychological reward in the shape of sympathy from one's family and friends. Declaring oneself to be a 'junkie', and thereby assuming a helpless victim status, might then be understood under the right circumstances as a form of 'attention-seeking'. It has been pointed out to us on more than one occasion that it is not unknown for a young offender to claim addict-status when appearing before a Court, thereby hoping to secure a sentence which involves 'help' rather than 'punishment'.

As a person becomes more deeply involved with a heroin using network, they also become increasingly identified with group activities which centre around drug use. In order to gain acceptance within this group of acquaintances, it might then be necessary to magnify one's familiarity with heroin. Tall stories abound in drug-using circles about so-and-so who took twenty 'dikeys' at one go and really 'gouched out'; about how awful it was the other day when you were 'turkeying' and couldn't get a 'bag' anywhere; or how someone had escaped from the clutches of the law by 'legging it' when the drug squad appeared around the corner.

Equally important in this respect is that the life of a heroin user is an extremely active one, in which a person needs to be constantly on their toes — knowing who is who in the drugs scene; who sells the best 'bag' and where to buy it; how to avoid getting 'burned' by a dealer, and how to know the difference between brick-dust and the real thing; constantly hustling for the money for the next bag. In a study of street addicts in New York, Preble and Casey (Paper 17) showed how this hectic cycle of activity could assume more importance in a person's life than the effects of the drug itself (cf. Auld *et al.*, 1984). This corresponds with the argument advanced by Peele (1985) that people become addicted to activities just as much as they become addicted to substances. And it also squares with the commonly reported experience by ex-users that 'staying off' heroin was much more difficult than 'coming off' the drug, because the day seems so empty without the drug and its associated flurry of activity.

One can see, then, that within this 'grey area' of transitional use there is ample scope for a person to adopt harmful self-identifications with the addict lifestyle prior to the actual onset of dependence, in such a way that these generate a 'self-fulfilling prophecy'. But it is equally true that a different kind of mistaken identity can be assumed, whereby addiction overtakes someone without them realising how deeply involved they had become with the drug. In some people's accounts of their transition into habitual use, their experience of how this came about was simply passed over in a sentence:

'I just got into it, buying a bag every day because I had money then, from the redundancy money and that, and before I knew it like, I was dependent on it . . . I needed it' (Malcolm, 23 years, Manchester)

The impression that is so often given in accounts of a heroin user's early experimentation and transition through the 'grey area' into addiction is one of inevitability. In retrospect, the transition no doubt feels that it was inevitable. But the 'grey area' of transitional use does not necessarily take this form, and people can and do arrest their involvement and so avoid what would otherwise be the inevitable consequences of daily heroin use.

It is reasonable to suppose that over a period of weeks and months certain conscious choices and decisions are made. And also that these decisions would sometimes involve various kinds of subterfuge, by which people hide from themselves the obvious consequences of their actions. Perhaps the most common form which these subterfuges take is revealed in the often repeated expression, 'One little toot won't do me any harm', a self-deception whereby someone says to themselves that they will do it again today, but not tomorrow. And then when tomorrow comes, the same act of bad faith: 'One more little toot. . . . Just one more little chase'.

One of the characteristics of accounts given by heroin users and ex-users is that they rarely embrace any recognition of their own motivation and agency. So that the drift into addiction is remembered only as something in which one played a passive role — as if the user were powerless in the face of a relentless pharmacological process, and then later driven by the overriding concern to avoid symptoms of withdrawal.

REFERENCES

Auld, J., N. Dorn & N. South (1985) 'Irregular Work, Irregular Pleasures', in R. Matthews & J. Young (eds), *Confronting Crime* (Sage).

Blackwell, J.S., (1983) 'Drifting, controlling and overcoming: opiate users who avoid becoming chronically dependent', *Journal of Drug Issues*, vol. 13, no. 2.

Peele, S. (1985) *The Meaning of Addiction: Compulsive Experience and its Interpretation* (Lexington).

Stimson, G.V. (1973) *Heroin and Behaviour* (Irish UP).

Stimson, G.V. & E. Oppenheimer (1982) *Heroin Addiction* (Tavistock).

Zinberg, N.E. (1984) *Drug, Set and Setting: The Basis for Controlled Intoxicant Use* (Yale UP).

Alcohol problems and the family

JIM ORFORD

Senior Lecturer in Clinical Psychology, University of Exeter

This paper explores the family perspective relating to substance abuse. It describes the stress-victim model and a family systems perspective, and outlines a range of family treatments that have been used in work with families where a problem has been identified. Recommendations for service provision to meet the needs of families are also made.

When considering the involvement of families in alcohol problems it is important to appreciate that this topic can be considered from a variety of very divergent perspectives.

The two most influential models for those involved in treatment are the *stress victim* and the *systems* perspectives, and the first two sections of this chapter will examine research that has been carried out within these two seemingly contradictory frameworks. The third section will then consider research on treatment involving family members and the chapter will conclude by making tentative recommendations about approaches to and treatment of families with alcohol problems.

STRESS-VICTIM MODEL

This view supposes that the drinking problem of one member has a stressful impact upon other members of the family who then search for ways of responding or coping, which in turn may be relatively functional or dysfunctional as the case may be. The non-excessively drinking members of the family are important, according to this model, because they themselves are at risk because of the stress they are under, and because the ways in which they react may have a bearing upon the future course of the drinking problem.

Modified from *Approaches to Addiction: Research Highlights in Social Work*. Joyce Irishman (ed.) (Kogan Page, 1985).

Marital unhappiness and separation

A number of investigators have assessed the degree of 'hardship' to which a spouse (almost always a wife married to an excessively drinking husband in these studies) has been exposed as a result of the partner's excessive drinking. Studies have found that women married to men with identified drinking problems very often describe a great deal of severe, and often longstanding, hardship. This includes concern over the husband's job and economic security, financial strain, social embarrassment, reduction of social contacts, failure to keep up personal appearances, rows and quarrels, a poor sex life and infidelity, possessiveness and jealousy directed towards the wife, damage to household objects or furniture, physical violence in the family, and involvement with police.[1]

It is equally clear from these studies, however, that this hardship is a variable quantity. It is important not to make sweeping generalisations about 'alcoholic marriages', just as it is important not to make unsupported generalisations about all 'alcoholics' or problem drinkers. In one study of 100 London couples, where the husbands were under treatment for drinking problems,[1] we discovered wide variation in the degree of marital cohesion. Some couples reported low levels of mutual affection, and wives expressed a generally negative view of their husbands using expressions such as: '. . . hate him . . . unable to forgive him . . . never loved him . . . my feelings are dead . . . feeling of deep revulsion . . . drinking is not the main problem . . . it's his person I don't like . . .'. These attitudes were often associated with pessimism about, and lack of understanding of, the husband's behaviour, combined with resignation about the future. These cases, however, were extreme ones along a dimension at the other end of which were those couples who reported high levels of affection and where wives made a clear distinction between their husbands' unacceptable behaviour when drinking and their appropriate behaviour when not drinking.

One research strategy has been to consider marital roles. Complaints on grounds of role failure are made over things large and small. Many problem drinking husbands were found in these studies to be less involved in housework, or in doing repairs around the home, than either they or their wives considered ideal. Many were accused of not 'being around' when needed by the family. Although there was a general under-involvement in family 'tasks', however, there was no such under-involvement (indeed in some cases a suggestion of over-influence) in family 'decisions' about social recreational life and about marital sexual behaviour. Again the existence of great variation between couples needs to be stressed. It is also important to bear in mind that the kinds of stresses and marital unhappiness described by those who have studied families with alcohol problems are not unique and occur in other families also.

The possible connection between excessive drinking and family violence is a matter that has attracted special research attention. In our study of 100 couples[1] 72 per cent of wives reported sometimes being threatened by their husbands, 45 per cent having ever been beaten by them, and 27 per cent ever having experienced their husband attempting to injure them seriously.

Research suggests that we are right to suppose that wives living with men with drinking problems are at risk of experiencing distress and disturbance themselves. In addition to the kinds of hardship already described, there is the uncertainty that many family members describe about knowing whether there really is a problem in the family or not, deciding whether it is a problem of their own making or of someone else's, deciding what exactly the problem is, and in then deciding how is the best way to respond.

Rates of marital breakdown are high when a serious drinking problem exists for one or other partner, indeed many observers of families with alcohol problems have expressed surprise that so many such marriages survive at all. Survival of marriages is less surprising, however, if one considers the many obvious barriers against marital breakdown such as felt obligations to children, moral restraints, external pressure from relatives or the local community, legal difficulties, and a wife's lack of independent source of income, and an absence of anyone to take the partner's place.

Although at least one in three of those seeking help for drinking problems are now women, there has been a regrettable lack of research on husbands married to women problem drinkers.

Children as victims

Until quite recently the possible stresses experienced by children living in families with alcohol problems had been relatively neglected. Indeed Margaret Cork entitled the report of the early interview study of 115 youngsters The Forgotten Children.[2] Recently a great deal more interest has been shown and research has at least begun to outline the links of stresses to which such children are particularly prone. One of the most obvious of these is chronic exposure to a poor family atmosphere, with much parental marital tension and discord, and disruption of joint family activities and rituals.[3]

There may be forms of stress which are unusually common amongst children of families with drinking problems. One candidate which has been suggested as a result of interviews with such young people is a restriction on meeting friends or reciprocating invitations because of embarrassment about parental behaviour.

Again it is important to remind ourselves that 'children of alcoholics' are far from being a homogeneous group: circumstances vary greatly and generalisations should be treated with great caution. For one thing, length of exposure to a parental drinking problem during childhood, and the age at which exposure takes place, are obviously variables of significance. Furthermore, excessive drinking patterns vary greatly. Some children are regularly exposed to parental drunkenness, whilst others are shielded from it although their parent may have a very serious problem. Another variable is the amount of violence experienced. As a group, children in families with drinking problems undoubtedly witness and personally experience more family violence than the average, but not all do so.

A whole range of ill-effects has been reported for children of excessively drinking parents. For example, compared to control groups, they have been found to show a high incidence of school problems, difficulty in concentrating, conduct problems and truancy from school, poor school performance, and need for special or remedial schools. They have also been reported to show elevated rates of emotional problems, such as anxiety and depression, and of developmental disorders, as well as fewer means of coping with emotional upset. Other reports have shown them to become intoxicated more often than controls, and themselves to have drinking and drug problems. On the other hand, others have been impressed at how small are the differences between groups; one report has found no difference between children of excessive drinkers and controls in terms of 'personality disturbance' as measured by anxiety, depression and social isolation, and another reported no difference in the rate of attendance at psychiatric clinics. Harmful effects appear to be more regularly reported for young children than for adolescents.

Quite apart from ill-effects upon young children and adolescents, there is evidence, largely from retrospective self-report studies with clinical groups, that children of excessively drinking parents are themselves more than usually at risk of developing drinking problems in adulthood. This work has been thoroughly reviewed by Goodwin[4] and Cotton[5] who concluded that alcohol problems do indeed run in families. Present evidence therefore suggests that children of problem drinkers represent an important high risk group both because of their proneness to problems during childhood and adolescence, and their proneness to problems in later life.

Genetic transmission may provide part of the explanation for any intergeneration transmission of drinking problems which exists. It is difficult to draw certain conclusions from research to date, but recent reviews[6,7] report that twin and adoption studies, although not entirely consistent in their findings, have produced some evidence for a genetic component at least in the determination of male drinking behaviour.

Again variability needs to be stressed. One important fact about children of problem drinking parents is that many, perhaps the majority, appear to escape obviously harmful ill-effects.[6]

A FAMILY SYSTEMS PERSPECTIVE

The stress-victim model assigns clear roles to different family members: one is the excessive drinker, the rest receive the impact and are at risk of suffering ill-effects as a result.

There are a number of research findings which are troublesome to such a viewpoint however: in some marriages roles and/or drinking behaviour are reported to be non-ideal early on in a relationship for example. Clinicians have also long reported that families with alcohol problems are frequently more complicated than the simple stress-victim model would suppose. They have, for example, suggested that family members can sometimes be as resistant to treatment progress as the identified excessive drinker.

A systems view of families with alcohol problems treats the family as an indivisible system of people playing interdependent roles and it eschews the idea of attributing to individuals any particular parts in the drama, such as 'problem person' or 'stress victim'. In systems perspective, the use of alcohol in the family is purposive, adaptive and meaningful. A proper assessment would consider what functions excessive drinking is serving for the family as a whole, not just for the individual identified problem drinker. According to Steinglass[8] whose name is most closely associated with this perspective, these functions include the family's attempts to deal with a problem in some other member of the family, a problem arising between two or more family members, or serious difficulties the family faces in making an adjustment to its immediate social environment. Thus, excessive drinking in one member could well be a signal of a family problem at one or another level. The idea of homeostasis is an important one here for understanding the way in which the family has become stuck in a repetitive pattern involving excessive drinking, and the difficulty the whole family may have in accepting and adjusting to change.

Although it is important to keep in mind that such

apparently different viewpoints as the systems and stress-victim viewpoints are possible, in practice it seems that those with direct experience of families complicated by alcohol problems work with elements of each.

The danger is probably in adhering too rigidly to one or another extreme viewpoint. Systems thinking alone carries the danger of losing sight of the commonsense approach that partners and children are victims of the excessive drinking with which they must learn to cope in the best possible way, whilst stress-victim thinking alone runs the risk of ignoring the interactional nature of family life and the possible family functions which continued excessive drinking may be serving.

INVOLVING FAMILIES IN TREATMENT
Naturalistic coping

Because the large majority of families with drinking problems do not come into direct contact with professional alcohol treatment agencies, it is important to consider the ways in which such families treat themselves. Research asking spouses how they have attempted to cope[9,10] has revealed a number of coping strategies including the following: pleading, threatening, and rowing; avoiding, keeping out of the way; withdrawing sexually; being indulgent (giving a drink to help with the hangover, going without to give the drinker money, etc.); controlling access to drink (pouring it away, making a rule not to allow it in the house, etc.); attacking or competing; taking greater control or responsibility (e.g. over money matters or child-care); seeking outside help; and taking steps towards separation.

Similar research with children living in families with alcohol problems[11] has shown that they use a very similar range of tactics, although avoidance, and other passive or self-directed responses may be more common than amongst spouses.

In our own research on 100 couples, husbands whose wives had been trying to reduce the availability of alcohol by pouring it away when they found it or by trying to make rules about drinking at home, did relatively well, and those whose wives had been adopting avoidance or withdrawal strategies did relatively badly.[9] As a result we tentatively recommend 'engaged

but discriminating' coping in which family members would remain involved in attempts to help the problem drinker but would direct their attempts at the drink rather than at the drinker. It may well be the case, though, that our results were an artifact, and the different outcomes merely the result of different levels of severity of problem, with wives who avoided their husbands doing so simply because they had more hardships to cope with.

Our conclusions were in any case not totally in line with the kind of advice fairly consistently given in books addressed directly to partners and children and by Al-Anon (a self-help organisation, allied to Alcoholics Anonymous, for relatives of excessive drinkers). An analysis of the content of the books by Meyer[12] and Seixas[13] shows that they recommend that spouses and children *be positive* (see the drinking as a symptom, understand the drinker's distress, not moralise, understand it is difficult to stop drinking), that they *do not protect or collude* (e.g. do not help supply alcohol, or make excuses to others, or otherwise soften the effects of over drinking), and that where possible they should use *constructive confrontation* (e.g. feed in correct information, leave pamphlets and books around, calmly confront after a crisis, let the excessive drinker know clearly the effects of drinking on you). However, they also recommend a certain detachment. Spouses should *take distance emotionally*, not carry the burden of thinking that they are the cause of the problem, and if necessary consider divorce as the most positive solution. Children should try and 'let go' of their parent's problem, find ways to get away for a while, not feel ashamed, and take responsibility for their own lives.

Members of Al-Anon are also taught to 'detach with love' which, according to Harwin[14] means:

'. . . the individual must try to unravel the tight knot of symbiosis, whereby the spouse's entire life revolves around futile attempts to change the alcoholic. Instead the partner is encouraged to achieve some measure of personal fulfilment so that the need to control the alcohol abuser is reduced and so that some pleasure is introduced into an otherwise unhappy situation' (pp. 232–3).

About the only study of how Al-Anon members cope with their problems, in Washington, USA,[15] found that the longer the wife had been a member, the less likely she was to use 'negative coping strategies'. These referred not only to such things as coaxing, nagging, pleading, and covering up, but also to such things as pouring drink away, which was found to carry a positive prognosis in our study. Meyer[12] also recommends that spouses do not attempt to control their partners' drinking, and specifically recommends that they not throw drink away ('Do realise he will only buy more' p. 87).

Treatment for families

The problems of carrying out conclusive research on family treatment are formidable. Quite apart from the usual problems of conducting treatment outcome research, there is in addition the difficulty of recruiting sizeable enough samples of cases in which two or more members of a family are willing to become engaged, and remain in treatment. The usual problems of satisfactorily defining 'outcome' are also made more difficult: is it a good outcome if excessive drinking continues but marital communication improves: or if problem drinking ceases but the family breaks up; or if drinking continues but spouse and children become less enmeshed in the problem and their health and happiness improves? These problems are such that reviewers of research on treatment for families with alcohol problems can offer us no very clear directions about which forms of family treatment are the most effective.

What these reviews do show, however, is the range of family treatments that have been used. These include:

(a) Groups for relatives held separately from but concurrently with treatment for the problem drinkers (concurrent groups).

(b) Groups involving a number of married pairs together (conjoint groups).

(c) Treatment for an individual pair or whole family (marital and family therapy).

(d) Assisting multiple problem families in problem-solving about both practical and emotional problems (ecological family treatment).

(e) Counselling for individual relatives when the problem drinker is unavailable for treatment (unilateral family treatment).

RECOMMENDATIONS FOR SERVICE PROVISION

1. Much more attention should be paid to the high levels of stress experienced by families with a drinking problem, and also to the role which family members can play in the continuation or successful resolution of such problems. The types of stresses experienced, and the changes of role which occur, are on the whole no different in kind from those experienced by other families in distress, but they are very often of major proportions. Children and other family members are as important as partners. This recommendation applies not only to specialist practitioners and service providers, but also to those whose work is not specially focussed on problem drinking.

2. It should be acknowledged that there are several different models of alcohol and the family, and people should be explicit about the model(s) with which they are operating. A combination of stress-victim and systems models is likely to be a strong contender for those involved in providing treatment.

3. The partner of an identified problem drinker should always be involved in the latter's treatment wherever possible. Special effort may have to be made to engage husbands.

4. The exact form in which families are involved is probably less important than their involvement per se, but conjoint groups have received most support from research. There are a number of different possibilities, and type of treatment should probably be matched with the particular needs of the family. Possibilities include treatment with a greater focus on drinking and a more educational style where family cohesion is relatively high: a greater focus on communication and interaction where there is greater family disturbance; and treatment with more of a focus on practical or ecological issues in the case of multiple problem families.

5. A comprehensive service should also make available counselling and advice services for partners alone when drinkers are unavailable for treatment. The balance of opinion, and what little research has been carried out on the subject, suggests that partners

may be helped *to reduce* the level of their criticism of the drinker, their encouragement of his/her drinking, their enmeshment in attempts to modify the drinker to the exclusion of pursuing their own life, and their own level of guilt, and *to increase* their level of engagement with the drinker in a constructively confronting manner.

6. The considerable needs of children living in families with drinking problems have been largely neglected, and service providers should make it a priority to consider ways of responding to these needs.

Although one major reviewer has concluded that:

'... there is strong indication that family treatment for alcoholism can be successful ... Treatment which begins with the family is apparently successful in producing change both in the alcoholic and the family'.[16]

the evidence is that the larger number of agencies which provide treatment for problem drinkers do not involve partners or children, and that when they do they are rarely involved in family or conjoint treatment.

REFERENCES

1. Orford, J., Oppenheimer, E., Egert, S., Hensman, C. & Guthrie, S. 'The Cohesiveness of Alcoholism. Complicated Marriages and its Influence on Treatment Outcome' *British Journal of Psychiatry*, 128, 1976, 318–339.
2. Cork, R.M. *The Forgotten Children: A Study of Children with Alcoholic Parents*. Alcoholism and Drug Addiction Research Foundation of Ontario, Toronto, 1969.
3. Wilson, C. 'The Impact on Children', in Orford, J. & Harwin, J. (Eds) *Alcohol and the Family*. Croom Helm, London, 1982.
4. Goodwin, D.W. *Is Alcoholism Hereditary?* Oxford University Press, New York, 1976.
5. Cotton, N.S. 'The Familial Incidence of Alcoholism: A Review' *Journal of Studies on Alcohol*, 40, 1979, 89–116.
6. Davies, J.B. 'The Transmission of Alcohol Problems in the Family', in Orford, J. & Harwin, J. (Eds) *Alcohol and the Family*. Croom Helm, London, 1982.
7. Murray, R. & Stabenau, J. 'Genetic Factors in Alcoholism Predisposition', in Pattison, E.M. & Kaufman, E. (Eds) *Encyclopedic Handbook of Alcoholism*, Gardner Press, New York, 1982.
8. Steinglass, P. 'The Roles of Alcohol in Family Systems' in Orford, J. & Harwin, J. (Eds) *Alcohol and the Family*. Croom Helm, London, 1982.
9. Orford, J., Guthrie, S., Nicholls, P., Oppenheimer, E., Egert, S. & Hensman, C. 'Self-Reported Coping Behaviour of Wives of Alcoholics and its Associations with Drinking Outcome', *Journal of Studies on Alcohol*, 36, 1975, 1254–67.
10. Schaffer, J.B. & Tyler, J.D. 'Degree of Sobriety in Male Alcoholics and Coping Styles Used by their Wives'. *British Journal of Psychiatry*, 135, 1979, 431–437.
11. Velleman, R. & Orford, J. *Adult Children of Problem Drinking Parents*. Final Research Report to DHSS, 1984.
12. Meyer, M. *Drinking Problems Equal Family Problems: Practical Guidelines for the Problem Drinker, the Partner and all those Involved*. Lancaster, Momenta, 1982.
13. Seixas, J. *How to Cope with an Alcoholic Parent*. Edinburgh, Canongate, 1980.
14. Harwin J. 'Alcohol, The Family and Treatment', in Orford, J. & Harwin, J. (Eds) *Alcohol and the Family*. Croom Helm, London, 1982.
15. Gorman, J.M. & Rooney, J.F. 'The Influence of Al-Anon on the Coping Behaviour of Wives of Alcoholics'. *Journal of Studies on Alcohol*, 40(11), 1979, 1030–38.
16. Janzen, C. 'Families in the Treatment of Alcoholism'. *Journal of Studies on Alcohol*, 38, 1977, 114–130.

Paper 14

Becoming a marihuana user

HOWARD S. BECKER

This classic work describes in detail the way in which people become marihuana users. Based on fifty interviews, the paper describes the way in which people learn the techniques involved in using marihuana, and then go on to learn how to perceive and enjoy the effects of its use.

An unknown, but probably quite large, number of people in the United States use marihuana. They do this in spite of the fact that it is both illegal and disapproved.

The phenomenon of marihuana use has received much attention, particularly from psychiatrists and law enforcement officials. The research that has been done, as is often the case with research on behavior that is viewed as deviant, is mainly concerned with the question: why do they do it? Attempts to account for the use of marihuana lean heavily on the premise that the presence of any particular kind of behavior in an individual can best be explained as the result of some trait which predisposes or motivates him to engage in that behavior. In the case of marihuana use, this trait is usually identified as psychological, as a need for fantasy and escape from psychological problems the individual cannot face.[1]

I do not think such theories can adequately account for marihuana use. In fact, marihuana use is an interesting case for theories of deviance, because it illustrates the way deviant motives actually develop in the course of experience with the deviant activity. To put a complex argument in a few words: instead of the deviant motives leading to the deviant behavior, it is the other way around; the deviant behavior in time produces the deviant motivation. Vague impulses and desires — in this case, probably most frequently a curiosity about

the kind of experience the drug will produce — are transformed into definite patterns of action through the social interpretation of a physical experience which is in itself ambiguous. Marihuana use is a function of the individual's conception of marihuana and of the uses to which it can be put, and this conception develops as the individual's experience with the drug increases.[2]

The research reported in this section deals with the career of the marihuana user. In this chapter, we look at the development of the individual's immediate physical experience with marihuana. What we are trying to understand here is the sequence of changes in attitude and experience which lead to *the use of marihuana for pleasure*. This way of phrasing the problem requires a little explanation. Marihuana does not produce addiction, at least in the sense that alcohol and the opiate drugs do. The user experiences no withdrawal sickness and exhibits no ineradicable craving for the drug.[3] The most frequent pattern of use might be termed 'recreational'. The drug is used occasionally for the pleasure the user finds in it, a relatively casual kind of behavior in comparison with that connected with the use of addicting drugs. The report of the New York City Mayor's Committee on Marihuana emphasizes this point:

A person may be a confirmed smoker for a prolonged period, and give up the drug voluntarily without experiencing any craving for it or exhibiting withdrawal symptoms. He may, at some time later on, go back to its use. Others may remain infrequent users of the cigarette, taking one or two a week, or only when the 'social setting' calls for participation. From time to time we had one of our investigators associate with a marihuana user. The investigator would bring up the subject of smoking. This would invariably lead to the suggestion that they obtain some marihuana cigarettes. They would seek a 'tea-pad', and if it was closed the smoker and our investigator would calmly resume their previous activity, such as the discussion of life in general or the playing of pool. There were apparently no signs indicative of frustration in the smoker at not being able to gratify the desire for the drug. We consider this point highly significant since it is so contrary to the experience of users of other narcotics. A similar situation occurring in one addicted to the use of morphine, cocaine or heroin would result in a compulsive attitude on the part of the addict to obtain the drug. If unable to secure it, there would be obvious physical and mental manifestations of frustration. This may be considered presumptive evidence that there is no true addiction in the medical sense associated with the use of marihuana.[4]

In using the phrase 'use for pleasure', I mean to emphasize the noncompulsive and casual character of the behavior. (I also mean to eliminate from consideration here those few cases in which marihuana is used for its prestige value only, as a symbol that one is a certain kind of person, with no pleasure at all being derived from its use.)

The research I am about to report was not so designed that it could constitute a crucial test of the theories that relate marihuana use to some psychological trait of the user. However, it does show that psychological explanations are not in themselves sufficient to account for marihuana use and that they are, perhaps, not even necessary. Researchers attempting to prove such psychological theories have run into two great difficulties, never satisfactorily resolved, which the theory presented here avoids. In the first place, theories based on the existence of some predisposing psychological trait have difficulty in accounting for that group of users, who turn up in sizable numbers in every study,[5] who do not exhibit the trait or traits which are considered to cause the behavior. Second, psychological theories have difficulty in accounting for the great variability over time of a given individual's behavior with reference to the drug. The same person will at one time be unable to use the drug for pleasure, at a later stage be able and willing to do so, and still later again be unable to use it in this way. These changes, difficult to explain from a theory based on the user's needs for 'escape' are readily understandable as consequences of changes in his conception of the drug. Similarly, if we

think of the marihuana user as someone who has learned to view marihuana as something that can give him pleasure, we have no difficulty in understanding the existence of psychologically 'normal' users.

In doing the study, I used the method of analytic induction. I tried to arrive at a general statement of the sequence of changes in individual attitude and experience which always occurred when the individual became willing and able to use marihuana for pleasure, and never occurred or had not been permanently maintained when the person was unwilling to use marihuana for pleasure. The method requires that *every* case collected in the research substantiate the hypothesis. If one case is encountered which does not substantiate it, the researcher is required to change the hypothesis to fit the case which has proven his original idea wrong.[6]

To develop and test my hypothesis about the genesis of marihuana use for pleasure, I conducted fifty interviews with marihuana users. I had been a professional dance musician for some years when I conducted this study and my first interviews were with people I had met in the music business. I asked them to put me in contact with other users who would be willing to discuss their experiences with me. Colleagues working on a study of users of opiate drugs made a few interviews available to me which contained, in addition to material on opiate drugs, sufficient material on the use of marihuana to furnish a test of my hypothesis.[7] Although in the end half of the fifty interviews were conducted with musicians, the other half covered a wide range of people, including laborers, machinists, and people in the professions. The sample is, of course, in no sense 'random'; it would not be possible to draw a random sample, since no one knows the nature of the universe from which it would have to be drawn.

In interviewing users, I focused on the history of the person's experience with marihuana, seeking major changes in his attitude toward it and in his actual use of it, and the reasons for these changes. Where it was possible and appropriate, I used the jargon of the user himself.

The theory starts with the person who has arrived at the point of willingness to try marihuana. He knows others use marihuana to 'get high', but he does not know what this means in any concrete way. He is curious about the experience, ignorant of what it may turn out to be, and afraid it may be more than he has bargained for. The steps outlined below, if he undergoes them all and maintains the attitudes developed in them, leave him willing and able to use the drug for pleasure when the opportunity presents itself.

LEARNING THE TECHNIQUE

The novice does not ordinarily get high the first time he smokes marihuana, and several attempts are usually necessary to induce this state. One explanation of this may be that the drug is not smoked 'properly', that is, in a way that insures sufficient dosage to produce real symptoms of intoxication. Most users agree that it cannot be smoked like tobacco if one is to get high:

Take in a lot of air, you know, and . . . I don't know how to describe it, you don't smoke it like a cigarette, you draw in a lot of air and get it deep down in your system and then keep it there. Keep it there as long as you can.

Without the use of some such technique[8] the drug will produce no effects, and the user will be unable to get high:

The trouble with people like that [who are not able to get high] is that they're just not smoking it right, that's all there is to it. Either they're not holding it down long enough, or they're getting too much air and not enough smoke, or the other way around or something like that. A lot of people just don't smoke it right, so naturally nothing's gonna happen.

If nothing happens, it is manifestly impossible for the user to develop a conception of the drug as an object which can be used for pleasure, and use will therefore not continue. The first step in the sequence of events that must occur if the person is to become a user is that he must learn to use the proper smoking technique so that his use of the drug will produce effects in terms of which his conception of it can change.

Such a change is, as might be expected, a result of the individual's participation in groups in which marihuana is used. In them the individual learns the proper way to smoke the drug. This may occur through direct teaching:

I was smoking like I did an ordinary cigarette. He said, 'No, don't do it like that.' He said, 'Suck it, you know, draw in and hold it in your lungs till you . . . for a period of time.' I said, 'Is there any limit of time to hold it?' He said, 'No, just till you feel that you want to let it out, let it out.' So I did that three or four times.

Many new users are ashamed to admit ignorance and, pretending to know already, must learn through the more indirect means of observation and imitation:

I came on like I had turned on [smoked marihuana] many times before, you know. I didn't want to seem like a punk to this cat. See, like I didn't know the first thing about it — how to smoke it, or what was going to happen, or what. I just watched him like a hawk — I didn't take my eyes off him for a second, because I wanted to do everything just as he did it. I watched how he held it, how he smoked it, and everything. Then when he gave it to me I just came on cool, as though I knew exactly what the score was. I held it like he did and took a poke just the way he did.

No one I interviewed continued marihuana use for pleasure without learning a technique that supplied sufficient dosage for the effects of the drug to appear. Only when this was learned was it possible for a conception of the drug as an object which could be used for pleasure to emerge. Without such a conception marihuana use was considered meaningless and did not continue.

LEARNING TO PERCEIVE THE EFFECTS

Even after he learns the proper smoking technique, the new user may not get high and thus not form a conception of the drug as something which can be used for pleasure. A remark made by a user suggested the reason for this difficulty in getting high and pointed to the next necessary step on the road to being a user:

As a matter of fact, I've seen a guy who was high out of his mind and didn't know it. [How can that be, man?] Well, it's pretty strange, I'll grant you that, but I've seen it. This guy got on with me, claiming that he'd never got high, one of those guys, and he got completely stoned. And he kept insisting that he wasn't high. So I had to prove to him that he was.

What does this mean? It suggests that being high consists of two elements: the presence of symptoms caused by marihuana use and the recognition of these symptoms and their connection by the user with his use of the drug. It is not enough, that is, that the effects be present; alone, they do not automatically provide the experience of being high. The user must be able to point them out to himself and consciously connect them with having smoked marihuana before he can have this experience. Otherwise, no matter what actual effects are produced, he considers that the drug has had no effect on him: 'I figured it either had no effect on me or other people were exaggerating its effect on them, you know, I thought it was probably psychological, see.' Such persons believe the whole thing is an illusion and that the wish to be high leads the user to deceive himself into believing that something is happening when, in fact, nothing is. They do not continue marihuana use, feeling that 'it does nothing' for them.

Typically, however, the novice has faith (developed from his observation of users who do get high) that the drug actually will produce some new experience and continues to experiment with it until it does. His failure to get high worries him, and he is likely to ask more experienced users or provoke comments from them about it. In such conversations he is made aware of specific details of his experience which he may not have noticed or may have noticed but failed to identify as symptoms of being high:

I didn't get high the first time . . . I don't think I held it in long enough. I probably let it out, you know, you're a little afraid. The second time I wasn't sure, and he [smoking companion] told me, like I asked him for some of the symptoms or something, how would I know, you know . . . So he told me to sit on a stool. I sat on — I think I sat on a bar stool — and he said, 'Let your feet hang', and then when I got down my feet were real cold, you know.

And I started feeling it, you know. That was the first time. And then about a week after that, sometime pretty close to it, I really got on. That was the first time I got on a big laughing kick, you know. Then I really knew I was on.

One symptom of being high is an intense hunger. In the next case the novice becomes aware of this and gets high for the first time:

They were just laughing the hell out of me because like I was eating so much. I just scoffed [ate] so much food, and they were just laughing at me, you know. Sometimes I'd be looking at them, you know, wondering why they're laughing, you know, not knowing what I was doing. [Well, did they tell you

why they were laughing eventually?] Yeah, yeah, I come back, 'Hey, man, what's happening?' Like, you know, like I'd ask, 'What's happening?' and all of a sudden I feel weird, you know. 'Man, you're on, you know. You're on pot [high on marihuana].' I said, 'No, am I?' Like I don't know what's happening.

The learning may occur in more indirect ways:

I heard little remarks that were made by other people. Somebody said, 'My legs are rubbery', and I can't remember all the remarks that were made because I was very attentively listening for all these cues for what I was supposed to feel like.

The novice, then, eager to have this feeling, picks up from other users some concrete referents of the term 'high' and applies these notions to his own experience. The new concepts make it possible for him to locate these symptoms among his own sensations and to point out to himself a 'something different' in his experience that he connects with drug use. It is only when he can do this that he is high. In the next case, the contrast between two successive experiences of a user makes clear the crucial importance of the awareness of the symptoms in being high and re-emphasizes the important role of interaction with other users in acquiring the concepts that make this awareness possible:

[Did you get high the first time you turned on?] Yeah, sure. Although, come to think of it, I guess I really didn't. I mean, like that first time it was more or less of a mild drunk. I was happy, I guess, you know what I mean. But I didn't really know I was high, you know what I mean. It was only after the second time I got high that I realized I was high the first time. Then I knew that something different was happening.

[How did you know that?] How did I know? If what happened to me that night would of happened to you, you would've known, believe me. We played the first tune for almost two hours — one tune! Imagine, man! We got on the stand and played this one tune, we started at nine o'clock. When we got finished I looked at my watch, it's a quarter to eleven. Almost two hours on one tune. And it didn't seem like anything.
I mean, you know, it does that to you. It's like you have much more time or something. Anyway, when I saw that, man, it was too much. I knew I must really be high or something if anything like that could happen. See, and then they explained to me that that's what it did to you, you had a different sense of time and everything. So I realized that that's what it was. I knew then. Like the first time, I probably felt that way, you know, but I didn't know what's happening.

It is only when the novice becomes able to get high in this sense that he will continue to use marihuana for pleasure. In every case in which use continued, the user had acquired the necessary concepts with which to express to himself the fact that he was experiencing new sensations caused by the drug. That is, for use to continue, it is necessary not only to use the drug so as to produce effects but also to learn to perceive these effects when they occur. In this way marihuana acquires meaning for the user as an object which can be used for pleasure.

With increasing experience the user develops a greater appreciation of the drug's effects; he continues to learn to get high. He examines succeeding experiences closely, looking for new effects, making sure the old ones are still there. Out of this there grows a stable set of categories for experiencing the drug's effects whose presence enables the user to get high with ease.

Users, as they acquire this set of categories, become connoisseurs. Like experts in fine wines, they can specify where a particular plant was grown and what time of year it was harvested. Although it is usually not possible to know whether these attributions are correct, it is true that they distinguish between batches of marihuana, not only according to strength, but also with respect to the different kinds of symptoms produced.

The ability to perceive the drug's effects must be maintained if use is to continue; if it is lost, marihuana use ceases. Two kinds of evidence support this statement. First, people who become heavy users of alcohol, barbiturates, or opiates do not continue to smoke marihuana, largely because they lose the ability to distinguish between its effects and those of the other drugs.[9] They no longer know whether the marihuana gets them high. Second, in those few cases in which an individual uses marihuana in such quantities that he is always high, he is apt to feel the drug has no effect on him, since the essential element of a noticeable difference between feeling high and feeling normal is missing. In such a situation, use is likely to be given up completely, but temporarily, in order that the user may once again be able to perceive the difference.

LEARNING TO ENJOY THE EFFECTS

One more step is necessary if the user who has now learned to get high is to continue use. He must learn to enjoy the effects he has just learned to experience. Marihuana-produced sensations are not automatically or necessarily pleasurable. The taste for such experience is a socially acquired one, not different in kind from acquired tastes for oysters or dry martinis. The user feels dizzy, thirsty; his scalp tingles; he misjudges time and distances. Are these things pleasurable? He isn't sure. If he is to continue marihuana use, he must decide that they are. Otherwise, getting high, while a real enough experience, will be an unpleasant one he would rather avoid.

The effects of the drug, when first perceived, may be physically unpleasant or at least ambiguous:

It started taking effect, and I didn't know what was happening, you know, what it was, and I was very sick. I walked around the room, walking around the room trying to get off, you know; it just scared me at first, you know. I wasn't used to that kind of feeling.

In addition, the novice's naive interpretation of what is happening to him may further confuse and frighten him, particularly if he decides, as many do, that he is going insane:

I felt I was insane, you know. Everything people done to me just wigged me. I couldn't hold a conversation, and my mind would be wandering, and I was always thinking, oh, I don't know, weird things, like hearing music different . . . I get the feeling that I can't talk to anyone. I'll goof completely.

Given these typically frightening and unpleasant first experiences, the beginner will not continue use unless he learns to redefine the sensations as pleasurable:

It was offered to me, and I tried it. I'll tell you one thing. I never did enjoy it at all. I mean it was just nothing that I could enjoy. [Well, did you get high when you turned on?] Oh, yeah, I got definite feelings from it. But I didn't enjoy them. I mean I got plenty of reactions, but they were mostly reactions of fear. [You were frightened?] Yes. I didn't enjoy it. I couldn't seem to relax with it, you know. If you can't relax with a thing, you can't enjoy it, I don't think.

In other cases the first experiences were also definitely unpleasant, but the person did become a marihuana user. This occurred, however, only after a later experience enabled him to redefine the sensations as pleasurable:

[This man's first experience was extremely unpleasant, involving distortion of spatial relationships and sounds, violent thirst, and panic produced by these symptoms.] After the first time I didn't turn on for about, I'd say, ten months to a year . . . It wasn't a moral thing; it was because I'd gotten so frightened, bein' so high. An' I didn't want to go through that again, I mean, my reaction was, 'Well, if this is what they call bein' high, I don't dig [like] it.' . . . So I didn't turn on for a year almost, accounta that . . .

Well, my friends started, an' consequently I started again. But I didn't have any more, I didn't have that same initial reaction, after I started turning on again.

[In interaction with his friends he became able to find pleasure in the effects of the drug and eventually became a regular user.]

In no case will use continue without a redefinition of the effects as enjoyable.

This redefinition occurs, typically, in interaction with more experienced users who, in a number of ways, teach the novice to find pleasure in this experience which is at first so frightening.[10] They may reassure him as to the temporary character of the unpleasant sensations and minimize their seriousness, at the same time calling attention to the more enjoyable aspects. An experienced user describes how he handles newcomers to marihuana use:

Well, they get pretty high sometimes. The average person isn't ready for that, and it is a little frightening to them sometimes. I mean, they've been high on lush [alcohol], and they get higher that way than they've ever been before, and they don't know what's happening to them. Because they think they're going to keep going up, up, up till they lose their minds or begin doing weird things or something. You have to like reassure them, explain to them that they're not really flipping or anything, that they're gonna be all right. You have to just talk them out of being afraid. Keep talking to them, reassuring, telling them it's all right. And come on with your own story, you know: 'The same thing happened to me. You'll get to like that after a while'. Keep coming on like that; pretty soon you talk them out of being scared. And besides they see you doing it and nothing horrible is happening to you, so that gives them more confidence.

The more experienced user may also teach the novice to regulate the amount he smokes more carefully, so as to avoid any severely uncomfortable symptoms while retaining the pleasant ones. Finally, he teaches the new user that he can 'get to like it after awhile.' He teaches

him to regard those ambiguous experiences formerly defined as unpleasant as enjoyable. The older user in the following incident is a person whose tastes have shifted in this way, and his remarks have the effect of helping others to make a similar redefinition:

A new user had her first experience of the effects of marihuana and became frightened and hysterical. She 'felt like she was half in and half out of the room' and experienced a number of alarming physical symptoms. One of the more experienced users present said, 'She's dragged because she's high like that. I'd give anything to get that high myself. I haven't been that high in years.'

In short, what was once frightening and distasteful becomes, after a taste for it is built up, pleasant, desired, and sought after. Enjoyment is introduced by the favorable definition of the experience that one acquires from others. Without this, use will not continue, for marihuana will not be for the user an object he can use for pleasure.

In addition to being a necessary step in becoming a user, this represents an important condition for continued use. It is quite common for experienced users suddenly to have an unpleasant or frightening experience, which they cannot define as pleasurable, either because they have used a larger amount of marihuana than usual or because the marihuana they have used turns out to be of a higher quality than they expected. The user has sensations which go beyond any conception he has of what being high is and is in much the same situation as the novice, uncomfortable and frightened. He may blame it on an overdose and simply be more careful in the future. But he may make this the occasion for a rethinking of his attitude toward the drug and decide that it no longer can give him pleasure. When this occurs and is not followed by a redefinition of the drug as capable of producing pleasure, use will cease.

The likelihood of such a redefinition occurring depends on the degree of the individual's participation with other users. Where this participation is intensive, the individual is quickly talked out of his feeling against marihuana use. In the next case, on the other hand, the experience was very disturbing, and the aftermath of the incident cut the person's participation with other users to almost zero. Use stopped for three years and began again only when a combination of circumstances, important among which was a resumption of ties with users, made possible a redefinition of the nature of the drug:

It was too much, like I only made about four pokes, and I couldn't even get it out of my mouth, I was so high, and I got real flipped. In the basement, you know, I just couldn't stay in there anymore. My heart was pounding real hard, you know, and I was going out of my mind; I thought I was losing my mind completely. So I cut out of this basement, and this other guy, he's out of his mind, told me, 'Don't, don't leave me, man. Stay here.' And I couldn't.

I walked outside, and it was five below zero, and I thought I was dying, and I had my coat open; I was sweating, I was perspiring. My whole insides were all . . . , and I walked about two blocks away, and I fainted behind a bush. I don't know how long I laid there. I woke up, and I was feeling the worst, I can't descibe it at all, so I made it to a bowling alley, man, and I was trying to act normal, I was trying to shoot pool, you know, trying to act real normal, and I couldn't lay and I couldn't stand up and I couldn't sit down, and I went up and laid down where some guys that spot pins lay down, and that didn't help me, and I went down to a doctor's office. I was going to go in there and tell the doctor to put me out of my misery . . . because my heart was pounding so hard, you know . . . So then all week end I started flipping, seeing things there and going through hell, you know, all kinds of abnormal things . . . I just quit for a long time then.

[He went to a doctor who defined the symptoms for him as those of a nervous breakdown caused by 'nerves' and 'worries'. Although he was no longer using marihuana, he had some recurrences of the symptoms which led him to suspect that 'it was all his nerves.'] So I just stopped worrying, you know; so it was about thirty-six months later I started making it again. I'd just take a few pokes, you know. [He first resumed use in the company of the same user-friend with whom he had been involved in the original incident.]

A person, then, cannot begin to use marihuana for pleasure, or continue its use for pleasure, unless he learns to define its effects as enjoyable, unless it becomes and remains an object he conceives of as capable of producing pleasure.

In summary, an individual will be able to use marihuana for pleasure only when he goes through a process of learning to conceive of it as an object which can be used in this way. No one becomes a user without (1) learning to smoke the drug in a way which will produce real effects; (2) learning to recognize the effects and connect them with drug use (learning, in other words,

to get high); and (3) learning to enjoy the sensations he perceives. In the course of this process he develops a disposition or motivation to use marihuana which was not and could not have been present when he began use, for it involves and depends on conceptions of the drug which could only grow out of the kind of actual experience detailed above. On completion of this process he is willing and able to use marihuana for pleasure.

He has learned, in short, to answer 'Yes' to the question: 'Is it fun?' The direction his further use of the drug takes depends on his being able to continue to answer 'Yes' to this question and, in addition, on his being able to answer 'Yes' to other questions which arise as he becomes aware of the implications of the fact that society disapproves of the practice: 'Is it expedient?' 'Is it moral?' Once he has acquired the ability to get enjoyment by using the drug, use will continue to be possible for him. Considerations of morality and expediency, occasioned by the reactions of society, may interfere and inhibit use, but use continues to be a possibility in terms of his conception of the drug. The act becomes impossible only when the ability to enjoy the experience of being high is lost, through a change in the user's conception of the drug occasioned by certain kinds of experience with it.

REFERENCES

1. See, as examples of this approach, the following: Eli Marcovitz and Henry J. Meyers, 'The Marihuana Addict in the Army', *War Medicine*, VI (December, 1944), 382–391; Herbert S. Gaskill, 'Marihuana, an Intoxicant', *American Journal of Psychiatry*, CII (September, 1945), 202–204; Sol Charen and Luis Perelman, 'Personality Studies of Marihuana Addicts', *American Journal of Psychiatry*, CII (March, 1946), 647–682.
2. This theoretical point of view stems from George Herbert Mead's discussion of objects in *Mind, Self, and Society* (Chicago: University of Chicago Press, 1934), pp. 277–280.
3. Cf. Rogers Adams, 'Marihuana', *Bulletin of the New York Academy of Medicine*, XVIII (November, 1942), 705–730.
4. The New York City Mayor's Committee on Marihuana, *The Marihuana Problem in the City of New York* (Lancaster, Pennsylvania: Jacques Cattell Press, 1944), pp. 12–13.
5. Cf. Lawrence Kolb, 'Marihuana', *Federal Probation*, II

(July, 1938), 22–25; and Walter Bromberg, 'Marihuana: A Psychiatric Study', *Journal of the American Medical Association*, CXIII (July 1, 1939), 11.

6. The method is described in Alfred R. Lindesmith, *Opiate Addiction* (Bloomington, Indiana: Principia Press, 1947), chap. 1. There has been considerable discussion of this method in the literature. See, particularly, Ralph H. Turner, 'The Quest for Universals in Sociological Research', *American Sociological Review*, 18 (December, 1953), 604–611, and the literature cited there.

7. I wish to thank Solomon Kobrin and Harold Finestone for making these interviews available to me.

8. A pharmacologist notes that this ritual is in fact an extremely efficient way of getting the drug into the blood stream. See R.P. Walton, *Marihuana: America's New Drug Problem* (Philadelphia: J.B. Lippincott, 1938), p. 48.

9. 'Smokers have repeatedly stated that the consumption of whiskey while smoking negates the potency of the drug. They find it very difficult to get "high" while drinking whiskey and because of that smokers will not drink while using the "weed".' (New York City Mayor's Committee on Marihuana, *The Marihuana Problem in the City of New York, op. cit.*, p. 13.)

10. Charen and Perelman, *op. cit.*, p. 679.

Smoking in pregnancy: the attitudes of expectant mothers

HILARY GRAHAM

Department of Sociology, University of York
(now *Head of Department of Applied Social Studies, Coventry (Lanchester) Polytechnic*)

This paper considers the way in which the issue of smoking in pregnancy is perceived by the mass media/medical profession, and by a group of expectant mothers. Although the paper describes research undertaken in 1974 and outlines the health education ideology of that time, it has important messages for present day health workers.

SMOKING IN PREGNANCY: THE SCIENTIFIC VIEWPOINT

The widespread acceptance by the medical establishment of a link between maternal smoking and foetal growth retardation has led to the progressive involvement of the mass media and particularly those elements with a strong pedagogic purpose, in this field of preventive health. Today, we find newspapers, books and women's magazines, posters, leaflets and television advertisements all warning the mother-to-be of the unforeseen consequences her smoking habits can have for her unborn child.

Over the last two decades new publications have begun to include exhortations against smoking in pregnancy. The 1970 edition of *You and Your Baby*, for example, had a sub-section headed 'Cut down smoking' where it advised readers (p. 30):

Don't smoke if you can possibly help it . . . Mothers who smoke have babies that weigh less at birth and are often less vigorous as well.

At the heart of this literature, and the ante-natal programmes which they complement, one can identify a

particular theoretical model of individual behaviour. This model, similar to that which provides the rationale for contemporary birth control campaigns, views patterns of individual behaviour as the outcome of a triadic sequence: knowledge—attitude—practice (K.A.P.). According to this schema, modifications in smoking practices are accomplished by transmitting what Donovan calls 'the facts about smoking in pregnancy' to the expectant mother, facts which will hopefully transform their attitudes, and thus their behaviour, in line with medical precepts.[1] This literature, and the associated anti-smoking programmes, draw their facts from one side of the smoking debate, underplaying the evidence of those who dispute the dominant, 'scientific', position. In the transmission of these facts, the educators — be they agents of the mass media involved in the production of tabloid and celluloid material or ante-natal personnel — make certain assumptions about their target population, the smoking mother-to-be. It is implicitly assumed that smoking in pregnancy is a problem, firstly, of the *ignorance* of the smoker concerning the consequences of her actions and secondly of her *irresponsibility* or even selfishness regarding the future well-being of her unborn child. In tackling the first problem, factual information is seen as the key ('This is what can happen if you smoke when you're pregnant'); in tackling the second, moral persuasion is seen as more appropriate ('Is it fair to your baby to smoke cigarettes?')

The substitution of *factual information* for folk

ignorance, the first aim of anti-smoking literature, rests upon instilling a sense of future orientation, an awareness of the long-term consequences of activities in pregnancy. This process is perceived to be handicapped by two features of the smoking population. On the one hand, the individual is seen as immersed in a traditional world, built around a fatalistic acceptance of the future and one's position in it. These traditionalistic attitudes are referred to by popular writers under the rubric of 'old wives' tales' which, in most publications, include not only proverbial theories about strawberry marks and hare lips, but any unpleasant information passed on by non-medical personnel. On the other, the individual is seen as particularly gullible to the images and ideals portrayed in television and press advertisements, images and ideals again seen as in conflict with those of preventive medicine.

Moral persuasion, the second component of anti-smoking literature, works upon the backcloth of factual information to develop, in the place of selfishness and thoughtlessness, a sense of responsibility and self-sacrifice in the expectant mother. Thus one practitioner recommends that those who, even when told 'the facts' are reluctant to give up smoking can be 'helped along' by saying 'Now Mrs Smith I'm sure we want to do the best for your baby'. The themes of unselfishness and responsibility are more forcefully evoked in the H.E.C. campaign in such slogans as 'Do you want a cigarette more than you want a baby?'

Although the ascription of ignorance and irresponsibility to the smoking population has been identified by health educators as crucial to both an understanding of the smoking problem and to its eradication, the way the smoking mothers actually perceive their smoking habit during pregnancy remains relatively uninvestigated. While the medical journals attempt to keep their scientific readership in touch with recent research, the mass media aim to provide a similar service for the public. The process of educational osmosis is thus unidirectional, with information passing from the scientific community to the lay public through the media of press and television. By contrast, relatively little is known by the scientific community about lay theories concerning smoking in pregnancy and particularly, about their susceptibility to modification and change in response to 'scientific fact'.

SMOKING IN PREGNANCY: THE EXPECTANT MOTHER'S VIEWPOINT

A study carried out into the experiences of pregnancy, based on a small sample of 50 expectant mothers, can perhaps throw a little light on this neglected area.[2]

During interview, all respondents were asked: 'What do you think about smoking in pregnancy?' The responses to this question related to the smoking behaviour of the respondents. *The non-smoking expectant mothers* tended to endorse the scientific assumptions about maternal smoking. These respondents generally accepted the medical view of foetal retardation:

They say smoking does all sorts to them, it makes them small and backward — or it kills them.

Their attitudes to their smoking sisters coincided with — and was probably reinforced by — the cultural stereotype portrayed in the anti-smoking literature. Smoking was frequently conceived as a moral issue, in which one could distinguish a right and a wrong course of action. Right and wrong were assessed, in line with medical thinking, in terms of the needs of two protagonists: mother and child.

It's wrong and I won't do it, it's selfish only to think of yourself and not the health of your child.

As these comments suggest, those who abstained accorded themselves such qualities as unselfishness and responsibility, while those who failed to curb their habit were denigrated either as weak-willed and selfish, or as ignorant.

The smoking expectant mothers contained a larger proportion of those who dissented from the mainstream medical opinion on smoking. However, a third of the smokers accepted the view that smoking was detrimental to the unborn child. Among these respondents, were the four who gave up in anticipation or as a result of their present pregnancy:

I smoked up to about a month before the baby was conceived. It's unfair on the child to smoke . . .

Others among this group continued smoking however,

despite their convictions concerning its deleterious consequences. Unlike the non-smokers, these mothers could not revel in their self-righteousness but were victim to feelings of inadequacy and guilt. The notion that foetal abnormality was maternally-induced, frequently through negligence, was widely held by the respondents. The advice they received on smoking confirmed their fears, and transformed pregnancy from the carefree and enjoyable time they had anticipated into one of anxiety and apprehension. As one smoker put it:

If you must know, I'm worried sick about it. I can't stop and there's an end to it. I wish I could just be left alone, my husband goes on, and my mother, and every time I open a magazine, I'm told I'm killing my baby, and now it's even on the telly. What're they trying to do? . . . They don't need to tell me, I know I'm harming him, don't they think I've got any feelings and worry myself sick over it?

Most smokers were in a more fortunate position, being able, despite their general conviction that foetal abnormality was maternally-induced, to discount cigarettes as a possible teratogen — for example by maintaining that the amount they smoked was unlikely to cause harm:

I do smoke, but not that many, maybe two a day and four on a weekend, something like that. I don't think that enough to bother about, do you?

Others, while acknowledging the malevolent effects of sexual intercourse or heavy housework, were able to enjoy a cigarette without shame or guilt by rejecting the scientific theory altogether:

I don't think it makes any difference. It's supposed to make them underweight but I've always smoked nearly 40 a day and mine were all around 11 lbs — that's with the smoking.

This brief consideration of the views of a group of non-smoking and smoking expectant mothers indicates a number of areas relevant to an understanding of smoking attitudes and behaviour. Respondents typically differed not in their knowledge or ignorance of the arguments against smoking, but in their assessment of the validity of the scientific case. While the non-smokers' views were relatively homogeneous, among the smokers there were those whose attitudes were consistent with their behaviour (smoking and maintaining it to be relatively harmless) and those whose attitudes and behaviour were discrepant (smoking when they believed it to be harmful). The existence of these two smoking patterns, which together can be seen to constitute the 'problem' of ante-natal smoking, raises the question of why, within one group, medical findings about foetal retardation are rejected and smoking is continued and why, within the other, respondents failed to give up smoking despite adherence to medical theory. The interview material suggests that the first question can be seen to turn upon the individual's perception of scientific knowledge and the second to revolve around the perceived personal functions that smoking serves.

SMOKING: A SCIENTIFIC FACT

It has been suggested that when respondents disputed the medical evidence concerning smoking they did so by making cigarettes an exception to their general beliefs about the influence of the maternal environment on foetal normality and development. Cigarettes were excepted a possible teratogen invariably on the basis of their personal experience — 'I've always smoked 40 a day and mine were all around 11 lbs'. The medical contention that smoking retards physical and mental development is treated as 'just another of those tales'. It is one of 'so many theories', 'a majority opinion . . . no one's proved it'. The distinction persistently made in the mass media between old wives' tales (bad knowledge) and scientific fact (good knowledge) communicated through trained doctors and midwives is abandoned in favour of one that discriminates between generalised second-hand knowledge and personal 'proof' built up by the individual over years of observation and experience. It is a distinction which appeared as crucial in the interpretation of other aspects of the pregnancy experience.

When investigating the sources of information that respondents drew on during pregnancy, it was found that although respondents relied on a range of informants it was personally-transmitted information, rather than information from non-personal sources, that was more highly valued and more readily adhered to. This finding had one important proviso, namely that advice given by clinic-personnel was treated as information from a non-personal source. In other words, respondents would more readily turn to and accept advice from relatives, friends and their family doctor than from books, magazines, television and the staff of the ante-natal clinic. These preferences reflected an antipathy towards standardised, pre-packaged types of information: firstly because such non-individualised advice rarely fitted the exigencies of the individual's pregnancy and secondly because such information was considered to gloss over and distort the realities of childbearing. By contrast, knowledge disseminated in face-to-face interaction with social contacts — including for some, the family doctor — not only contained specific, problem-oriented advice tailored to the individual's needs, but minimised the possibility of exaggerating either the glamours or the horrors of the reproductive process.

This pattern was most marked among those who lived in the area of their childhood in close proximity to their family of origin. Those who had moved away from their childhood contacts to take up residence in a new area — a predominantly but not exclusively middle-class group — tended to rely on the mass media and the medical profession to a greater extent for guidance on the child-bearing process.

SMOKING: A PERSONAL DILEMMA

It was not only that the case against smoking rested, from the point of view of many smokers, on the 'wrong' type of proof also it failed to relate to or take account of the reality of the individual's daily life. By presenting the issue as a moral choice between the mother's (present) happiness and the child's (future) health, based on the imputation of a single set of motives (selfishness and ignorance), the media abstracted the individual, and her smoking patterns, from the everyday context in which it was sustained and found meaning. When viewed in this everyday context, the decision to continue smoking can be seen to rest on a range of dilemmas and decisions over and above that between maternal happiness and foetal health.

One such dilemma related to the moral conflict between the needs of one's present family and the needs of the future addition. In the non-smokers' perspective, as in the mass media, the mother-to-be is rarely pictured with a family, or even a husband. By contrast, smoking mothers discussed the smoking issue in the context of their husband and children, for it was they, as well as the mother herself, who was seen to pay a price if she decided to sacrifice her cigarettes for the sake of the new baby:

I'm always more scratchy when I'm carrying. I fly off the handle more and over little things . . . It's hard enough for Dave [husband] and Louise [daughter] as it is. I gave up the smoking for a bit, and I was even more irritable, and I don't think I can ask that of them again. Besides, I reckon if I get much worse, Dave'll move out!

Respondents, in deciding on their smoking behaviour, felt they had to weigh up the risks for the unborn child of continuing smoking against the detrimental effects upon the family if they were to give up. Although the choice, when made in a clinical context, may be simple and clear-cut, for these mothers it was considerably more complicated and problematic.

Similar complications were evident even when the smoking issue was perceived, in line with the media's image, as a conflict between the desires of the mother and the needs of the child. However, while in the media, smoking is portrayed as a solitary activity, pursued, apparently, simply for reasons of personal enjoyment, in respondents' accounts, smoking took on an additional significance. The functions of smoking extended beyond the simply pleasurable: smoking became a way of marking out the day into 'work' and 'rest', a method of achieving a momentary autonomy from one's domestic role.

Smoking appeared as a ritual activity engaged in at certain prescribed periods — at coffee time, after lunch, during the afternoon and in the evening. This is not to underestimate the addictive qualities of nicotine, but rather to suggest the way in which individuals, whether they smoked two or 20 cigarettes a day, structured their smoking so as to provide a sense of escape from the perceived rigours of daily life. Smoking functioned in this way whether the mother worked in the home or in employment.

The smoking of one, or several, cigarettes, appears as a way of delineating periods of the day as both a time for relaxation (putting the feet up) and a time for social intercourse (having friends in). These are times when the harassed mother can temporarily escape from the exactions of full-time motherhood. During such interludes, the children are expected to entertain themselves, for the mother is not oriented to them but to herself or to her peer group. The existence of these periods was considered essential by the individuals if they are to keep 'their strength up' and perform their role with equanimity. One mother, describing a 'typical day' put it this way:

... after lunch, I clear away and wash up and put on the telly for Stevie. I'll have a sit down on the sofa, with a cigarette and maybe a cup of tea. It's lovely, it's the one time in the day I really enjoy and I know Stevie won't disturb me ... [what do you do?] I just sit and enjoy being on my own.

Smoking provides both a sense of body autonomy and role distance, a time when children are forbidden to climb on mother's knee and to demand attention. It emphasises her adult status and her independence from her children, a function it serves not only with respect to her peers but also her husband:

Now I smoke four or five a day, mostly in an evening with Alec. It's part of our time together, having a cigarette ...

SUMMARY

This paper considered the way in which the media, and a group of expectant mothers, perceive and portray the issue of smoking in pregnancy. It suggested that within the popular literature aimed at the expectant mother, there is a tendency to view the problem as a function of ignorance, fanned by traditionalism and advertisements, and of irresponsibility.

The paper indicated that among one group of expectant mothers it was not ignorance of 'the facts' that was the crucial variable, but rather the credibility the individual accorded to these facts in particular and to scientific knowledge in general.

The interpretations of smoking attitudes and behaviour in this paper are based, at present, only on a small sample of expectant mothers. If their validity is confirmed, they have serious implications for the way in which anti-smoking programmes are managed in prenatal clinics and in the mass media — and by extension, for the way pregnancy care in general is organised. These implications relate, in particular, to the general tendency to impute ignorance and/or irresponsibility as primary motivating factors among smoking expectant mothers. The paper has suggested that, before ascribing these twin attributes, both the mass media and the medical profession should take account of four aspects of the individual's approach to, and experience of, pregnancy. It argues for a recognition of:

(i)   the general preference for and importance of personal over non-personal sources of information among expectant mothers;
(ii) the way in which non-personal knowledge, scientific and traditional, is routinely apprehended, with a distinction between the two only emerging when the preferred lay system of guidance is unavailable or inoperative;
(iii) the multiple dimensions to the question of the individual's responsibility and obligations in pregnancy: with responsibilities not only to her unborn child, but to her other offspring, to her husband, to her friends and to herself;
(iv) the way women, and particularly mothers, structure and achieve autonomy (and thus realise their responsibilities to themselves) within their working day. Particular recognition should be given to the symbolic role of smoking in this structuring and autonomy-giving process.

REFERENCES

1. Donovan, J.W., Burgess, P.L., Hossack, D.M. and Tudkin, G.D. *J.R. Coll. gen. Practitioners* **25**, 264, 1975. This is a study of an ante-natal anti-smoking programme, based on telling the patient 'the facts about smoking in pregnancy'.
2. The research on which this paper is based was carried out in 1974 and was based on a random sample of 50 pregnant women, 25 expecting their first, and 25 expecting a second or subsequent, baby. Although based on a small number of women, it is felt that, in view of the dearth of information in this area, the findings are important and relevant to the smoking debate. However, the small size of the sample and the unverified nature of the data should be borne in mind.

Paper 16
Historical and political perspective: women and drug use

EDITH S. LISANSKY GOMBERG

Institute for Social Research, University of Michigan

This paper explores the political and historical factors contributing to the different usage of drug substances for men and women. Gender is linked to the use of drugs for both therapeutic and recreational purposes. Some possible reasons for the differences between the sexes are discussed in the paper.

The story may be apocryphal but there is a history surrounding the cacao bean that is interesting and illuminating. Cacao beans were among the curiosities of the New World brought back to Europe by Columbus. The tree on which the beans grew was considered to be of divine origin by the Aztec people of Mexico, and a beverage derived from the bean, cocolatl (choco, meaning foam, and atl, water) was the favorite of the Emperor Montezuma (Cacao, 1954). The apocryphal part of this story is the attribution of aphrodisiac quality to the beverage and the response of the Europeans who promptly forbid its use by women. The original drink was quite bitter but, in very little time, someone had figured a spectacular improvement: the addition of sugar. At this point, it may well be that cocoa was the most abused drug of its time because women, particularly upper class women who could afford it, drank cups of the forbidden stuff, even having it brought by servants while they were at their devotions (Taylor, 1968). The drink was delicious, desirable, and presumably a sexual stimulant. Eventually the ban was lifted and we view cocoa with equanimity, although to this day there are legends about the aphrodisiac characteristic of various foods or drugs.

The story may be a myth but it does carry certain

messages. People have sought to regulate the use of substances and they have often ended up with differences in the regulations for men and women. This paper explores some of the historical and political factors contributing to the difference. The work of Child, Barry and Bacon (1965) in the cross-cultural study of sex differences in drinking norms suggests that increased *familiarity* with a substance like alcohol leads to clearer, more differentiated normative rules for sexes. Societies with definite sex differences in the use of alcohol were significantly more often those societies that had used alcohol aboriginally; among societies with no evidence of normative sex differences, postcontact introduction to alcohol was more likely than aboriginal use. This, of course, may lead to some interesting questions about the usage of alcohol and other substances in the history of colonialization (Lisansky, 1967).

If we are to discuss such a vast area as women's use of drug substances, we must limit the focus. The focus here is the use of legal, socially acceptable drugs by women.

Within the classification of legal drugs, there are the *medicinal drugs* including both prescribed and over-the-counter (OTC) medications. In the category of medicinal drugs would be included herbal infusions, homemade medications and folk remedies including chicken soup and camomile tea. Second, there are *social drugs* which include alcohol, caffeine and nicotine. There may be tax laws that modify the use of these substances,

From *Journal of Social Issues*, Vol. 38, No. 2, 1982, pp. 9–23. Reprinted with permission from Society for the Psychological Study of Social Issues and Plenum Publishing Corporation.

and there are laws relating to minimum age and restricting sale of alcoholic beverages, but legal limitations are few and the use of alcoholic beverages is more or less sanctioned by American society which — like all mankind — has had an ambivalent, love-hate relationship with alcohol for centuries. Of the three 'social drugs', alcohol is the oldest, having been around, we think, since Neolithic man. It occurs in nature, fermentation being a process observed and utilized by almost all peoples. It probably is the 'social drug' most widely used since it occurs in so many forms: fermented fruit juices, grain, honey, etc. In history, drinking wine or beer has been, probably, less of a risk in many times and places than drinking the water.

MEDICINAL DRUGS

Prescription drugs can be readily defined: They are those drugs and medications which, at least by law, cannot be obtained without a prescription. There are also over-the-counter (OTC) or proprietary drugs, traditionally used for self-medication. The OTC drugs are heirs of the traveling medicine show products and the home remedies of the past. Items such as Lydia E. Pinkham's Vegetable Compound or Mrs Winslow's Soothing Syrup were presented as painkiller, health tonic, 'women's friend', just as OTC medications such as Midol or Geritol are advertised currently. The medicine show products and drugs sold over the counter in the nineteenth century included a good dollop of alcohol, or sometimes a quantity of an opiate drug. A widely used 'doctor book' of the late eighteenth and nineteenth century recommends tincture of opium or liquid laudanum for treating a variety of common ailments. During that period, cocaine, too, was in a number of proprietary medications. These practices were halted by passage of the Pure Food and Drug Act in 1906 which classified drugs as either proprietary or prescription and set up methods of monitoring and control (Chambers, Inciardi & Siegal, 1975). The passage of the Harrison Act in 1914 added the final touch and women, who had been the largest consumers of opiate drugs, at this point shifted their medication habits. There is little record of these events.

There are several other drugs, organic compounds that occur in nature and have been known for many centuries, e.g. atropa belladone or datura stamonium (Jim-

son weed). Knowledge about the preparation and use of these substances was probably linked at several points in history to witchcraft, to orgies, and to sorcerers' brews. These substances are still around and in use: currently, derivatives of these compounds appear in medical practice as Atropine or scopalamine, and in some OTC medications such as sleep inducers and medicine for nervous tension, nasal congestion or diarrhea.

If we confine ourselves to those societies about which we have some information about men, women and drugs, it would appear that *gender and the use of drugs for medicinal/therapeutic purposes are inextricably linked*. One theme that runs through the nineteenth and twentieth centuries is a sex difference, in which women use substances in medicinal/therapeutic ways more than men do, and in which men use substances as recreation and for pleasurable purposes more than women do.

Women are bigger users of psychoactive drugs. In a twentieth-century duplication of nineteenth-century opiate-in-tonic usage, women are much more likely than men to use medically prescribed psychoactive drugs (Chambers, 1971; Cooperstock, 1976; Mellinger, Balter, Parry, Mannheimer & Cisin, 1974; Verbrugge, Note 1) and to be heavier users of minor tranquilizers, stimulants, hypnotics and antidepressants. Over-the-counter drug usage is more variable: Women use nonprescription sleeping medication and tranquilizers more than men, and men, particularly under the age of 25, report more frequent use of nonprescription stimulants (Chambers et al., 1975).

What are some of the possible reasons for this differential in the use of medication? There are a number of possibilities, not mutually exclusive by any means: the physiological events in women's lives, the relative health status of men and women, different aspects of sexually assigned roles, and socially determined double standards in the substances prescribed and proscribed.

The physiological events in women's lives

Perhaps anatomy is not destiny but the fact remains that stages in women's lives are more clearly marked by physiological events than is true of men's lives.

Menstruation, pregnancy, childbirth, lactation, menopause, are unmistakable markers of life stage and hormonal status. Assuming no pathology, these are natural events. But it is not so simple: These events are surrounded by mythologies and beliefs and while one may argue for 'human cycles' for both men and women (Unger & Denmark, 1975), popular conceptions of menstruation as 'the curse' and negative descriptions of 'change of life' do not seem to have changed very much. Attempts have been made to study the relation of menstrual cycle to efficiency of performance, to depression and suicide and psychiatric symptomatology, and the relations are unclear. Nevertheless, it is clear that many women turn to analgesics, diuretics or tranquilizers at stages of the menstrual cycle, it is women who take 'the pill' for contraception, and it is women for whom estrogen and similar substances have been prescribed for menopause. This is not to deny that there are real stresses and real pain associated with some of the normal physiological events in women's lives, but one may question whether the amount of medication consumed is in proportion and whether tea and sympathy might not very often work as well. It is obviously true that there are physiological events, markers that occur in the lives of women, and the social norms may carry the message to women: You may not indulge in use of this or that substance for pleasure or for 'highs' or for erotic enhancement but you may take medicine. If *illness* then includes not only disease and organic pathology, but the discomfort associated with menstruation or childbirth, we can begin to understand the popularity of tonics and remedies for 'women's troubles'. If the concept of illness is further extended to include unhappiness, loneliness, boredom and other psychic malaise, we have arrived at the situation in which we find ourselves now: Women as the major consumers of psychoactive drugs.

The relative health status of men and women

Women apparently experience more acute illness and men have more serious chronic conditions and more injuries than women (Verbrugge, Note 1). The data on chronic medical conditions are mixed, actually, since women after age 45 have more chronic illness, although males have higher prevalence rates for 'killer' conditions, i.e., major causes of death. The importance of

socialization and attitudes toward health and sickness are apparent in data from interviews and health behavior surveys. Women use medical services more than men do, and '. . . data repeatedly show that females use more prescription and nonprescription drugs than men do' (Verbrugge, Note 1). Does this sequence of events relate to women's greater longevity? Are men more stoic or less aware of symptoms or less willing to seek medical care?

Differences in 'real' illness are one factor but possibly more significant in medication is the question of which of the sexes reports feeling more ill? The survey data are consistent: Women consistently report worse health status than men do. It is perhaps these reported perceptions that result in more female use of outpatient medical services and in more female use of medication. And these two may be related: Perhaps women use prescribed drugs more than men do because they are in physicians' offices and clinics more frequently. Some of the greater female use of medication is based on more total visits to physicians. The question has been raised, too, whether — other things being equal — physicians tend to prescribe more readily for women patients than for men patients. The trend of evidence is that this is true (Cooperstock, 1971; Sims, Note 2). Both factors are operating: more office visits, more tendency to prescribe — thus, more medication.

Different aspects of sexually assigned roles

There may be societies in which much of male/female roles are interchangeable but we know few, if any, such societies. And rules about substance use may be related to gender assignment of work; Child et al. (1965) point out that taboos about intoxication are related to women's and men's work roles:

Under the generally prevailing conditions of human life, temporary incapacity of a woman is more threatening than is temporary incapacity of a man. For example, care of a field can be postponed for a day, but care of a child cannot. The general social role makes drunkenness more threatening in women than in men.

Knupfer (Note 3), seeking to explain the greater distaste and rejection of female intoxication, suggests that impairment in the nurturing, caretaker role — the work role — of women is anxiety-provoking and threatening.

Two links to sexual role may be suggested. Once the female has achieved adult, i.e., wife and mother, status, there are not many avenues through which she can search for gratification of her own dependency needs. One socially sanctioned way to be taken care of is to be sick. The caretaker may have to nurture herself via sickness, medical care, and medicine. A second hypothetical link may be between women's role as caretakers of the sick and their own use of medications. In this caretaker role, she has responsibility, including medication, for the ill and the elderly. Might these responsibilities heighten her awareness and responsiveness to medication?

Socially determined double standards in substances prescribed and proscribed

Most societies develop rules about the use of substances. And those norms will spell out, more or less clearly, who may use a particular substance, in what amount, on what occasion. It was those preliterate peoples who were familiar with alcoholic beverages *before* contact with Europeans who had established gender differentiations in the norms of drinking (Child et al., 1965).

Linked to physiological events in women's lives and linked to sex role functions, societies set up standards about the utilization of recreational drugs. In the United States, alcohol has been the major recreational drug, and indeed saloons and bars were set up as primary need constructions when the Americans moved westward; these saloons and bars were for male use. If women were to have alcohol, they were more likely to get it from the tonics bought from the peddlers and medicine show people also moving westward.

A current picture of double standards may be derived from analysis of contemporary drug company advertising and the models used for drug company ads. It is true that the drug companies may be reflecting current viewpoints in picturing women more frequently in tranquilizer advertisement but the whole situation is circular and self-perpetuating: stereotype—advertisement —confirmed stereotype—self-fulfilling prophecy.

A note on illegal drug use

'Street drugs' include not only illegal drugs but drugs that are ordinarily obtained by prescription but have

found their way to illegal channels of distribution. A percentage of pharmaceuticals from respectable drug companies disappear and find their way to these channels. Illegal use of drugs also includes the taking of drugs prescribed for someone else: If adolescents are playing Russian roulette by popping pills at parties, these pills may often be from family medicine cabinets. It is also drug abuse when people collect a number of prescriptions from different physicians, whether the drug is sanctioned, e.g., a minor tranquilizer, or not.

Women are less frequent users of illegal 'street drugs' than are men. This may be a matter of relative accessibility since women spend more time at home. It may be that women are more law-abiding than men: they do indeed have lower crime rates. Or it may simply be that there are alternative substances available for their use which are socially approved, e.g., medications.

'Street drugs' are more likely to be involved in the search for a 'high' experience rather than as medication per se. Consistent with the hypothesis that women are more likely than men to be using substances medicinally, it is significant that the women of the nineteenth century who were using opiates were using them in tonics, i.e., as medicine. It is also noteworthy that there was an iatrogenic use, and that after the opiates became unavailable in tonics, there was the phenomenon of 'medical addiction.' Some women and men would become addicted to morphine after it was used in medical treatment: One famous example is Eugene O'Neill's mother, described in his *Long Day's Journey Into Night*.

When women do become involved with illegal 'street drugs', stigma appears to be greater for the woman addict than for the male. The female heroin addict may be socially punished, as the bearer of 'addicted babies', as a prostitute, as a petty thief. Sympathy for addicts is minimal, and apparently less for women addicts. Considering on the one hand the punitive, rejecting attitude toward women addicts, and the kinder, more accepting attitude toward the female user (and abuser) of medication, the outcome is predictable.

SOCIAL DRUGS

Examination of the differential expectations for men and women related to the use of social drugs highlights the influence of social norms. The usage of two of the three social drugs, alcohol and nicotine, has traditionally been greater among males than among females. And, of course, attitudes toward women's smoking and drinking have undergone much change in the last half century (the cigarette advertisement campaign that shows the earlier disapproval of women's smoking, states it flatly: 'You've come a long way, baby.')

People have had a love/hate relationship with alcohol for millennia. Alcohol, interestingly, has been viewed in many different ways. Alcohol has a venerable history as a *medicinal* drug (Williams, 1980), and it is still in medical usage in a limited way. It may be used, for example, during the process of childbirth, and it is often in use in geriatric wards. It is also present in many over-the-counter drugs. But alcohol has a complicated history in that it has also been considered at certain times and places, as a beneficial *food*. Among working class people in Chile and in other parts of South America, breakfast often consists of beer mixed with a kind of toasted whole wheat flour (harina tostada), a breakfast considered particularly good for nursing mothers (Marconi, Varela, Rosenblat, Solari, Marchesse, Alvarado, & Enriquez, 1959). Wine is considered a food in many parts of Italy and other countries of Europe.

As for women's drinking, it is rewarding to look back at historical descriptions. In the first book of Samuel in the Bible, there is a description of Hannah, apparently intoxicated, praying and weeping and possibly hallucinating:

. . . therefore Eli thought she was a drunkard. So Eli said to her: How long will you be drunken? Get yourself free of your wine (Keller, Note 4).

In ancient Greece, a symposium was usually a convivial meeting following dinner for the purpose of drinking and intellectual conversation. If women were present, it usually would be to provide entertainment. The Greek states were heavy drinking with the exception of Sparta where wine was much more watered than in the other states. It is interesting to note that the Greeks had a word for 'the headache that follows a debauch' (McKinlay, 1959). In the later stages of the Roman Empire, women were apparently free to drink and McKinlay describes the heavy drinking of highborn women, 'tippling old ladies', nurses and servingmaids.

The early Church writers from St. Paul on have left evidence, too, that the Christian authorities were indeed concerned with the heavy drinking of some women. Both the church and the ancient Hebrews were *not* concerned about women drinking moderately, they were concerned about heavy drinking and intoxication. Thus, it says in the Talmud:

One cup of wine is good for a woman;
Two are degrading;
Three induce her to act like an immoral woman;
And four cause her to lose all self-respect and sense of shame.

This message to women, that it is all right to drink but not in excess is still the message to this very day. The message that it is *not* all right to drink, the message of Prohibition, is directed toward men and women alike.

A notable moment in the history of women and alcohol is 'the gin epidemic' of eighteenth-century London. To increase revenues, Parliament lifted restrictions on the production of domestic gin leading to the orgy of drinking pictured by Hogarth in 'Gin Lane'. Much of the outraged response was directed toward women who produced sickly offspring in the first place, and neglected their children in the second. As in our current concern about 'the fetal alcohol syndrome', there was much anxiety about defective offspring. In the past and in the present, women substance abusers have received short shrift and little sympathy. The message in outraged England was: You have failed in your primary function, you are a bad mother.

Early American history

A recent historical work suggests that between 1790 and 1840, Americans drank very heavily and that this was true universally, crossing regional, racial, social class and gender lines. The reasons for the pervasiveness of alcohol were several: a belief that alcoholic beverages were nutritious and healthful, the bad taste of competing beverages, and the rising abundance of grain and economic conditions that created a large supply of cheap whiskey. Rorabaugh (1979) believes that this national binge ended in the 1830's when a new national grain market appeared. This interpretation suggests that the high alcohol consumption and the subsequent decline in consumption parallels the transition from an agricultural economy into the industrial revolution. It is about the same period dur-ing which the temperance movement started expand-ing, and Gusfield (1962) has suggested that one byproduct of industrialization was an advocacy of abstinence by industrialists as a means of improving the efficiency of the labor force. The doctrine of the Women's Christian Temperance Union was a humanitarian one, a moral reform movement bent on improving the lot of the working class (Gusfield, 1959).

Whether the 1790–1840 drinking of Americans was a national binge or the earthy behavior of an emerging colonial people, there does not seem to have been much anxiety about women drinking, women appear-ing in taverns, women drinking with men, even women owning and running taverns. Behavior and attitudes were reflections of English customs and running a tavern was an acceptable way for a widowed woman to support her family. Women probably drank less than men but there was no fuss raised about their drinking. As the shift into industrialization began in the early nine-teenth century, family organization and middle class role definition for men and women changed, and with this change, the role of the tavern shifted. It had serv-ed as community and social center for both men and women during the colonial era and up to the early nine-teenth century, but as the century moved on and the country expanded westward, the early New England and Eastern seaboard view of the tavern or 'pub' under-went a change. The tavern was now the *saloon* and this was male territory. Furthermore, in the cities it was often the territory of working class males, often foreign-born immigrants. The urban saloon was not only 'the poor man's club' (Kingsdale, 1980), it was also perceived as a center of maleness, foreign behaviors, and wickedness, the nemesis of the women's temperance advocates. While few went as far as Carrie Nation, it is clear that the saloon was enemy territory.

In a study of women and the temperance movement, Levine (1980) argues that women's role in the move-ment needs to be understood in the context of two major social shifts that occurred in the first half of the nineteenth century: a change in the structure and organization of the family and a new view of alcohol as a dangerous drug. The latter view seems to have been linked to growing ascetic Protestantism on the one hand, and to a pervasive Victorian morality on the other. The image of alcohol was changed from the

Puritan's term, 'the Good Creature of God', to Demon Rum, a shift that clearly spells out America's love/hate relationship with alcohol. From God's gift, it had become the Devil's work. At the same time, family organization and sex roles were changing, with increas-ing emphasis on woman as homemaker and mother. Women had little economic or political power but one power was vouchsafed them: They were creatures of gentility and virtue and they symbolized *moral force*. Since the woman drunkard could hardly be held up as a symbol of gentility and virtue, the temperance move-ment chose to ignore the existence of such persons and there was very rare reference to women with drinking problems. The primary emphasis was on the male drunkard and the woman as helpless victim of his debauchery.

The gentle picture of American womanhood cherish-ed by the temperance movement was contradicted by the very existence of the movement. For one thing, women turned out to be superb organizers, admini-strators and activists. For another, the leadership of the Women's Christian Temperance Union was, at times, quite militant, and during Frances Willard's tenure as leader, supported not only temperance but women's suffrage, the fight against child labor, and the strug-gles of the beginning trade union movement.

Clearly, however, the first enemy was the saloon, and in its campaigns the WCTU and other temperance groups were early feminists:

In many towns and cities, the saloon was the antithesis of the home. It was a male institution, and it was not simply a place where men went but part of the system of privileges and freedoms that men enjoyed and women did not. To attack the saloon was to attack both a symbol of male power and privilege and also an institution that contributed to the system (Levine, 1980).

There is some current work that suggests that the temperance movement, 'the largest enduring secular mass movement in nineteenth-century America' (Levine, 1980) offered expression to many of the anx-ieties and hostilities of women (Epstein, 1980). The movement developed out of a combination of historical events: developing capitalism, Victorian morality, the changed view of the family and woman's place at home, and a native-born distrust of foreigners. Women organized themselves as the 'moral agents' who would bring about social change, and American attitudes about drinking are probably influenced to the present moment by the American experiment. This experiment included in rapid succession: heavy drinking up to 1840, growth of the temperance movement, the experiment in Prohibition, the consequences of the law in stimulating organized crime, and finally the repeal of the Noble Experiment. It is an ironic footnote to history, but while women were fighting Demon Rum with such enthusiasm, many women — possibly including temperance workers — were sustaining themselves on opiate-laced tonics.

Alcohol: social norms of the twentieth century

At the end of the Prohibition period and before World War II, it was estimated that approximately 38 per cent of American women drank alcoholic beverages and the remaining 62 per cent were abstainers. Significant changes followed World War II. By 1947, it was estimated that 56 per cent of women used alcohol (Riley & Marden, 1947). During the 1960's and 1970's, per capita consumption increased in the United States and then leveled off; during the same period, the percentage of American women who drink also increased and at a rate somewhat higher than the male increase. There is still a gap in the percentages, and there are still more male drinkers. But the gap is smaller. The percentage of American women who drink varies by generation, with younger women showing relatively high percentages and women over 50 relatively low percentages. We have gone from one-third to two-thirds in a 50-year period; about a third of American women drank before World War II and about two-thirds drink at the present time. Still, in spite of the increase, it is still more characteristic of males to drink than females: their percentage is larger, the quantity is larger, the frequency is larger, and the alcohol-related problems are larger.

There are, therefore, two important questions: First, how may one account for the last half century increase in the percentage of American women who drink? Second, how may one account for the fact that in spite of this increase, there are still more men who drink and they more often drink heavily and present alcohol-related problems?

How may one account for the increase over the last half century in the percentage of American women who drink? At the present time, it is not only more socially acceptable for women to drink alcoholic beverages, they may drink in gender-mixed company (Pfautz, 1962) and in public places. But social drinking is part of a general pattern of social behavior, and there have been changes in norms of acceptability in other areas of social behavior as well: in dress, in language, in sexual assertiveness, and the like.

The relation between changes in drinking behavior and the two phenomena of recent decades, the increasing proportion of women in the work force and the rise of feminist consciousness, is complex. An increasing percentage of American adult women work at jobs outside the home. But social drinking is more characteristic of housewives than of married women working outside the home. Yet, the proportion of drinkers who are heavy or problematic drinkers is greater for women working outside the home (Johnson, Note 5). There also appears to be a higher proportion of heavy or problem drinkers among women living out-of-role life styles than in-role life styles (Johnson, Note 5), and adolescent girls who reject traditional femininity are reported to 'drink more, more symptomatically and with more problem consequences' than more traditional-minded adolescent girls (Wilsnack & Wilsnack, 1978).

It is very important that a distinction be made between *attitudes toward women's social drinking and attitudes toward women's heavy drinking, intoxication and alcoholism*. There seems to be little change in the direction of greater tolerance for the latter. Female intoxication has been almost universally viewed as more distasteful and more reprehensible than male intoxication (Laurence & Maxwell, 1962; Knupfer, Note 3). While public attitudes about viewing alcoholism as 'a disease' are more sophisticated, there still appears to be less tolerance for women alcoholics than for men alcoholics. And there is no question but that 'lady drunks' are still more negatively judged than their male counterparts. Getting drunk is still considered in many groups a male rite of passage to adulthood, but getting drunk is *not* an acceptable rite of passage for adolescent girls and young women. The double standard and the possible reasons for it reveal much about attitudes toward women and substance use. The negative attitude toward female drunkenness appears to stem from two sources. The first is a general perception of woman's impaired effectiveness in her nurturant role. The Child et al. report (1965) spoke of women's impaired ability to care for a child, and Knupfer (Note 3) emphasizes the impaired functioning of women as caretakers. In this view, women who have had a lot to drink are behaving self-indulgently and irresponsibly. The second basis for the negative view of female intoxication is linked to loss of sexual inhibitions. It has taken a quarter of a century to dissociate female alcoholism from sexual promiscuity, an illogical pairing considering that most middle class female alcoholics drink at home. Female alcoholism is sometimes linked to prostitution, particularly if one studies women prisoners; but, like narcotic addicts, the prostitution for alcohol abusers is a source of income rather than a manifestation of unbridled sexuality. It is a good guess that drunkenness in a public place probably renders a woman more vulnerable to rape than to uninhibited expression of her sexual drives.

How may one account for the fact that the percentage of men who drink and who have problems related to drinking is larger than the percentage of women? The larger proportion of men who drink may be noted from all the surveys of American drinking; the larger proportion of male alcoholics may be inferred from surveys and from sex ratios in treatment facilities. Although the male-to-female ratio may vary depending on whether the information is from private hospitals, physicians' offices, state hospitals, Skid Row centers, or other sources, there are more males. Although the temperance movement did emphasize *male* drunkenness and alcoholism, we cannot attribute the sex ratio just to the American experience with the temperance movement and with Prohibition because similar sex ratios appear in every country and society about which we have information.

Explanation might well lie in three factors: differential socialization of men and women, sexual taboos, and the use of alternative substances. A cross-cultural survey of some sex differences in socialization (Barry, Bacon & Child, 1957) suggests that, almost universally, girls are socialized with 'greater pressure toward nurturance, obedience, and responsibility.' The relation of taboos on sexuality to different norms for drinking seems clear. At high levels of intoxication man may be impotent, the female will be sexually available — if not

cooperative — at high levels of alcohol intake. Anxiety about pregnancy and venereal disease may be a deterrent. Again, there are linkages between drinking and sexuality, in that women may be very vulnerable to rape when they have been drinking (Marolla & Scully, 1979). Finally there is the availability of alternative substances, substances that are more clearly designated by society as medicinal: prescription drugs and over-the-counter medications. Women use more of these, by medical mandate and with female cooperation.

EPILOGUE

In the history of men, women and substance usage, there are gender differences in the sanctions for medicinal use and for recreational use of substances, and in attitudes toward drug abuse. These differences may account for the greater use of prescription drugs, particularly psychoactive drugs, by women, and for the greater use of alcohol by men.

Drug and alcohol abuse among women is a political issue, linked to gender roles, power, ambivalence, and hidden angers and fears. The idea that intoxication produces sexual acting out among women is part of a set of social attitudes toward women and their sexuality. The idea that intoxication impairs women's primary responsibility, her nurturing role, reaches its current expression in campaigns of fear about 'neonatal addiction' and 'the fetal alcohol syndrome'. It is not that these phenomena do not exist. But it is sad to see them made the basis for further rejection of a group of women badly in need of help and sympathy.

REFERENCE NOTES

1. Verbrugge, L.M. Sex differentials in health and mortality, 1980. To be published in A.H. Stromberg (Ed.), *Women, Health and Medicine*, Palo Alto CA: Mayfield Publishing Company, 1981.
2. Sims, M. *A comparison of the prescribing of psychoactive drugs by outpatient clinics and by physicians in private practice.* Substudy No. 534, Addiction Research Foundation, Toronto, 1973.
3. Knupfer, G. *Female drinking patterns*. Selected papers presented at the 15th Annual Meeting of the North American Association of Alcoholism Programs, Washington, D.C., 1964, 140–160.

4. Keller, M. *Women alcoholics*. Paper presented at the Business and Professional Women's Club, New Brunswick, New Jersey, 1970.
5. Johnson, P.B. *Working women and alcohol use. Preliminary national data*. Paper presented at the meeting of the American Psychological Association, Toronto, Canada, September 1978.

REFERENCES

Barry, H., Bacon, M.K. & Child, I.L. A cross-cultural survey of some sex differences in socialization. *The Journal of Abnormal and Social Psychology*, 1957, *55*, 327–332.

Cacao: The Chocolate tree, Washington, D.C.: Pan American Union, 1954.

Chambers, C.D. *Differential drug use within the New York State labor force*, Albany: New York Narcotics Addictions Control Commission, 1971.

Chambers, C.D., Inciardi, J.A., & Siegal, H.A. *Chemical coping: A report on legal drug use in the United States*, New York: Spectrum Publications, Inc., 1975.

Child, I.L., Barry, H., & Bacon, M.K. Sex differences. In *A Cross-Cultural Study of Drinking, Quarterly Journal of Studies on Alcohol*, Supplement No. 3, 1965, 49–61.

Cooperstock, R. Sex differences in the use of mood-modifying drugs: An explanatory model, *Journal of Health and Social Behavior*, 1971, *12*, 238–244.

Cooperstock, R. Psychotropic drug use among women, *CMA Journal*, 1976, *115*, 760–763.

Epstein, B.L. *Women, evangelism, and temperance in nineteenth-century America*, Middletown, CT: Wesleyan University Press, 1980.

Gusfield, J.R. Social structure and moral reform: A study of the WCTU. In R.G. McCarthy (Ed.), *Drinking and intoxication*, Glencoe, IL: The Free Press, 1959.

Gusfield, J.R. Status conflicts and the changing ideologies of the American temperance movement. In D.J. Pittman & C.R. Snyder (Eds), *Society, culture, and drinking patterns*, New York: Wiley, 1962.

Kingsdale, J.M. The 'poor man's club': Social functions of the urban working-class saloon. In E.H. Pleck & J.H. Pleck (Eds), *The American man*, Englewood Cliffs, NJ: Prentice-Hall, Inc., 1980.

Laurence, J.J. & Maxwell, M.A. Drinking and socio-economic status. In D.J. Pittman & C.R. Snyder (Eds), *Society, culture, and drinking patterns*, New York: Wiley, 1962.

Levine, H.G. Temperance and women in 19th-century United States. In O.J. Kalant (Ed.), *Alcohol and drug problems in women. Research advances in alcohol and drug problems*, Volume 5, New York: Plenum Press, 1980.

Lisansky, E.S. Drinking and alcoholism. Psychological aspects. In the *International encyclopedia of the social sciences*. Volume 4, New York: Crowell Collier and Macmillan, 1967.

McKinlay, A.P. The Roman attitude toward women's drinking. In R.G. McCarthy (Ed.), *Drinking and intoxication*, Glencoe, IL: The Free Press, 1959.

Marconi, J., Varela, A., Rosenblat, E., Solari, G., Marchesse, I., Alvarado, R., & Enriquez, W. The working class in Santiago de Chile. In R.G. McCarthy (Ed.), *Drinking and intoxication*, Glencoe, IL: The Free Press, 1959.

Marolla, J.A., & Scully, D.H. Rape and psychiatric vocabularies of motive. In E.S. Gomberg & V. Franks (Eds.), *Gender and disordered behavior: Sex differences in psychopathology*. New York: Brunner/Mazel, 1979.

Mellinger, G.D., Balter, M.B., Parry, H.J., Manheimer, D.I., & Cisin, I.H. An overview of psychotherapeutic drug use in the United States. In E. Josephson & E.E. Caroll (Eds.), *Drug use: Epidemiological and sociological approaches*. Hemisphere Publishing Corp., 1974, pp. 333–366.

Pfautz, H.W. The image of alcohol in popular fiction: 1900–1914 and 1946–1950. *Quarterly Journal of Studies on Alcohol*, 1962, *23*, 131–146.

Riley, J.R., Jr., & Marden, C.F. The social pattern of alcoholic drinking. *Quarterly Journal of Studies on Alcohol*, 1947, *8*, 265–283.

Rorabaugh, W.J. *The alcoholic republic: An American tradition*, New York: Oxford University Press, 1979.

Taylor, N. *Narcotics: Nature's dangerous gifts*, New York: Dell Paperbacks, 1968.

Unger, R.K., & Denmark, F.L. *Woman: Dependent or independent variable*? New York: Psychological Dimensions, Inc., 1975.

Wilsnack, R.W., & Wilsnack, S.C. Sex role and drinking among adolescent girls. *Journal of Studies on Alcohol*, 1978, *39*, 1855–1874.

Williams, S.E. The use of beverage alcohol as medicine, 1790–1860, *Journal of Studies on Alcohol*, 1980, *41*, 543–566.

Taking care of business — the heroin user's life on the street

EDWARD PREBLE* and JOHN J. CASEY, JR.†

* Associate Research Scientist, Drug Addiction Unit, Manhattan State Hospital, and Associate Professor of Anthropology, The New York School of Psychiatry; † Department of Economics, Georgetown University

This report is a description of the life and activities of heroin users in New York City in the context of their street environment. The report emphasizes the active nature of the lifestyle involved, and outlines the economic and social networks in which heroin users operate.

It is often said that the use of heroin provides an escape for the user from his psychological problems and from the responsibilities of social and personal relationships — in short, an escape from life. Clinical descriptions of heroin addicts emphasize the passive, dependent, withdrawn, generally inadequate features of their personality structure and social adjustment. Most sociological studies of heroin users make the same point. Thus Chein et al. (1964) reported that street gang members are not likely to become heroin users because they are resourceful, aggressive, well-integrated boys who are 'reality-oriented' in their street environment. They held that it is the passive, anxious, inadequate boy who cannot adapt to street life who is likely to use heroin. Similarly, Cloward and Ohlin (1960) referred to heroin users as 'retreatists' and 'double failures' who cannot qualify for either legitimate or illegitimate careers. Unaggressive 'mamma's boys' is the usual stereotype these days for the heroin addict, both for the students of narcotic use and the public at large. Experienced researchers and workers in the narcotics field know that there is no such thing as 'the heroin addict' or 'the addict personality'. However, most attempts to generalize — the goal of all scientific investigation — result in some version of the escape theory.

The description which follows of the activities of lower class heroin users in their adaptation to the social and economic institutions and practices connected with the use of heroin contradicts this widely held belief. Their behavior is anything but an escape from life. They are actively engaged in meaningful activities and relationships seven days a week. The brief moments of euphoria after each administration of a small amount of heroin constitute a small fraction of their daily lives. The rest of the time they are aggressively pursuing a career that is exacting, challenging, adventurous, and rewarding. They are always on the move and must be alert, flexible, and resourceful. The surest way to identify heroin users in a slum neighborhood is to observe the way people walk. The heroin user walks with a fast, purposeful stride, as if he is late for an important appointment — indeed, he is. He is hustling (robbing or stealing), trying to sell stolen goods, avoiding the police, looking for a heroin dealer with a good bag (the street retail unit of heroin), coming back from copping (buying heroin), looking for a safe place to take the drug, or looking for someone who beat (cheated) him — among other things. He is, in short, *taking care of business*, a phrase which is so common with heroin users that they use it in response to words of greeting, such as 'how you doing?' and 'what's happening?' *Taking care of biz* is the common abbreviation.

Modified from *The International Journal of the Addictions*, 4(1), pp. 1–24, March 1969. Reprinted by courtesy of Marcel Dekker, Inc.

For them, if not for their middle and upper class counterparts (a small minority of opiate addicts), the quest for heroin is the quest for a meaningful life, not an escape from life. And the meaning does not lie, primarily, in the effects of the drug on their minds and bodies; it lies in the gratification of accomplishing a series of challenging, exciting tasks, every day of the week.

Much of the life of the heroin user on the street centers around the economic institutions of heroin distribution. Therefore, this report features a description of the marketing processes for heroin, from importation to street sales. The cost of heroin today is so high and the quality so poor that the street user must become totally involved in an economic career. A description of typical economic careers of heroin users will be presented.

The economic pressures on heroin users today are so great that they prey on each other as well as on their families and on society at large. An addict with money or drugs in his possession runs a good risk of being *taken off* (robbed) by other addicts. An addict who has been robbed or cheated by another addict usually takes his loss philosophically, summed up by the expression, 'that's the name of the game'. Referring to a fellow addict who had cheated him, one victim said, 'he beat me today, I'll beat him tomorrow'. Another addict who specializes in robbing other addicts said, 'I beat them every chance I get, which is all the time'. Sociability even among partners extends no farther than that suggested by the following excerpt: 'You might be hanging out with a fellow for a long time, copping together and working as crime partners. You might beat him for a purpose. You might beat him because maybe you bought a bag together and you know it's not going to do both any good, so you beat him for it. But then you try to go and get some money and straighten him out; make it up to him'. Another informant summed up the attitude between partners this way: 'I'm looking out for myself — I might be sick tomorrow; anyway, he's got something working for him that I don't know about'. Sometimes a distinction is made between a hustling partner and a crime partner (*crimey*), where it is suggested that the latter is more dependable; however as one informant put it, 'there are larceny minded crimeys'. The causes of these changes in the relationships of heroin users to each other, to family members,

and to other members of the community are to be found in the economic practices of heroin distribution.

THE DISTRIBUTION OF HEROIN IN NEW YORK CITY

Heroin contracted for in Europe at $5,000 per kilo (2.2 pounds) will be sold in $5 bags on the street for about one million dollars, after having passed through at least six levels of distribution. The following description of the distribution and marketing of heroin from the time it arrives in New York until it reaches the hands of the heroin user in the street is a consensus derived from informants in the hospital and in the street representing different ethnic and racial groups from different parts of the city. There are many variations to the account given here at all levels of the marketing process. For example, as in the marketing of any product, a quantity purchase can be made at a lower price, and a dealer who makes a rapid turnover of the product for a wholesaler will receive higher benefits for his work. All the way down the line, the *good customer* is the key to a successful operation. He is one who buys regularly, does a good volume of business, does not ask for credit or try to buy short (offer less than the established price) and can be trusted. The following account does not include all the many variations, but can be taken as a paradigm.

Opium produced in Turkey, India, and Iran is processed into heroin in Lebanon, France, and Italy and prepared for shipment to the East Coast of the United States. A United States importer, through a courier, can buy a kilogram of 80% heroin in Europe for $5,000. The quality is represented to him in terms of how many cuts it will hold (that is, how many times it can be adulterated). In earlier days, when the marketing of heroin was a more controlled operation, the word of the European seller was accepted. Now, it is customary for the importer to test it, either by means of scientific instruments, or through a reliable tester — an addict who makes experimental cuts, uses the drug and reports on its quality. The importer, who usually never sees the heroin, sells down the line to a highly trusted customer through intermediaries. If it is a syndicate operation, he would only sell to high level, coded men, known as *captains*. These men are major distributors, referred to as *kilo connections* and, generally, as *the people*.

Major distributors

The *kilo connection* pays $20,000 for the original kilogram (kilo, kee), and gives it a one and one cut (known as *hitting it*), that is, he makes two kilos out of one by adding the common adulterants of milk sugar, mannite (a product from the ash tree used as a mild laxative) and quinine. The proportions of ingredients used for the cutting varies with the preferences of the cutter. One may use 5 parts milk sugar, 2 parts quinine and 1 part mannite, while another may use 2 parts milk sugar, 3 parts quinine and 1 part mannite. All three of these products are quickly soluble with heroin. A match lit under the *cooker* (bottle cap) will heat and dissolve the mixture into a clear liquid in a few seconds. The milk sugar contributes the bulk, the mannite inflates the volume — described as *fluffing* it up — and the quinine heightens the sensation of the *rush*, when, upon injection into the vein, the mixture first registers on the nervous system. In the cutting procedure the substance to be cut is placed under a fine sieve, often made from a woman's nylon stocking stretched over a coat hanger. The adulterants are sifted on top of it, then the new mixture is sifted through several more times. After the cut, the kilo connection sells down the line in kilos, half kilos and quarter kilos, depending upon the resources of his customers. He will get approximately $10,000 per half kilo for the now adulterated heroin.

The customer of the kilo connection is known as *the connection* in its original sense, meaning that he knows *the people*, even though he is not one of them. He may also be called an *ounce man*. He is a highly trusted customer. (One common variation here is that the kilo connection may sell to a third line man, known, if a syndicate operation, as a *soldier* or *button man*. He in turn, will make a one and one cut and sell to the connection.) Assuming that the connection buys directly from a kilo connection, he will probably give the heroin a one and one cut (make two units of each one), divide the total aggregate into ounces, and sell down the line at $700 per ounce. In addition to the adulteration, the aggregate weight of the product is reduced. Known as a *short count*, this procedure occurs at every succeeding level of distribution. At this stage, however, it is called a *good ounce*, despite the adulteration and reduced weight.

The next man is known as a *dealer in weight*, and is probably the most important figure in the line of distribu-

tion. He stands midway between the top and the bottom, and is the first one coming down the line who takes substantial risk of being apprehended by law enforcement officers. He is also the first one who may be a heroin user himself, but usually he is not. He is commonly referred to as one who is *into something* and is respected as a big dealer who has put himself in jeopardy by, as the sayings go, *carrying a felony with him* and *doing the time*; that is, if he gets caught he can expect a long jail sentence. It is said of him that 'he let his name go', or 'his name gets kicked around', meaning that his identity is known to people in the street. This man usually specializes in *cut ounces*. He may give a two and one cut (make three units of each one) to the good ounce from the connection and sell the resulting quantity for $500 per ounce. The aggregate weight is again reduced, and now the unit is called a *piece* instead of an ounce. Sometimes it is called a *street ounce* or a *vig ounce* (*vig* is an abbreviation for *vigorish*, which is the term used to designate the high interest on loans charged by loan sharks). In previous years 25 to 30 level teaspoons were supposed to constitute an ounce; today it is 16 to 20.

The next customer is known as a *street dealer*. He buys the *piece* for $500, gives it a one and one cut and makes *bundles*, which consists of 25 $5 bags each. He can usually get seven bundles from each piece, and he sells each bundle for $80. He may also package the heroin in *half-bundles* (ten $5 bags each), which sell for $40, or he may package in *half-loads* (fifteen $3 bags), which sell for $30 each. This man may or may not be a heroin user.

The next distributor is known as a *juggler*, who is the seller from whom the average street addict buys. He is always a user. He buys bundles for $80 each and sells the 25 bags at about $5 each, making just enough profit to support his own habit, day by day. He may or may not make a small cut, known as *tapping the bags*. He is referred to as someone who is 'always high and always short', that is, he always has enough heroin for his own use and is always looking for a few dollars to get enough capital to cop again. The following actual account is typical of a juggler's transactions: He has $25 and needs $5 more to buy a half-load. He meets a user he knows who has $5 and would like to buy two $3 bags; he is short $1. The juggler tells him he needs only $5 to cop, and that if he can have his $5, he will buy a half-load and give him his two $3 bags — $1, in effect, for the use of the money. When the juggler returns he gives the person his two bags. In the example here, the person had to wait about two hours for the juggler's return, and it was raining. For taking the risk of getting beat for his money by the juggler, for the long wait and the discomfort of the weather, the juggler was expected to go to the *cooker* with him (share the use of some of the herion), with the juggler putting in two bags to the other person's one bag and sharing equally in the total. The juggler had his fix and now has 11 bags left. He sells three bags for $9. From the eight bags he has left he uses two himself to get straight — not to get high, but enough to keep from getting sick so that he can finish his business. Now he sells four bags for $12 and has three left. He needs only $7 more to cop again, so he is willing to sell the last three bags for the reduced price, and he can begin a similar cycle all over again. He may do this three or four times a day. The juggler leads a precarious life, both financially and in the risks he takes of getting robbed by fellow addicts or arrested. Most arrests for heroin sales are of the juggler. Financially he is always struggling to stay in the black. If business is a little slow he may start to get sick or impatient and use some of the heroin he needs to sell in order to re-cop. If he does this he is in the red and temporarily out of business. A juggler is considered to be doing well if he has enough money left over after a transaction for cab fare to where he buys the heroin. One informant defined a juggler as a 'non-hustling dope fiend who is always messing the money up'.

THE STREET BAG OF HEROIN

The amount of heroin in the street bag is very small. A generous estimate of the aggregate weight of a $5 bag is 90 milligrams, including the adulterants. Assuming, as in the above account, that the original kilo of 80% heroin is adulterated 24 times by the time it reaches the street, the amount of heroin would be about 3 milligrams. There is considerable fluctuation in the amount of heroin in the retail unit, running the range from 1 to 15 milligrams, which depends mainly upon the supply available in the market. The important point is that no matter how small the amount, heroin users are never discouraged in their efforts to get it. The consensus figure of 3 milligrams is a good approximation for an average over a one year period.

The amount of heroin in the street unit has resulted in an institution known as *chasing the bag*. In a community with a high incidence of heroin use there will be two, three, or four competing bags on the street; that is, bags which have come down through different distributorship lines. Because of the low quality of the heroin, users want to get the best one available on a given day. The number of times it has been cut and the ingredients that were used to cut it are the main considerations. The dealer who has the best bag on the street at a given time will sell his merchandise fast and do a big volume of business. A dealer with a good bag who works hard can sell 40 to 50 bundles a day. A good bag dealer can sell 75 to 100 bags a day. By keeping the quality relatively high — for example by giving a one and a half cut to a quantity represented as being able to hold two cuts — he makes less profit on each unit. However, this loss can be offset by the greater volume and the reduced price he gets from his wholesaler as a result of buying more often and in large quantities.

ECONOMIC CAREERS OF HEROIN USERS

Virtually all heroin users in slum neighborhoods regularly commit crime in order to support their heroin use. In addition to the crimes involving violation of the narcotic laws heroin users engage in almost all types of crime for gain, both against property and the person. Because of the greatly inflated price of heroin and because of its poor quality, it is impossible for a heroin user to support even a modest habit for less than $20 a day. Since the typical street user is uneducated, unskilled, and often from a minority racial group, he cannot earn enough money in the legitimate labor market to finance his drug use; he must engage in criminal activity.

As with non-addict criminals, addict criminals tend to specialize in certain activities, depending upon their personalities, skills, and experience.

The heroin user is an important figure in the economic life of the slums. In order to support a $20 a day habit, he has to steal goods and property worth from $50 to $100. Usually he steals outside his neighborhood, not out of community loyalty but because the opportunities are better in the wealthier neighborhoods, and he brings his merchandise back to the neighborhood for sale at high discounts. This results, to some extent, in a redistribution of real income from the richer to the poorer neighborhoods. Although non-addict residents in the slums may deplore the presence of heroin users, they appreciate and compete for their services as discount salesmen. The user, in turn, experiences satisfaction in being able to make this contribution to the neighborhood.

The type of criminal activity he engages in, and his success at it, determine, to a large extent, the addict's status among fellow addicts and in the community at large. The appellation of *real hustling dope fiend* (a successful burglar, robber, con man, etc.) is a mark of respect and status. Conversely, *non-hustling dope fiend* is a term of denigration applied to users who stay in the neighborhood begging for money or small tastes of heroin, renting out works, or doing small time juggling. There are also middle status occupations, such as *stealing copper*, where the person specializes in salvaging metal and fixtures from vacant tenement buildings and selling to the local junkman. About the only kinds of illegal activity not open to the heroin user are those connected with organized crime, such as gambling and loan sharking. Users are not considered reliable enough for work in these fields. They may be used as a lookout for a dice game or policy operation, but that is about as close as they can get to organized criminal operations.

It can be seen from the account in this section that the street heroin user is an active, busy person, preoccupied primarily with the economic necessities of maintaining his real income — heroin. A research subject expressed the more mundane gratifications of his life this way: 'When I'm on the way home with the bag safely in my pocket, and I haven't been caught stealing all day, and I didn't get beat and the cops didn't get me — I feel like a working man coming home; he's worked hard, but he knows he done something, even though I know it's not true'.

CONCLUSIONS

Heroin use today by lower class, primarily minority group, persons does not provide for them a euphoric escape from the psychological and social problems which derive from ghetto life. On the contrary, it provides a motivation and rationale for the pursuit of a meaningful life, albeit a socially deviant one. The activities these individuals engage in and the relationships they have in the course of their quest for heroin are far more important than the minimal analgesic and euphoric effects of the small amount of heroin available to them. If they can be said to be addicted, it is not so much to heroin as to the entire career of a heroin user. The heroin user is, in a way, like the compulsively hardworking business executive whose ostensible goal is the acquisition of money, but whose real satisfaction is in meeting the inordinate challenge he creates for himself. He, too, is driven by a need to find meaning in life which, because of certain deficits and impairments, he cannot find in the normal course of living. A big difference, of course, is that with the street user, the genesis of the deficits and impairments is, to a disproportionate degree, in the social conditions of his life.

In the four communities where this research was conducted, the average median family income is $3500, somewhat less than that of family Welfare Department recipients. Other average population characteristics for the four communities include: public welfare recipients — four times the city rate; unemployment — two times the city rate; sub-standard housing — two times the city rate; no schooling — two times the city rate; median school years completed — eight years. Neither these few statistics nor an exhaustive list could portray the desperation and hopelessness of life in the slums of New York. In one short block where one of the authors worked, there was an average of one violent death a month over a period of three years — by fire, accident, homicide, and suicide. In Puerto Rican neighborhoods, sidewalk *recordatorios* (temporary shrines at the scenes of tragic deaths) are a regular feature.

Given the social conditions of the slums and their effects on family and individual development, the odds are strongly against the development of a legitimate, non-deviant career that is challenging and rewarding. The most common legitimate career is a menial job, with no future except in the periodic, statutory raises in the minimum wage level. If anyone can be called passive in the slums, it is not the heroin user, but the one who submits to and accepts these conditions.

The career of a heroin user serves a dual purpose for the slum inhabitant; it enables him to escape, not from purposeful activity, but from the monotony of an existence severely limited by social constraints, and at the same time it provides a way for him to gain revenge on society for the injustices and deprivation he has experienced. His exploitation of society is carried out with emotional impunity on the grounds, for the most part illusory, that he is *sick* (needs heroin to relieve physical distress), and any action is justified in the interest of keeping himself well. He is free to act out directly his hostility and at the same time find gratification, both in the use of the drug and in the sense of accomplishment he gets from performing the many acts necessary to support his heroin use. Commenting on the value of narcotic maintenance programs, where addicts are maintained legally and at no cost on a high level of opiate administration, one informant said: 'The guy feels that all the fun is out of it. You don't have to outslick the cop and other people. This is a sort of vengeance. This gives you a thrill. It's hiding from them. Where you can go in the drug-store and get a shot, you get high, but it's the same sort of monotony. You are not getting away with anything. The thing is to hide and outslick someone. Drugs is a hell of a game; it gives you a million things to talk about'. This informant was not a newcomer to the use of heroin, but a 30-year-old veteran of 15 years of heroin use on the street. *Soldiers of fortune* is the way another informant summed up the lives of heroin users.

Not all, but certainly a large majority of heroin users are in the category which is the subject of this paper. It is their activities which constitute the social problem which New York City and other urban centers face today. The ultimate solution to the problem, as with all the problems which result from social injustice, lies in the creation of legitimate opportunities for a meaningful life for those who want it. While waiting for the ultimate solution, reparative measures must be taken. There are four major approaches to the treatment and rehabilitation of heroin users: (1) drug treatment (opiate substitutes or antagonists), (2) psychotherapy, (3) existentialist oriented group self-help (Synanon prototype), (4) educational and vocational training and placement.

To the extent that the observations and conclusions reported in this paper are valid, a treatment and rehabilitation program emphasizing educational and vocational training is indicated for the large majority of heroin users. At the Manhattan State Hospital Drug Addiction Unit an intensive educational and vocational program supported by psychological and social treatment methods has been created in an effort to prepare the patient for a legitimate career which has a future and is rewarding and satisfying. The three year program is divided into three parts: (1) eight months of education, vocational training, and therapy in the hospital, (2) one month in the night hospital while working or taking further training in the community during the day, (3) twenty-seven months of aftercare which includes, where needed, further education and training, vocational placement, and psychological and social counseling. With this opportunity for a comprehensive social reparation, those who have not been too severely damaged by society have a second chance for a legitimate, meaningful life.

REFERENCES

Chein, Isidor *et al. The Road to H*. Basic Books Inc., New York, 1964.
Cloward, Richard A. and Ohlin, Lloyd E. Delinquency and *Opportunity*. Free Press, Glencoe, Illinois, 1960.

Section IV

Section IV

Tackling drug misuse: a summary of the government's strategy

EXTRACTS FROM THE REPORT OF THE MINISTERIAL GROUP ON THE MISUSE OF DRUGS

> These extracts cover only a small part of the Government's overall strategy for combating drug misuse. The overall strategy is outlined and some details of the controls, deterrence and enforcement of strategy are described.

THE STRATEGY

1   The Government has drawn up a comprehensive strategy for tackling drug misuse. The objective is to attack the problem by simultaneous action on five main fronts:

- reducing supplies from abroad
- making enforcement even more effective
- strengthening deterrence and tightening domestic controls
- developing prevention
- improving treatment and rehabilitation.

2   This strategy recognises that the different aspects of the problem are interrelated and that it is necessary to tackle both the supply of, and demand for, drugs. Thus, although supplies of drugs may come to this country initially to meet an existing demand, the high profits to be made encourage further supplies and the seeking of new markets. At the same time the greater availability of drugs may encourage experimentation by new misusers. As the ACMD noted in its report on prevention:

Experience suggests that, when the numbers of existing users are low, as is the case with illegal drugs, an increase

in the availability of drugs increases the opportunity for non-users to be offered a drug for the first time (paragraph 2.10)

This, in turn, may create further demand and lead to increased supplies. Similarly, greater availability may encourage established users to increase their level of use, possibly by quite considerable amounts — which, again, serves to fuel demand and encourage yet more supplies.

3   The Government's strategy aims to reduce the supply of drugs by

- supporting international efforts to curb the production and trafficking of drugs
- strengthening Customs and police enforcement
- tightening the controls on drugs produced and prescribed in this country so that there is no 'leakage' to the illicit market
- deterring drug traffickers and dealers by high maximum penalties and by depriving them of the proceeds of their crimes.

4   Demand for drugs is being tackled by

- discouraging those who are not misusing drugs from doing so
- helping those who are already misusing to stop doing so.

5   An interdepartmental Ministerial Group on the Misuse of Drugs has been established to review, develop and oversee the implementation of this

Taken from *Tackling Drug Misuse* (HMSO, 1986). Copies of the complete Strategy Document are available free of charge from C5 Division, Room 236, Home Office, 50 Queen Anne's Gate, London SW1. Reproduced with permission of the controller of Her Majesty's Stationery Office.

strategy. The Group meets regularly and has considered a range of issues including the development of preventive education and information campaigns.

6 The Advisory Council on the Misuse of Drugs provides valuable assistance to the Government in the formulation of its policies. The Advisory Council, which is established under the Misuse of Drugs Act 1971 is a distinguished body of independent experts drawn from many fields. It offers advice to the Government and has undertaken a number of longer-term studies such as those on treatment and rehabilitation and on prevention. . . .

ENFORCEMENT

The Government attaches high priority to effective enforcement action, by Customs and the police, to try to prevent drugs from actually entering the country and reaching the streets.

HM Customs and Excise

(i) Responsibilities HM Customs and Excise are responsible for preventing and detecting the illegal import and export of controlled drugs, the investigation of organisations and individuals engaged in international drug smuggling, and their prosecution. They are concerned not only with current smuggling activities but also with gathering intelligence about trafficking routes and techniques which may be used in future smuggling operations. In addition they follow up drugs which have evaded Customs controls and where there is a clear link with the importation.

(ii) Organisation There are two principal aspects of control. First, there is preventive control by staff at ports, airports, container depots and parcel post depots, and on coastal surveillance. Secondly, there is investigation by specialist investigation officers working on information and intelligence gathered from various sources at home and overseas in order to anticipate, target and intercept consignments.

(iii) Methods It would be impossible to prevent smuggling entirely, no matter how many Customs staff were provided. Moreover, the sheer volume of passenger and freight traffic, and the inconvenience and expense which would result, make it impracticable to carry out searches on every occasion. So, much importance is attached by Customs to the effective use of intelligence.

Aircraft and vessels arriving in the United Kingdom have to report their arrival and are liable to be boarded and searched. The decision whether to board or search is normally based on general or specific intelligence. Particular attention is given to the risk from private craft and aircraft.

Passengers may be selected for questioning, and their belongings and persons searched, for a variety of reasons. Particular attention is paid to drug smuggling and, again, Customs staff are guided by intelligence information.

The examination of freight presents special problems given the huge volume and the practical difficulties of searching loaded containers and lorries. Selection for searching is therefore largely based on intelligence. Drug detector dogs are used routinely in the examination of freight.

Various new enforcement measures are in hand

- fifty additional specialist drugs investigators were recruited in 1985. Seven more investigators are being posted overseas to liaise with foreign law enforcement agencies
- one hundred and sixty officers were appointed for local information gathering and analysis and mobile task forces during 1984/85. Another 150 staff will be provided in 1986 to enhance this work. Of these, 75 will be deployed in mobile teams, 35 will be used to enhance practical training and to boost technical guidance and the remainder will join specialist teams to strengthen control at smaller ports and airports considered at risk
- two hundred more posts will be allocated to Customs work to maintain levels of control over passengers and freight
- £10 million will be provided over the next three years to develop and introduce technical aids
- provision has been made to improve the reference and information computer system, which has already greatly assisted with the identification of smugglers

- aerial surveillance will be enhanced with the injection of £850,000 over the next three years
- the number of drugs detector dogs is being increased from 30 to 37 and the need for a further increase is under review
- urgent action is being taken to strengthen controls of importation of foreign mails by channelling the flow of foreign mail.

Police

(i) Responsibilities The police are responsible for investigating offences of unlawful supply, manufacture and possession of controlled drugs. Prosecutions will become the responsibility of the area chief crown prosecutor. In Scotland the responsibility for prosecuting such offences lies with the Crown Office and Procurator Fiscal Service and in Northern Ireland with the Director of Public Prosecutions for Northern Ireland. Police and Customs work closely together in the investigation of drugs offences and often mount joint operations.

(ii) Organisation Each chief officer of police is responsible for deciding what arrangements are needed in his force to tackle drug misuse and trafficking. These naturally vary according to the perceived size and nature of the problem in different areas and in relation to other priorities. But over the country as a whole the police operational response is at three broad levels:

uniform and plain clothes officers deal with offences involving the individual misuser which arise in the normal course of their duties. The local links which the police have in a community enable officers to refer misusers to other agencies for advice and treatment as necessary

drugs squads and CID deal with the more serious cases of misuse of drugs and trafficking offences occurring within the force area

Regional Crime Squads (8 in England and Wales outside London, one in Scotland and the Central Drug Squad in London) provide a mobile network of experienced detective officers who are able, by virtue of their organisational structure, to investigate drug trafficking networks involving more than a single force area and which might stretch across the country. On average

about half their activity at present is concerned with the investigation of drugs offences or drug-related crime.

There are over 1,000 police officers, in force drugs squads and in the Regional Crime Squads, with a major commitment to drugs work.

(iii) Action taken On 18 July 1985, in his response to the Report of the Association of Chief Police Officers (ACPO) on drug-related crime, the then Home Secretary, Mr Brittan, announced a package of new measures to increase the effectiveness of the law agencies in fighting drugs trafficking. This comprised

- the addition of dedicated drugs 'wings' to Regional Crime Squads in England and Wales, envisaging an increase of more than 200 officers
- the creation of a new National Drugs Intelligence Unit (NDIU) to supersede the existing Central Drugs Intelligence Unit
- the appointment of a new senior post of National Drugs Intelligence Co-ordinator (NDIC) to head the new unit and co-ordinate drugs intelligence with the operation of Regional Crime Squads
- the establishment of a top level Steering Group to review the working of the new arrangements and to give the Home Secretary assessments of the nature and extent of the drugs threat.

As from 1 January 1985 all forces in England and Wales have had specialised drugs squads.

All officers study the control of drugs as part of general police officer development training. Specialist drugs courses are offered to drug squad officers.

DOMESTIC CONTROLS AND DETERRENCE

1 Two other important elements of the Government's strategy to reduce the supply of drugs are

- tightening the controls on drugs produced and prescribed in this country so that there is no 'leakage' to the illicit market
- deterring drug traffickers and dealers by high maximum penalties and by depriving them of the proceeds of their crimes.

Tightening domestic controls

2 Most drugs that are currently being misused are illegally imported from abroad. But this has not always been the case. In particular, the increase in heroin misuse in the 1960s resulted principally from over-prescribing by a few doctors.

3 The Government considers it essential that efforts to reduce supplies of drugs from abroad are not undermined by 'leakage' from the licit market in this country, whether by thefts from pharmacies and other premises or by irresponsible prescribing on the part of doctors. For the more successful Customs and the police are in restricting the availability of supplies from abroad, the greater is the pressure that can be expected to be exerted on domestic controls.

4 The Home Office Drugs Inspectorate and DHSS (Northern Ireland) are responsible for supervising the legitimate production and distribution of controlled drugs. Manufacturers, wholesale chemists and others are visited regularly to ensure that standards of security, handling procedures and record-keeping are satisfactory. (Inspection of retail pharmacies is normally undertaken by the police, working in close liaison with Home Office inspectors and DHSS (Northern Ireland inspectors.) The Inspectorate is also responsible for investigating cases of suspected irresponsible prescribing. In 1983 their investigations led to three cases being referred to the Misuse of Drugs Tribunal and to directions being made by the Home Secretary restricting the right of those doctors to prescribe controlled drugs. Four more directions were made in 1984 and two in 1985.

5 The main legislative controls are to be found in the Misuse of Drugs Act 1971. During the past two years the Government has taken the following steps to strengthen these controls

- *dipipanone* is now more strictly controlled. This pain-killing drug, already controlled under the Act, had become increasingly popular among drug misusers. In 1982 it was responsible for more overdose deaths than heroin and, after heroin, was the most commonly reported drug of addiction. Since 1 April 1984 only doctors specially licensed by the Home Office have been able to prescribe it for the treatment of addiction

- *barbiturates* have been brought under the control of the Misuse of Drugs Act. These drugs, which at one time were widely prescribed as sedatives, have always been popular with drug misusers. They are highly addictive, and the risk of overdose is considerable. On 1 January 1985 medium and long-acting barbiturates were made controlled drugs. Manufacturers and suppliers now require authorisation from the Home Office and imports and exports are monitored. Prescriptions must be handwritten by the prescribing doctor

- *benzodiazepine tranquillisers* and eight other drugs controlled under the United Nations Convention on Psychotropic Substances 1971 became controlled drugs under our legislation as from 1 April 1986, as a result of the Government's decision to ratify the Convention. These drugs are not currently widely misused in this country, but the controls which are to be exercised over their production, supply, export etc enable the United Kingdom to comply with its new treaty obligations.

6 The ACMD, in a review of the requirements governing the safe custody of controlled drugs, has made a number of recommendations for improving security which the Government has examined very carefully in the light of its consultation with trade and professional organisations and of its other priorities within the overall strategy for tackling drug misuse. As a result action is being taken to

- encourage the police to make greater use of their powers to exempt pharmacies from present statutory arrangements where adequate non-standard security precautions are taken
- issue revised guidelines to NHS hospitals
- carry out a review by the Home Office Drugs Inspectorate of the security arrangements of premises of persons and organisations licensed to possess, supply or manufacture controlled drugs
- implement a range of detailed recommendations in the report.

Deterring drug traffickers

7 The Government is determined that traffickers in drugs should be punished severely and should not profit from their illegal activities, and it has taken a number of important steps to achieve this.

8 To strengthen further the deterrent effect of the law the then Home Secretary announced in October 1983 his decision that parole should be severely restricted for those sentenced to more than 5 years' imprisonment for drug trafficking.

9 The Government announced in October 1984 that it intended to introduce legislation to increase the maximum penalty for trafficking in Class A drugs (e.g. heroin and cocaine) from 14 years' to life imprisonment, and it subsequently supported a Private Member's Bill, introduced by Mr Keith Raffan, MP, designed to effect this change. The resulting Controlled Drugs (Penalties) Act 1985 came into force on 16 September 1985. The Lord Chief Justice had already indicated that the most serious trafficking offences merited very long sentences up to the previous maximum of 14 years'. The introduction of life imprisonment enables the courts to impose even longer sentences in cases where, for example, the offender has been responsible for trafficking drugs worth several million pounds.

Drug Trafficking Offences Bill

10 Lengthy sentences of imprisonment may not in themselves be an adequate deterrent. Many drug traffickers make vast profits from their illegal activities. Because of shortcomings in the existing law, they are often able to enjoy those illegal profits on their release from prison. To remedy these shortcomings, the Government has introduced legislation for England and Wales to provide new powers for tracing, freezing and confiscating the proceeds of drug trafficking. The Government's proposals were set out in a Statement published on 11 November 1985.

11 Under the provisions of the Bill, when a person is convicted in the Crown Court of a drug trafficking offence, in addition to whatever sentence is otherwise imposed the court will also impose a confiscation order. This will require the offender to pay an amount equal to the full value of the proceeds from his drug trafficking activities. For this purpose the court will be able to assume, unless the offender can prove otherwise, that the whole of his assets at the time of conviction, and any property which has passed through his hands during the previous six years, represent the proceeds of drug trafficking.

Paper 19
British drug policies in the 1980s

GERRY STIMSON

Principal Lecturer, Sociology Department, Goldsmith's College, University of London

This paper attempts an assessment of recent developments in British drug policies. It shows the transition from the central role of the medical approach to drug policies, towards a more diffuse response involving a broader range of agencies and ideas. The more active role played by central government with its emphasis on enforcement and control is discussed.

An immense gulf seems to separate the understanding of the addict as a 'sick person' in the 1960s, from the understanding in the 1980s of the 'problem drug taker'. When we read reports from the two periods, it is as though their authors are seeing and describing very different phenomena. In 1965, during a time of considerable public concern about the relatively new drug problems then being encountered in Britain, the Interdepartmental Committee on Drug Addiction described the problem in the following terms:

addiction is after all a socially infectious condition and its notification may offer a means for epidemiological assessment and control. We use the term deliberately to reflect certain principles which we regard as important, viz. that the addict is a sick person and that addiction is a disease which (if allowed to spread unchecked) will become a menace to the community.[1]

Seventeen years later the Advisory Council on the Misuse of Drugs in its 1982 *Report on Treatment and Rehabilitation* chose very different terms to describe the drug problems of the day:

Most authorities from a range of disciplines would agree that not all individuals with drug problems suffer from a disease of drug dependence. While many drug misusers do incur medical problems through their use of drugs some do not. The majority are relatively stable individuals who have more in common with the general population than with any essentially pathological sub-group.[2]

The Report went on to describe the 'problem drug-taker' as someone who experiences social, psychological, physical or legal problems associated with drug use.

These two reports epitomize the different conceptions of drug problems in the 1960s and the 1980s. But if we look further at the twenty years or so that have passed since the major policy changes in the late 1960s, it is not just the conceptualization of problems that has changed. There have been both major changes in the scale of the misuse of drugs in the United Kingdom, and marked developments in the British response to drug problems at a national and local level. In the 1980s British drug policies appear to be undergoing a major transformation.

The paper will focus mainly on heroin, not because its use is the only drug problem in the UK, but because it is around the issue of heroin and other opiates that the major strands of British policy have been framed and discussed. British drug policies have often been synonymous with policies for opiates.

THE 'BRITISH SYSTEM' FOR DEALING WITH DRUG PROBLEMS

The special features of British drug policy have been the attention of a number of writers (see e.g. refs. 3, 4). It was the idea that there was a unique 'British system' for dealing with opiate problems that was the subject of many of these accounts. In particular some US observers thought that Britain had a system that was special and preferable to other approaches.

Many commentaries on the 'British system' have tended to indicate that two things distinguished the British response. First, that the balance swung more to the medical side — both in rhetoric and practice — rather than to the legal and penal, and was thus benign rather than punitive. The essence of the British approach was that the interests of treatment and prevention were best served by regarding the addict as a patient.[5] Some observers have suggested that it was not just Britain's medico-centric approach that distinguished it from other countries, but that it had a particular type of medical approach that allowed for the prescription of opiate drugs to addicts. This has been a key differentiating practice since the 1920s, and perhaps one that has enabled doctors to remain central to debate and policy. Second, the British medical approach, as well as helping the individual, was thought to limit the social problems of addiction, for example by preventing the spread of addiction, and reducing the financial and criminal problems often associated with it. It was early realized that medical treatment had benefits for society as well as (and sometimes instead of) the individual addict. (The analysis tended to ignore the fact that non-medical use of opiates was subject to strict legal penalty; that a continuing part of the British response has been through policing, the courts and the prison system; and that a wide range of controlled drugs were outside of the medico-centric domain.)

There have been several transformations of the British approach since its basic form was established under the 1920 Dangerous Drugs Act and the subsequent Rolleston Committee Report.[6] Most readers will be familiar with the major changes which established the Drug Treatment Centres (the 'Clinics') in 1968. A brief recapitulation of the period since then will set the scene for discussing the present position. As is now well known, rapid changes in patterns of drug use in the 1960s — the appearance of young, recreational heroin addicts — led to questions about the effectiveness of the then British policy that allowed any medical practitioner to prescribe for addicts. Evidence given to the Second Interdepartmental Committee on Drug Addiction[1] (known after its chairman as the Brain Committee) suggested that the system which had allowed any practitioner to prescribe for addicts appeared (in 1965) to be a policy that actually facilitated the spread of addiction. It must be made clear to those who do not have experience of that time, that the vast bulk

of heroin and cocaine available illicitly in London in the 1960s was pharmaceutical heroin that had been legitimately supplied to addict patients by doctors and then resold. There was no illicit market in smuggled heroin and cocaine.

The Brain Committee saw addiction as a 'socially infectious condition' and believed that control of the drug problem could be exercised through control of treatment. In this new formulation, medicine was seen in functional relation with the black-market — if doctors could get the right balance then addicts would come for treatment, be prescribed just the right amount to prevent them having recourse to the black-market, and so the development of a major black-market would be curtailed. Thus was born the notion of 'competitive prescribing' or, prescribing to 'keep out the Mafia'. This task was given to specialist hospital doctors (mainly psychiatrists), who would have more colleague support and over whom some (subtle) oversight could be exercised.

The ensuing period was dominated, at the level of debate and to a large extent in practice, by a clinic-based medical response, supplemented by some agencies in the non-statutory (i.e. outside the NHS) sector, such as 'concept' houses (e.g. Phoenix House) and a handful of drop-in centres. One major preoccupation for clinic workers in this period was the social control of the drug problem.[3] Many clinic workers were concerned to limit the spread of addiction through the treatment given to individual patients.

There was considerable variety in methods of treatment and treatment aims in the clinics, which included heroin maintenance, in- and out-patient withdrawal, therapeutic wards, and methadone substitution. The principles that generally emerged were first that patients should, where possible, be transferred from heroin to methadone, and second, that doses should go down (and almost never up). The main switch from heroin to methadone occurred from the first year or two of the clinics. There was eclectic borrowing from the experience of others. Significant here was the British experience with methadone, which was sometimes used to wean people from heroin, sometimes to maintain them on drugs, and sometimes as part of an abstinence programme. At first it was quite common for injectable methadone to be prescribed. At this time, as in later years, there were few studies of treatment or good descriptions of treatment practice. Reviewing the first ten years of the clinics *Druglink*[7] remarked on the 'almost overwhelming silence on what actually happens in a clinic . . .'

Around the mid-1970s there were some misgivings within clinics and a change of treatment philosophies. The Hartnoll–Mitcheson[8] work compared the outcome for patients offered injectable heroin versus oral methadone. Despite the authors' reservations about the results, the study was widely taken to show that oral methadone treatment was preferable. This study coincided with a new version of methadone treatment in clinics: it was now to be given on a short-term, contract basis, in a confrontational therapeutic climate. The major treatment philosophy was now abstinence oriented.[9] This policy shift was not dictated from central government, nor was it adopted wholesale by all clinics for all patients. Clinic consultants have an extremely high level of autonomy in deciding their clinic practices.

This move from social control to treatment had several impetuses. First was the feeling of greater safety about the nature of the drugs problem. The number of addicts grew only slightly between 1973 and 1976 and there was a feeling that things were under control, and therapists could therefore be more energetic. Second was the growing disillusionment regarding the lack of success of maintenance prescribing — the continued multiple drug-taking, high morbidity and mortality among long-term patients. Third was criticism about the limits of social control through competitive prescribing.[10] Fourth, the clinics were beginning to be filled with ageing addicts and long-term patients. The shorter-term contract treatment enabled a faster throughput without an increase in resources.[11,12] By the mid-1970s most of the clinics had switched most of their patients to some sort of methadone (IV or oral).

A survey of clinics in 1982[13] showed that most were restricted by a lack of staff, few had consultants working on a full-time basis, they lacked support services, and the majority did not come close to the guidelines on staffing policy and resources in the Advisory Council on the Misuse of Drugs report on *Treatment and Rehabilitation*.[2] Many were still based in the cramped accommodation in which they had been established.[9]

With isolated exceptions, there has been a marked lack of research on treatment, then and now. Treatment policies proceed largely without empirical investigation.

CHANGES IN THE CHARACTER OF DRUG PROBLEMS

This account of the British approach, emphasizing the medico-centric debate and practice, sets the scene for understanding developments in the 1980s. First it is necessary to review changes in the characteristics of drug problems. Despite the relative complacency and security felt by many workers in the late 1970s, a longer-term view indicates considerable alterations in the size and pattern of drug use since the 1960s, with major changes occurring since the end of the 1970s. We have limited information to work from, and our basic data still come primarily from the Home Office, supplemented by information from the DHSS, surveys and more anecdotal reports. Despite the known shortcomings of the official statistics the changes that are indicated are so massive that few could deny that we now face a problem of a new magnitude.

Number of regular users

In the 1960s there were few regular users. By 1966, after what was then seen as a major increase in the extent of heroin addiction, the total number of addicts known to the Home Office was only 1349.[14] When the Vera Institute of New York estimated in 1967 that Britain would have 11 000 addicts by 1972 this was dismissed by many British observers as belonging to the realms of fantasy rather than scientific projection.

By 1984 the number of addicts known to the Home Office was 12 489.[15,16] Notifications to the Home Office rose by 20 to 30 per cent a year from 1980, more steeply than at any time since the 1960s. Estimating a notional 'real' number of regular users (i.e. both those known and unknown to the Home Office) is a matter of guesswork, but refinements introduced by drug indicators projects suggest that official notifications may be multiplied by five to give an approximation of the number of regular users.[17] This would give an estimated 60 000 regular users. Some drug workers estimate that as many again may use opiates on an occasional basis.[17]

Seizures

In the 1960s seizures of illicitly imported heroin were insignificant, and the major heroin market was in prescribed pharmaceutical heroin. The first major seizure of smuggled heroin came in 1971 when 1.14 kg was seized. In 1984, the customs seized 312 kg and the police seized a further 49 kg.

Convictions

In 1966 there were 2613 convictions for drug offences (1119 for cannabis, the rest for other drugs). By 1984 the total number of convictions for drug offences was 25 022. Most of these were for cannabis offences (20 529), but convictions concerning heroin, at 2446, were almost as great as the total for all drug offences in 1966.

Price

In the 1960s pharmaceutical heroin was sold at £1 for 60 mg (the standard retail unit of one pharmaceutical grain made up of six 10 mg pills). Price rose after 1968, stabilized in the mid-1970s and dropped from 1978. Illicitly imported heroin (in 1986) retails at about £80 for a gram. Relative to inflation, the real price of heroin on the illicit market has halved since 1978.[17,18] Retail purity is high at around 45 to 55 per cent though there have been some recent local reports of a drop in purity.

Geographical spread

In the 1960s heroin use was mainly concentrated in London and the South-East, with a handful of users in other major cities. In the 1980s heroin use can be found in most parts of the UK and is no longer confined to urban environments.

Changes in mode of administration

In the 1960s most regular heroin users injected the drug. In the 1980s, it is probably true that the majority use various methods of inhalation such as 'chasing the dragon' (inhaling the fumes of heroin heated on tinfoil), 'snorting' (sniffing) or smoking with tobacco.

After many years of relative silence in the media, 1984 was the year that Britain heard again about heroin.

Press and TV began running stories on new, young heroin users, often, but not always, living in run-down parts of large cities. The changed pattern of use has led some researchers to hypothesize a 'normalization' of drug use.[19,20] This thesis proposes that heroin use is now a commonplace activity that many young people will encounter, and which is no longer at the extreme end of a self-conscious youth culture. Barker[21] commenting on drug use in South London, noted that there is no longer a 'drug scene' but a 'local scene' where illicit drug use has become part of the character of the community. In parts of London '. . . it is impossible to grow up without being exposed to or involved in illicit drugs and substance abuse'. Some commentators have suggested that the reaction has also been normalized. As Banks and Waller put it: 'In the days of the Brain Committees the country panicked over an increase in known addicts from 470 in 1961 to 631 in 1963 — now we shrug off what is probably a 20-fold increase'.[22] In other words, whilst heroin is not accepted and tolerated, there is scepticism about measures to control its spread.

IDENTIFYING THE THEMES OF CONTEMPORARY BRITISH POLICY

Accompanying these changes in the extent and pattern of drug use have come numerous changes in the perception of drug problems and the nature and level of response. Indeed since 1985 there have been more initiatives and more debate about drugs than at any previous time. This section of the paper attempts to identify a number of themes that characterize this new response. Given the lack of research on contemporary drug policy these should be viewed as working hypotheses about the new directions being taken by British policy.

Theme 1: The decline of the clinic

As was indicated at the beginning of this paper, a major trend appears to be a shift from a medico-centric to a more diffuse response. The first change is that clinics appear to be less central than in previous years. This was anticipated in a succinct review of the clinic system in *Druglink*[7] which argued that 'To an extent the clinics (not all of them) have become a backwater of our social response to drug abuse dealing with a problem that no longer reaches the heart of the UK drug scene'. An indication of this is that notifications of new addicts from clinics now (1984 figures) make up only 30 per cent of the total, the rest come from general practice (independent and NHS) (55 per cent) and prisons (15 per cent). Many others are seen outside the medical/notification system.

From being seen as a central hub of the response to drug problems, doctors in clinics are now but one of numerous groups working in the field, and their views are among many different — sometimes complementary and sometimes conflicting — views.

Theme 2

Earlier discussions of the 'addict' or the 'drug dependent' have been replaced by the 'problem drug taker'. This term received its official warrant in the ACMD Report on *Treatment and Rehabilitation*[2] which defined a problem drug taker as 'any person who experiences social, psychological, physical or legal problems related to intoxication and/or regular excessive consumption and/or dependence as a consequence of his own use of drugs or other chemical substances (excluding alcohol or tobacco)'. This definition broadens the scope of concern for treatment and rehabilitation services and suggests that drug problems are wide-ranging, and do not always involve dependence and a medical response.

Theme 3: The rise of the 'community'

A third theme, also linked to the suggestion that the clinics are becoming less central is the 'community' response to drug problems. The focus is changing, as one commentary put it, as '. . . non-statutory and community resources outside the clinic system have replaced heroin maintenance inside . . .'. This response is also linked to a demedicalization of drug problems.[23]

In this context 'community' means first the voluntary sector. The voluntary agencies have been present to a greater or lesser extent since the 1960s but have rarely figured prominently in policy debate. They are now seen as a crucial part of the response. They include residential rehabilitation projects; advice, information and counselling agencies; and self-help and

community groups. In England, 162 projects were funded under the DHSS central initiative by February 1986, ranging from clinics, drug-screening equipment, nurse training courses, counselling services, telephone help lines, rehabilitation hostels, and therapy services for drug takers and their families. A recent listing of projects is given added kudos with a foreword by the Princess of Wales.[24]

Theme 4: The shift from specialists to generalists

The fourth linked trend is the shift of emphasis from specialists to generalists in recent DHSS circulars.[25] This seems to be based on an assessment that the spread of drug problems has overloaded specialist services, and that many such services are inappropriate for the treatment of the problem drug taker.

Many different groups of workers come into contact with people with drug problems (e.g. social workers, community and youth workers, general practitioners, general medical workers and psychiatrists in the NHS, health visitors, clergy, teachers, probation officers) and an increasing proportion of their work is concerned with such clients. In some cases clients' major problems might be with drugs, or drugs can be incidental to other welfare and health problems.

'Community' has yet a third meaning. There has been greater attention to the role of families and parents. This is indicated in the 1986 anti-heroin media campaigns which were targeted at parents as well as young people.

Theme 5: A role for the 'responsible' general practitioner

Another shift from specialists is the encouragement given to the 'responsible' general practitioner to become involved in the treatment of addiction. The last twenty years has of course seen the continuation of the private prescribing practitioner, an attempt by such practitioners to improve their status through the Association of Independent Doctors, and continued controversy about their role.[26]

Recently it has been argued that the general NHS practitioner has a new and important role to play. This reverse of earlier policy has come about in part because of the limitations of specialist resources in the face of high levels of drug misuse. Encouragement has come in the form of various local guidelines for GPs[27] and in the national *Guidelines of Good Clinical Practice in the Treatment of Drug Misuse*[28] issued by the DHSS and sent in 1984 to every general practitioner and hospital doctor in the UK, and subsequent DHSS circulars.[25] All GPs of course have a responsibility for the general medical care of patients, including those who are addicts. It is now suggested that GPs take some responsibility for their drug-related problems, including detoxification. Doctors are advised in the guidelines not to undertake long-term prescription of opiates to addicts unless in conjunction with specialist support. This encouragement has happened without much information available on the extent of GP involvement in drug problems.

Theme 6: A new role for central government

A marked feature of state intervention in drugs in the UK has been the lack of detailed central direction. But since 1984 the government has taken a new major interest in drug problems. The level of government involvement is greater than has hitherto been seen in this country. This is the first government to have seriously considered the problem of drug-taking at many levels; it has set up inter-Ministerial collaborative machinery at ministerial level (a recognition that the issues concern and cut across government departments). Drugs are no longer the concern of just the Home Office and the DHSS, but also Customs and Excise, Department of Education and Science, Foreign and Commonwealth Office, Overseas Development Administration, Department of the Environment, Scottish Office, Welsh Office, DHSS Northern Ireland.[29] This Ministerial Group on the Misuse of Drugs has developed a strategy for *tackling drug misuse* and the government has put money into numerous law enforcement, educational, preventive and treatment projects.

Theme 7: The debate on law enforcement and control

A further indication of the changes that are occurring is in the character of the new debate on drugs. Whilst professional debate focuses on treatment and rehabilitation, discussions about control through legal and penal measures have recently become prominent. This new debate has emerged from central government and Parliament rather than the caring professions. This shift in debate came in 1985. It is typified by the report of the Home Affairs Select Committee[29] which argued for the Royal Navy and the Royal Air Force to help the customs and the police. The committee called for intensified law enforcement efforts, sequestration of the assets of drug traffickers, extradition of suppliers from other countries, a reform of the banking laws to trace drug money, more efforts for crop substitution and eradication, and an increase in the penalty for systematic dealing in drugs to 'no less than the penalty for premeditated murder'. The new approach to drugs — the Home Affairs Committee report described the problem as 'the most serious peacetime threat to our national well-being' — was echoed in Prime Minister Margaret Thatcher's visits to the Customs at Heathrow and to the Central Drugs Intelligence Unit at Scotland Yard. She made it clear that there was now a war on traffickers and smugglers, and warned 'We are after you. The pursuit will be relentless. We shall make your life not worth living.' The new approach to drug issues has been called the 'war on drugs' (see Paper 20).

Theme 8: The politicization of drugs

In seeing the emergence of this new debate, we are seeing the politicization of drug problems. The Ministerial Group on the Misuse of Drugs, the Prime Minister's interest, numerous ministerial statements, a government hosted international conference of foreign ministers, reports from the House of Commons Home Affairs and Social Services Select Committees — all these indicate that the arena for debate is no longer confined to professional and advisory committees, but that centre stage may for the moment be taken by central government and Parliament. Along with prominent statements from politicians in all parties, it appears that drugs are now on the agenda as a political issue. The next election is likely to be the first where each of the major parties has a drug strategy to offer the electorate.

CONCLUSION

In so far as we can make some preliminary assessment

of what has happened, it appears that the British approach to drugs is in the process of undergoing a marked transformation.

Responsibility for dealing with drugs has been spread out. Where once medicine was central to debate and practice, there is now no clear centre. The response has diversified and includes a more prominent place for government, law enforcement, the legal and penal system, and the community.

In the long term, the contribution of policy studies is not just through an analysis of past events, and of the gradual transformation from the British 'system' to some new pattern of response.

The key question is What are the policy options for the future? Are we able to develop new measures for controlling drugs and reducing the social and health costs of their use and control? What package of policies offers the best buy? Such questions require examination of policies directed at the whole range of drugs capable of misuse, and of the relationship between policies for drug misuse, and policies for alcohol, tobacco and prescribed drugs. Given scarce resources for responding to drug problems, policy studies are not an optional extra, but an essential part of planning the response. The task has barely begun.

REFERENCES

1. Interdepartmental Committee on Drug Addiction (1965) *Second Report*. London: HMSO.
2. Advisory Council on the Misuse of Drugs (1982) *Treatment and Rehabilitation*. London: HMSO.
3. Stimson, G.V. and Oppenheimer, E. (1982) *Heroin Addiction: Treatment and Control in Britain*. London: Tavistock.
4. Edwards, G. (1967) Relevance of American experience of narcotic addiction to the British scene, *British Medical Journal*, **3**, 425–9.
5. Edwards, G. (1969) The British approach to the treatment of heroin addiction, *Lancet*, 768–72.
6. Departmental Committee on Morphine and Heroin Addiction (1926) *Report*. London: HMSO.
7. Institute of the Study of Drug Dependence (1980). Controlling addiction: the role of the clinics, *Druglink*, **13**, 1–6.
8. Hartnoll, R.L., Mitcheson, M.C., Battersby, A., Brown,

G., Ellis, M., Fleming, P. and Hedley, N. (1980) Evaluation of heroin maintenance in controlled trial, *Archives of General Psychiatry*, **37**, 877.
9. Ghodse, A.H. (1983) Treatment of drug addiction in London, *Lancet*, 636–9.
10. Edwards, G. (1978) Some years on: evolutions in the 'British System', in D.J. West (ed.), *Problems of Drug Abuse in Britain*. Cambridge Institute of Criminology.
11. Ghodse, A.H. (1982) Drug addiction: British system failing, *Lancet*, 83–4.
12. Strang, J. (1984) Abstinence or abundance — what goal? *British Medical Journal*, **289**, 604.
13. Smart, C. (1985) Drug dependence units in England and Wales. The results of a national survey, *Drug and Alcohol Dependence*, **15**, 131–44.
14. Spear, H.B. (1969) The growth of heroin addiction in the United Kingdom, *British Journal of Addiction*, **64**, 245.
15. Home Office (1985) *Statistics of the Misuse of Drugs in the United Kingdom*, 1984, Home Office Statistical Bulletin 23/85. London: Home Office.
16. Home Office (1985) *Statistics of the Misuse of Drugs, United Kingdom, Supplementary Tables 1984*. London: Home Office.
17. Institute for the Study of Drug Dependence (1984) *Surveys and Statistics on Drug-taking in Britain*. London: ISDD.
18. Lewis, R. (1985) Serious business — the global heroin economy, in A. Henman, R. Lewis and T. Malyon, *Big Deal: the Politics of the Illicit Drugs Business*. London: Pluto Press.
19. Pearson, G., Gilman, M., and McIver, S. (1985) *Young People and Heroin Use in the North of England*. Mimeo. London: Health Education Council.
20. Strang, J. (1984) Changing the image of the drug taker, *Health and Social Service Journal*, 1202–4.
21. Barker, J. (1985) The local situation, in *Proceedings of the Conference on London's Drug Problems*. London: Greater London Council.
22. Banks, A. and Waller, T.A.M. (1983) *Drug addiction and polydrug abuse: the role of the General Practitioner*. London: Institute of the Study of Drug Dependence.
23. Institute for the Study of Drug Dependence (1985) *On Heroin*. London: ISDD.
24. Standing Conference on Drug Abuse (1986) *Drug Problems, Where to get Help*. London: BBC Drugwatch and SCODA.
25. Department of Health and Social Security (1986) Health Service Development Services for Drug Misusers: Circular HC(86)3.
26. Bewley, T. and Ghodse, A.H. (1983) Unacceptable face of private practice: prescription of controlled drugs to addicts, *British Medical Journal*, **286**, 1876–7.
27. Strang, J. (1985) The generalists' guide to the assess-

ment and treatment of the problem drug-taker, *Update*, 979–87.

28. Department of Health and Social Security (1984) *Guidelines of Good Clinical Practice in the Treatment of Drug Misuse*. London: DHSS.

29. UK House of Commons (1985) Fifth Report of the Home Affairs Committee, *Misuse of Hard Drugs (Interim Report)* Session 1984/5.

Can a war on drugs succeed?

GERRY STIMSON

Principal Lecturer, Sociology Department, Goldsmith's College, University of London

This paper questions current policies and describes the new penalties that are used for drug offences. It argues strongly that tougher law enforcement is not enough on its own to cope with the problems of drug abuse.

As everyone knows, there has been a huge increase in the successful smuggling of heroin into this country. In the mid-1960s, at the height of the last great scare about hard drugs, there was hardly any smuggled heroin in Britain. Twenty years later, there are few places where you can't find it. Is it really possible to stop or slow this supply? What problems face a country trying to control drug smuggling? The government thinks that a tougher approach is the answer: but is it?

The question of how to curb the supply might seem to have an easy answer. Being an island, all we need do is strengthen our customs control, or even — as the Commons home affairs select committee has suggested — bring in the navy and the air force to help the customs and the police.

Let's look at how heroin gets to Britain. The chain of supply starts in some poor country. Most of the heroin now coming to Britain originates in Afghanistan and Pakistan. The rest comes from south east Asian countries like Burma, Thailand and Laos, and the Middle East.

Heroin is, of course, derived from the opium poppy. Opium growing is a major source of income for many poor farmers. A Pathan farmer may give an acre over to poppies. This will produce about seven kilograms of opium, which will sell (depending on the general success of the crop that year) at between £22 and £100 a kilo. Opium growing needs a lot of labour. The size of the crop is limited by the supply of labour and by the need to put some land over to foodstuffs to feed the workforce. Ten kilos of opium make a kilo of heroin. Opium is converted to heroin in simple local refineries. The local wholesaler in the North West Frontier Province of Pakistan sells it for export at between £3,000 and £4,000 a kilo.

Since the 1970s, there have been many attempts by western countries to persuade producer countries to stop growing opium. This has worked with some former suppliers — Yugoslavia and Turkey, for example. But it has failed in south west and south east Asia.

Two approaches have been tried: crop eradication and crop substitution. Eradication means burning or spraying the growing plants. But this leaves peasant farmers worse off than before. It is, anyway, difficult to carry out. Despite satellite monitoring and sophisticated surveillance, the United States has not eradicated marijuana growing even in its own country. Hence the alternative tack — crop substitution. This means encouraging farmers to grow alternative cash crops, like sugar beet, coffee or flowers. But the difficulty is that the growers are often a long way from the markets for these crops. Transport is hazardous, and the cash returns are much lower. No other crop returns so great a yield per acre as the opium poppy.

What is more, these areas are often beyond the reach of government. In the Golden Triangle of south east Asia, they are controlled by tribal warlords or anti-government rebels. In the North West Frontier region

Previously published in *New Society*, 15 November 1985, pp. 275–278, and reproduced with their permission.

of Afghanistan and Pakistan — the so-called Golden Crescent — they are controlled by fiercely independent tribal groups. In South America, many cocaine-growing areas are controlled by the drug producers themselves. They have private armies that are better equipped than the national armies.

So, these areas are poorly policed, inaccessible, and hostile to government officials and to officials from other countries. The US Drug Enforcement Agency has 20 officials in Pakistan, but they are mostly in the cities, rather than in the growing areas. Visits to growing areas can only be undertaken with heavily armed guards. In Columbia, the six ruling coca families threatened to kill three Drug Enforcement Agency men for each drug producer arrested. In February this year they carried out that threat.

It is no coincidence that the main opium-growing areas have been, and remain, politically unstable. They are often right-wing and anti-communist. They depend on trafficking bands, tribal groups and private armies for border security. Western governments have often supported these people as a buffer against communism.

Quite simply, many people in these countries do not share the western governments' view on the need to control a traditional crop which brings in money. Imagine the response if the Pakistan government sent emissaries here to persuade our distillers to stop producing whisky because whisky drinking was causing a social problem in Pakistan.

Drug production in the third world relies on poverty, a suitable climate and an abundance of labour. It gives poor peasants some extra income. However, this is no place to get romantic. The peasants are exploited, just like most growers of raw materials for export. The big profits are made by the refiners and the exporters. These profits are often taken out of the country, and rarely benefit its economy. Drug production reproduces, in an alarming way, the traditional exploitation of poor countries. Bolivia, a main cocaine producer, is a prime example. Cocaine is now the main dollar-earning export. Its production employs one in ten of the population. Despite pockets of affluence, this has not raised the living conditions for the mass of the people. The history of former drug-producing countries — China, Yugoslavia and perhaps Iran — is that drug production only ceases when there are major economic, political and social changes.

The next stage of the journey taken by the heroin that worries us here is when it is smuggled into Britain. Each year, 36 million passengers arrive from foreign destinations. What are the chances of getting through customs without being searched? The returning holidaymaker may think the search level is high. In fact, very few people are searched by customs, perhaps only one in 100.

The difficulty for the customs men comes not only from passengers, but also from motor vehicles, ships and aircraft. Heroin smugglers are more and more using the cover of commercial freight to bring in large consignments. The customs policy on goods from the EEC is that only 2 per cent are subject to random searches. In 1983 only 6 per cent of all freight brought into the United Kingdom was examined.

Then there are private yachts. On the south coast alone, there are thousands of boats, many capable of sailing to other countries: 6,000 at Chichester harbour, 4,000 on the Hamble, 4,000 at Lymington. The Society of Civil and Public Servants, pressing a claim for more customs staff, reports that on a Sunday night up to 60 yachts on the Hamble may report their arrival from abroad, and a similar number not bother. There are not enough customs officers even to deal with those asking for customs attention.

But contrary to the popular impression, random searches are not the main thrust of the customs effort. Probably less than a fifth of seizures come from random search, and these are likely to hit the one-off independent importer, rather than the large-scale trafficker. Much of the customs work is in intelligence. Drugs are now the largest single part of the operations of the Customs Special Investigation Division. The intelligence men work from both ends of the supply chain — in producer countries (Britain has now stationed a customs official in Pakistan), and in this country. Some of the most spectacular seizures result from this. Despite these successes, the customs would be the first to admit that they have a tough job. As the Commons select committee acknowledged: 'No amount of law enforcement can stop the great bulk of supplies getting through'. Seizures have increased. But they probably remain minimal, compared with what is missed.

The Chief Investigation Officer for Customs and Excise is reluctant to estimate success rates. But no law enforcement agency anywhere in the world credibly claims more than a 10 per cent interception rate.

After heroin has come into Britain for distribution, control becomes a police responsibility.

Intelligence for all these activities is provided at New Scotland Yard by the recently created National Drugs Intelligence Unit. This has replaced the former Central Drugs Intelligence Unit. It is staffed by both police and customs. The seriousness of the Home Office's view of drug distribution is indicated by the fact that the new coordinator heading the national unit is a very senior policeman, Colin Hewett, who has previously headed the Metropolitan Police Special Branch and its anti-terrorist squad.

The police make many more seizures than the customs (2,800 seizures of heroin in 1984). But the seizures are much, much smaller. In terms of quantity, the total police seizures amount to only 10 per cent of those of the customs. Seizing one kilo at import is clearly much cheaper than seizing that kilo when it has been divided up into 1,000 separate one-gram packets at a street level. Despite attempts to move up the chain of supply, most convictions are at the user and user/dealer ends. In 1983, two thirds of police seizures were for less than one gram.

The government continues to try to tighten the screw. Parole has been removed for major drug traffickers, and the government has increased the maximum penalty for trafficking in Class A drugs from 14 years to life imprisonment. But it is unlikely that even this will deter major importers while the profits remain so high.

Sequestration of assets is another of the government's current proposals. It could be one way of increasing the costs of heroin distribution, which might make heroin a less attractive proposition for criminals. The hurdle here is that a successful policy would require close international cooperation in controlling the flow of capital, and tighter national controls. The government's policies on free exchange control run against this.

What, then, can we make of this labour? Last year, at best, all the time, effort and money put into British customs and police work resulted in the interception of perhaps 10 per cent of imports. If we want to be pessimistic about this, it is a 90 per cent failure rate. And even this had no impact on the price and purity of drugs in Britain. These are sensitive indicators of supply — low price and high purity indicate high supply. With a combination of poor producer countries, and a high demand for heroin at home, all the customs and police efforts cannot stop the import of heroin. At best, they can slow it down a bit. Against this must be set the undoubted (but uncalculated) deterrence effect. Without controls, it is likely that imports would have been much higher.

Could things be done better? There are no easy solutions. What if we put more men and money into policing and customs work: would a doubling of present resources double the seizures?

It is inconceivable that any government — however determined in its fight against drugs — could put enough money in to reduce seriously the amount of heroin coming here.

If you don't believe in the free availability of dangerous drugs — and few people seriously entertain that idea — then controls over supply are inevitable. But the question remains: What is the best way?

Let us think again about the first link in the chain, the producer country. Many crop control schemes may have failed, but there is room for a more vigorous and imaginative approach. The British government is spending £200,000 a year for the next five years from 1986 towards a crop substitution and rural development programme in the North West Frontier Province. But this still compares poorly with the money the farmers get for producing the raw material for the three tons of heroin that come to Britain from Pakistan each year. Third world drug production must be seen in the light of the dependent position of these countries in the world economy. As a minimum, western governments could pay farmers a decent price for crop substitution.

An alternative might be for western governments to accept the fact that opium growing will continue so long as these countries remain poor and underdeveloped, and to purchase opium at source for later destruction.

It would cost the British government between £600,000 and £3 million to buy the opium from the Pakistani peasant farmers (or between £9 million and £12 million from the wholesaler). This would guarantee them an income. By analogy with the EEC's Common Agricultural Policy, it would create an opium mountain. And it would interrupt supply at source. It would be a cheap buy, compared with the £100 million a year that London addicts alone are estimated to spend on heroin.

Better still, perhaps, would be to encourage a third world pharmaceutical industry, based on locally grown drugs. This would legitimise controlled production and help economic development.

EDUCATION AND PREVENTION

And what of the other two links in the chain, importa-tion and distribution within this country? We need some public accountability for resources and effectiveness. The 'value for money' calls now made over other state services are equally applicable to law enforcement, as the new Home Secretary, Douglas Hurd, has indicated. What is the best way to control supply through law enforcement? Is there a better return from more money spent on the police; or is the customs better value? The figures on seizures suggest a greater return from customs work.

Law enforcement alone is unlikely to be the answer. We need to find the right balance between public expenditure on education, prevention and treatment — not just on enforcement. Education and information campaigns and 'pump-priming' for local treatment and rehabilitation projects are welcome. But these measures look small by comparison with expenditure on enforcement.

The rise and fall of the solvents panic

RICHARD IVES

Development Officer at the National Children's Bureau

In this paper the rise and fall of the solvent-sniffing panic is chronicled. Although acknowledging that solvent misuse can be a serious problem, the paper details the ways in which the surrounding 'moral panic' obscured the most important issues and may even have attracted more potential sniffers than it deterred.

Societies appear to be subject, every now and then, to periods of moral panic. A condition, episode, person or group of persons emerges to become defined as a threat to societal values and interests; its nature is presented in a stylised and stereotypical fashion by the mass media; the moral barricades are manned by editors, bishops, politicians and other right-thinking people; socially accredited experts pronounce their diagnoses and solutions; ways of coping are evolved or (more often) resorted to; the condition then disappears, submerges or deteriorates . . . Sometimes the object of the panic is quite novel and other times it is something which has been in existence long enough, but suddenly appears in the limelight. Stanley Cohen, *Folk devils and moral panics*.

Before the 'solvents problem' waxed and then waned in the media and among the public, a similar cycle had been completed with respect to the young 'deviants' of the '60s.

In his book *Folk devils and moral panics*,[1] Stanley Cohen used material gathered from the public response to the mods-and-rockers' clashes of the mid-1960s to develop a theory of 'moral panic' as a response to emerging threats to society's values and interests.

Media reports of various seaside incidents portrayed the fairly homogeneous mass of young people as polarised into these rival gangs, encouraging their polarisation in reality. Public panic came to be out of all proportion to the size of the problem. Young people of all descriptions were turned back from seaside resorts on Bank Holiday weekends, and the fines and other punishments imposed were disproportionate to the relatively minor offences committed.

Coverage of these events encouraged people, including young people themselves, to see mods and rockers in opposition to one another, attracting more young people to the resorts on Bank Holiday weekends and giving a new shape to their presence there: they were 'looking for trouble' instead of 'doing nothing'.

Adult opinion was outraged by this apparently new phenomenon, and many and various causes and solutions were postulated. These were often extremely punitive and included, among others, forcing mods to smash up their own scooters with hammers.

Eventually the moral panic died away. What stopped it? From the point of view of the public and mass media, it was largely a waning of interest. The mod phenomenon had developed before receiving widespread public attention and the disturbances continued after reporting of them had ceased. Mods and rockers as folk devils were replaced by other new and newsworthy youth phenomena — notably drugs, student militancy, hippies and football hooligans.

The rise and fall of the 'glue sniffer' can be looked at in similar terms. Glue sniffing was born as a social phenomenon in Britain in the late 1970s. Although not at first the prerogative of any particular youth subculture, sniffing was adopted by punks (and later by skinheads) because public perceptions of sniffing fitted in with what punk subculture 'had to say'.

This paper previously appeared in *Druglink*, November/December 1986, and is reproduced by permission of the author and the Institute for the Study of Drug Dependence.

Punk was opposed to consumption and to adults' solutions to problems. Political allegiance, if any, was to anarchy — a political form most opposed to all conventional solutions to structural problems, and significantly the one best suited to shock adults. As a response to youth unemployment and renewed threats of nuclear extinction, its slogan was 'no future'.

Dick Hebdige's notion that subcultures are constructed, however obliquely, out of headlines[2] gives an important clue to the origins of the punk movement. By presenting themselves as degenerate, punks were dramatising Britain's highly publicised decline. Punk was a spectacle. It became important to members of the subculture itself, as much as for adults outside it, for punk to be oppositional to adult concerns. As a result, these aspects of punk subculture became 'amplified'.

WHY GLUE SNIFFING?

By using household products as intoxicants, punks were certainly giving objects and events fresh meaning by re-assembling them in novel ways, one definition of the creation of a 'style'.[3] But from the start there must have been something about these objects that fitted punk's self-image.

For many years, experimental sniffing (and sometimes a bit more than experimental) had been fairly random individual and small group behaviour. Sniffing was taken up by a few punks, probably at first as a cheap 'high'. Adults who saw them were outraged, hostile, and often concerned: sniffing became a 'problem'.

Because sniffing was singled out for adult repulsion, punks came to see sniffing as useful 'oppositional behaviour', and adult emphasis on 'sniffing kills' resonated well with the punk theme of 'no future'. For adults and punks alike, sniffing became a potent sign of punk's deviant image, arousing yet higher collective emotions spilling over into outrage against anything (such as the innocent scented rubbers) seen as encouraging sniffing.

Sniffing was both a useful and a practical part of punk 'sign-language' for several reasons.

- Sniffing was visible drugtaking which (being legal) could take place on the street, fitting well with punk's *emphasis on street life* and making it easy to *shock adults* by sniffing in front of them.

- Sniffing provided a swift 'high', fitting in with the value punks placed on *immediacy*. This same emphasis on immediacy called for a drug that was not only cheap but easily and widely available — not one (like illegal drugs) that required forethought to obtain and might be in short supply. Solvents fitted the requirement.

- Use of a readily available consumer product to achieve intoxication strengthened punk's statement about its *relationship to consumer society*. Punks saw themselves as outcasts from consumer society and rejected consumerist values. Sniffing transmuted the products offered by society for practical, unglamorous purposes into items of illicit pleasure.

- The objects of sniffing could be used to provide hallucinatory experiences which *distinguished* the sniffer from adults and from other young people, and could even perform a *sacramental* role. These experiences could also be used to give at least the illusion of *control* and *power*, which sniffers actually lacked (see below).

- *Disgust* is one of the most noticeable features of adult reaction to solvent sniffing, perhaps due to the confusion of consumer categories. If familiar household products are not used for their manufacturer-ordained purpose, then nothing is sacred. If glues can become intoxicants, what can be done with a packet of Persil! This disturbing dissonance made glue sniffing a particularly effective way for punk to shake up the adult 'establishment'.

- To most adults today sniffing from a plastic bag is a dramatically different way of becoming intoxicated, although in the last century snuff-taking and the inhalation of nitrous oxide or ether were all fairly common. So sniffing served to emphasise the *difference* between members of the subculture and the rest of humanity.

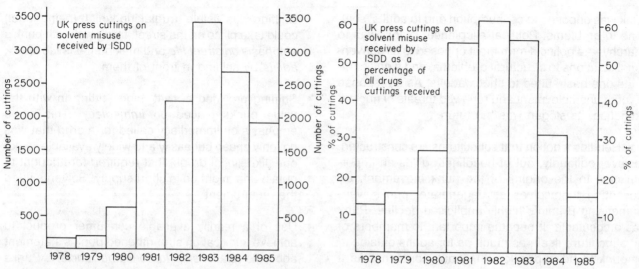

How 'the solvent sniffer' rose and fell in the British press.

- Solvents are an effective way of becoming '*completely out of it*', often for considerable periods of time, a potentially desirable prospect for unemployed youngsters with time to kill.

- Sniffing solvents can be *dangerous*, an attraction to many people. And the more adults told young people that 'sniffing kills', for some youngsters, the more attractive it became.

The hallucinations experienced by many solvent users helped provide a sense of shared 'communion' among the small group of sniffers.[4] At the same time these mystic experiences helped mark out the sniffer as someone special in a society where individuality is often not recognised. Hallucinations also offered youngsters scope to control a small part of their world. Sniffers report exerting considerable control over the course of their experiences and groups have reported that they can collectively control jointly experienced hallucinations. Hallucinations often have themes of power of flying or swooping over territory — taking 'symbolic possession' of it.

MORAL PANIC DEVELOPS

The constantly changing elements of punk style were partly a response to the internal demands of the sub-culture and of the individuals who composed it. But changes were also due to the response of adults. Much

of that response was visible through newspaper reports. In the constant interplay between public concern and media response, the media reflected and wrote large society's concerns, providing a graphic record of the development of the moral panic over sniffing.

- Glue deaths became material for lurid front page stories in both local and national newspapers: 'Glue Trip Punk In Death Leap' (*Islington Gazette*, 4 April 1985).

- Minor offences linked to glue sniffing became 'news' and received punitive responses: 'Glue Sniffers Used Bad Language' — they were fined £25 plus costs (a Scottish local newspaper in 1984). Meantime over-the-top responses by parents and others were portrayed as desperate attempts to combat the grip of glue: 'Glue Sniffer Locked In A Cage For A Year' (*Daily Telegraph*, 13 May 1985).

- Media carried exaggerated warnings of dangers and over-the-top descriptions: 'Death Games — As Deadly As Heroin, Yet As Easy To Buy As A Bar Of Chocolate', headlined the *News of the World* magazine in July 1984: 'It takes a tanker load of glue a week to keep up with the demands of the children in Wiltshire. That's how much they sniff . . . gulping it into their lungs, wrecking their bodies, doing untold, and in many cases permanent damage to their health and endangering their lives'.

- Panic was heightened by discovering ever younger sniffers — 'Mohican Aged Five. Head Says Boy Has Sniffed Glue. Robert Was A Skinhead At Three' (*Sun*, 6 September 1984) — and by implicating glue as the primary cause of various kinds of adolescent misbehaviour.

- Deviant images of sniffers were presented. A poster advertising a Scottish solvent helpline counter-productively depicted an evil-looking sniffer and press photos featured sniffers with their eyes blanked out, like criminals required to hide their identity.

- Media campaigns reported and promoted many and various calls for legislation, some claiming success with the passing of the Intoxicating Substances Supply Act of 1985.

- Sniffing was linked to up-and-coming moral panics: 'Glue And Heroin Link Feared . . . the Bishop of Norwich . . . was given government backing in the Lords yesterday for his suggestion that research should be done on the link between glue sniffing and the availability of cheap heroin near ports' (*Eastern Daily Press*, July 1984).

- Accredited experts appeared on the scene and their most frightening prognostications were seized on by the media. So-called 'signs and symptoms' of sniffing were repeated to worried parents. One list included: 'Giggling with no apparent reason . . . Inability to answer questions sensibly . . . Staying out late at night . . . Not buying school meals, asking for extra money'. An even longer list threw in 'Dialogues with God and Devil . . . Possession by evil entities'. Clearly, such 'symptoms' are as likely to be caused in other ways.

THE PANIC EBBS

As the panic began to die away, the various unthinking reactions tended to be replaced by a more questioning attitude. There had been too much crying wolf,

the papers and those who read them became bored, no new angles could be found and there were other more newsworthy and current moral panics.

Youth culture, too, moved on and developed new concerns. Society was and is left with a 'mopping-up exercise', to inform those still confused about the problem, and ensure young sniffers are helped to stop and that other young people do not start.

Concern and outrage about solvent misuse not only 'amplified' sniffing's role in punk subculture, but can also encourage experimentation by other young people. As punk died out, some members of the new generations of young people took up sniffing. To some, it became a useful metaphor which emphasised the role of the outcast, the loner, the reject. It remains an easy way to achieve a 'high' for those on low incomes or when illegal drugs are in short supply, and for those (especially younger adolescents) without access to other drugs or alcohol.

Although this article has ignored the real effects of solvents on the life and health of some young people, it is important to stress that solvent misuse is still a significant and serious problem. But public outrage served merely to reinforce the place of sniffing in punk culture and obscure any real damaging effects under a barrage of hyperbole that probably attracted more potential sniffers than it deterred. The lesson is a general one — drug problems need to be taken seriously and tackled appropriately. Tackling them appropriately does not involve panic.

REFERENCES

1. Cohen, S. *Folk devils and moral panic*. MacGibbon & Kee, 1972.
2. Hebdige, D. Subculture: image and noise. *In* Dale *et al. Education and the state*. Volume II. Falmer/Open University, 1981.
3. Clarke, J. Style. *In* Hall, S. and Jefferson, T. *Resistance through ritual*. Hutchinson, 1976.
4. Hall, K. Crossing the divide. *Youth in Society*: 1984, 96.

Misuse of Drugs Act

ISDD INFORMATION SERVICE

> This short paper aims to explain and clarify some of the complexities of the Misuse of Drugs Act. It has been produced by the ISDD Information Service, which provides regular material for updating legal information on drug-related issues.

First we describe what the Misuse of Drugs Act aims to do and the main prohibitions it establishes to achieve these aims. Then explore the regulations classifying drugs according to the extent to which they are excused from these prohibitions. To complicate matters, 'controlled' drugs (shorthand for drugs controlled under the Misuse of Drugs Act) are divided up in a different way to set maximum penalties for offences involving them.

Tables 1, 2 & 3 are explained in the text. Together they outline the Misuse of Drugs Act as it currently stands, concentrating on those features that most affect the general public (as opposed to the doctor, pharmacist, pharmaceutical industry, etc). Those involved in Misuse of Drugs Act prosecutions will need much more detailed guidance, of the kind that can be obtained from Release (01-603 8654) or from text books that cover case law as well as the statutes.

AIMS AND PROHIBITIONS

In its own words, the Misuse of Drugs Act aims to prevent the unauthorised use (misuse) of 'drugs which are being or appear . . . likely to be misused and of which the misuse is having or appears . . . capable of having harmful effects sufficient to constitute a social problem . . .'. It is also the way the UK fulfills its obligation to control drugs in accordance with international agreements. To the man or woman in the street, the Misuse of Drugs Act is the law which makes it illegal to use (sic) a wide range of drugs without a prescription — drugs like heroin, cocaine, LSD, cannabis, amphetamines.

The Act begins by defining the things it is illegal to do with the drugs it controls. Surprisingly (except for prepared opium) these prohibited activities do *not* include using the drugs. But they do include:

— possession (i.e., just having the drug);
— possession with the intention of supplying the drug to another person;
— production (including cultivation);
— supply or offer to supply to another person (including giving, selling, sharing, bartering, etc);
— import or export;
— allowing premises you occupy or manage to be used for supplying or offering to supply drugs.

Possession, the first of these offences, is penalised less severely than the rest. Except for the last in the list, these more serious offences are known as 'trafficking' offences.

EXEMPTIONS

Most controlled drugs have medical uses, others may be of scientific interest, so the Act allows the government to authorise possession, supply, production and import or export of drugs to meet medical or scientific needs. These exemptions to the general prohibitions are in the form of 'regulations' made under the Act. It is these regulations that have recently been reorganised and extended to accommodate the benzodiazepine tranquillisers. (The new regulations are available from HMSO — ask for Statutory Instrument 1985 number 2066, *The Misuse of Drugs Regulations 1985*.)

Table 1   Misuse of drugs regulations[1]

| | Drugs in schedule | | | | |
	1	2	3	4	5
Available to the general public on ...					
Unrestricted sale	NO	NO	NO	NO	NO
Sale at pharmacies without a prescription	NO	NO	NO	NO	YES
Prescription	NO	YES	YES	YES	YES
Anyone can legally ...					
Possess without a prescription or other authority	NO	NO	NO	YES[2]	YES
Import or export without a licence	NO	NO	NO	YES	YES
Administer to another person without special authority[3]	NO	YES	YES	YES	YES

But only as directed by a doctor or dentist

For all controlled drugs (schedules 1, 2, 3, 4 and 5) it is illegal to:
— supply, offer to supply, or possess intending to supply them to another person;
— allow supply or offers of supply on premises you occupy or manage;
— produce by cultivation, manufacture or any other method.

1. The regulations also give detailed instructions to manufacturers, suppliers, doctors and pharmacists regarding records, labelling, the writing of prescriptions, etc. This table outlines only those provisions that most affect the general public. For more detailed guidance turn to the Regulations or phone the Home Office Drugs Branch (01-213 4247).
2. But only in the form of a medicinal product.
3. In the Regulations, administration is distinct from supply. So, for instance, a mother may administer a dose of kaolin and morphine (a schedule 5 controlled drug) to her child without authorisation, but could commit an offence of supply if she gave the bottle to her husband.

Schedule 1

The Misuse of Drugs Regulations now divide controlled drugs into five schedules (see *Table 1*). Drugs in schedule 1 are the most stringently controlled. These drugs (such as LSD and cannabis) are not authorised for medical use and can only be supplied, possessed or administered in accordance with a Home Office

licence. Such licences are issued only for research or other special purposes. Outside these rare exceptions there are no circumstances in which possessing, supplying, producing, etc. these drugs is permitted. Doctors cannot prescribe them nor pharmacists dispense them. This is the closest British law comes to absolute prohibition.

Schedule 5

At the other end of the scale is schedule 5, listing preparations of drugs considered to pose minimal risk of abuse. Some of these dilute, small-dose, non-injectable preparations are allowed to be sold over-the-counter at a pharmacy without a prescription, and all may be possessed by anyone with impunity. But once bought they cannot legally be supplied to another person, a restriction that is probably ignored more often than it is enforced. Among these schedule 5 preparations are some well-known cough medicines, anti-diarrhoea agents and mild painkillers.

Schedules 2, 3 and 4

Between the extremes of schedules 1 and 5 are schedules 2, 3 and 4, including the vast majority of controlled drugs. These drugs are available for medical use, but can only be supplied or administered in accordance with a prescription or other authority. Here we find heroin, a drug that can still legally be prescribed by any doctor to any patient for the treatment of physical disease or injury.

It is illegal to possess drugs in schedules 2 and 3 without a prescription or other authority; but so long as they are in the form of a medicinal product, the benzodiazepine tranquillisers in schedule 4 *can* legally be possessed, even *without* a prescription. So it is an offence for Mr X to give (i.e. 'supply') Ms Y some of the Valium his doctor prescribed him, but Ms Y would be in the clear as she merely possessed the drug.

PENALTIES AND CLASSES

Drugs divided in the Regulations to define what counts as an offence, are divided up *differently* in the Act itself, according to the maximum penalties for these offences.

Table 2   Maximum penalties

Offence	Type of trial	Class of Misuse of Drugs Act		
		A	B[4]	C
Possession	Summary[2]	6 months + £2000 fine	3 months + £500 fine	3 months + £200 fine
	Indictment[3]	7 years + unlimited fine	5 years + unlimited fine	2 years + unlimited fine
'Trafficking'[1]	Summary[2]	6 months + £2000 fine	6 months + £2000 fine	3 months + £500 fine
	Indictment[3]	Life + unlimited fine	14 years + unlimited fine	5 years + unlimited fine

1. Includes supply, offer to supply, production, import and export. The same penalties apply to allowing premises to be used for supply. Unauthorised import or export are prohibited by the Misuse of Drugs Act but offences under the Customs and Excise Management Act, so fines on summary conviction can reach three times the value of the goods seized.
2. That is, when tried before a magistrates court.
3. That is, when tried before a Crown court.
4. Any class B drug in injectable form is treated as a class A drug.

Table 3   Main types of controlled drugs by schedule and class

Schedule	Class of Misuse of Drugs Act		
	A	B	C
1	Active ingredients of cannabis Hallucinogens Raw opium Coca leaf	Cannabis and cannabis resin	
2	Strong opiates and opioids (heroin, morphine, etc) Cocaine Phencyclidine (PCP)	Strong stimulants (amphetamine, methylphenidate, etc) Weaker opiates and opioids (codeine, etc) Methaqualone and mecloqualone	Dextropropoxyphene
3		Pentazocine Barbiturates	Weaker stimulants (diethylpropion, phentermine, etc) Some sedatives and hypnotics (e.g. meprobamate)
4			Benzodiazepine tranquillisers
5[2]	Preparations containing opium, morphine, certain opioids, and cocaine	Non-injectable preparations containing codeine and other weak opiates and opioids	Preparations containing dextropropoxyphene to be taken by mouth

1. Any class B drug in injectable form is treated as a class A drug
2. Includes dilute and/or small dose preparations of certain of the drugs listed in schedule 2.

Class A drugs are thought to be the most harmful when misused, so the penalties are the highest; then comes class B and finally class C, with the least potential for harm and the lowest maximum penalties. In injectable form, drugs listed in class B count as class A.

Within each class, penalties are highest for 'trafficking' offences, less high for possession. Although maximum penalties are severe, they can only be imposed by a judge in a Crown court, where contested cases are tried by jury. Magistrates must either satisfy themselves with the limited penalties available to them or refer the case to a Crown court. Hence the distinction in *Table 2* between maximum penalties on 'indictment' (i.e. in a

Crown court) or after 'summary' trial (i.e. in a magistrates court).

The $2 \times 2 \times 3$ matrix of maximum penalties, depending on the class of the drug, the seriousness of the offence, and the court trying the offence, is reflected in *table 2*.

CONTROLLED DRUGS

Table 3 shows in general terms which types of drugs are in which schedule to the Regulations, and which class of the Act.

Drink and political economy

NICHOLAS DORN

Assistant Director (Research), ISDD

This paper examines the political economy of the alcohol industry, and explores the position of the drinks industry as part of total economic policy for the country as a whole.

The process of capitalisation, decline and revigoration of the alcohol industry shows this process to be an integral part of the uneven development of the broader economy, and illustrates how state policy towards production of this commodity is conditioned by this historical fact. The lesson to be drawn is that whatever political muscle may be put behind arguments about what the state 'ought' to do to restrict production and total consumption, the state's policies on alcohol production are *actually* conditioned by its broader concerns with private production, profitability, and electoral and fiscal considerations. Whilst historically, the state has consistently pursued policies *within the spheres of distribution and consumption* that aim to minimise the extent and reform the nature of working class drinking, translation of this restrictive intent *into the sphere of production* has been impeded by an equal commitment to freedom of private investment. The balance between liberal and restrictive alcohol control policies has shifted one way and then the other, but always between these parameters.

Whilst these shifts took place within the context of (at times quite acute) class struggle during the nineteenth century, it is not possible to assign any particular 'alcohol politics' to whole social classes, since there were quite characteristically splits within the classes, and cross-class alliances grew up around specific issues. Within the land-owning classes (which were in the process of becoming integrated with the newer business classes), the historically generated concern

about drinking, vagabondage and labour indiscipline was offset by interest in supplying the raw materials required by alcohol production. Within the rising industrial middle classes, the 'protestant ethic' and its temperance correlates found itself at odds with the commitment to free trade. Within the working class, concern about the dehabilitating consequences of over-indulgence sat side-by-side with a continuing attachment to public and often boisterous drinking occasions — reminders of previously-enjoyed leisure rites and customs, and resources in the fight to assert a collective identity within urban environments. Women's organisations were frequently involved closely in temperance politics (Sebestyen, 1980). It is by no means surprising, therefore, that complex alliances sprang up, and that the political parties were often split on 'the drink question'. The consequence of this is that, although alcohol politics in previous centuries can be quite closely equated with class politics, by the nineteenth century this was no longer the case.

Economic policy during the post-Second World War period has been marked by the adoption of, and subsequent retreat from Keynesian economic policies of expansion of demand (Stewart, 1970). These policies were for two decades fairly successful in stabilizing the previously chaotic conditions in which business operated, in increasing profitability, and in providing 'full' employment (i.e. within 2% of the pool of those available for wage work where this excludes approximately half the number of married women). Also, partly because of the generally favourable position of male labour in this situation of 'full' employment, and partly because it was not difficult for capitalists to pass on increased costs to consumers, wages were good in

Extract from *Alcohol, Youth and the State*, Croom Helm, 1983.

relation to the pre-war years — though at the cost of increasing inflation (Glyn & Harrison, 1980; 16–17). The combination of high employment and high wages increased the level of expendable income, and expenditure on non-durables — including alcohol — increased (Brewers Society, 1980; 45). The increase in demand stimulated new investment and innovation in the production and distribution ends of the alcohol industry. There were a series of brewery mergers, especially in 1959–61, leading to rationalisation of production, the bringing into service of very large production units, and a subsequent reduction in labour costs of production. 'The fall in the index of Unit labour costs reflects increases in productivity as fewer employees operate larger blocks of capital equipment' (Hawkins & Pass, 1979; 100). Brewing is today one of the most capital-intensive industries in Britain (ibid; 104). The development of keg beers, together with a new emphasis on promotion of bottles and cans, met the criteria of mass production, easy distribution, long shelf life, and retail by unskilled labour, and it is these products that have been most heavily advertised and which now dominate the market (Protz, 1978). In this connection it may be mentioned that, whether or not advertising contributes to expansion of total sales, it is essential to an industry whose profit rests upon the adoption by the public of those types of products most suitable for mass production and distribution.

The *pattern* of demand is, however, conditioned not only by the needs of the industry but also by social, demographic and cultural changes in the population, and these have been shaped by more general changes in the economy. The main change in the structure of capital during this century has been the relative stagnation of industrial capital and the growth of the service sector of the economy. This trend, which has been most marked in the south of England, has had consequences for inner city working class areas: de-industrialisation, mobility of labour, and post-war rehousing policies have combined to dislocate the pattern of community based upon local work and extended families and associated cultural traditions (Cohen, 1972). Population has been decanted to the New Towns, and more generally, to the suburbs, where social life has focussed upon the nuclear family, and the home is increasingly regarded as a place of leisure, recreation and consumption. It is in this context that off-licence sales have become more important. The 1961 Licensing Act relaxed restrictions on the opening of off-licences, and the 1964 Licensing Act facilitated supermarket sales. By the late 1970s, most beer was still sold in public houses, but one third of all wine and half of spirits were consumed at home (Thurman, 1981; 4).

The development of the drinks industry in the post-war period has meant that it has regained its place as a leading section of UK capital. The Brewers Society estimates that the industry provides over £2200 million in farmers' income; uses about half the total number of bottles produced in the country; employs three-quarters of a million people in production, distribution and retail; contributes almost £500 million to the balance of trade; and the government receives over 5% of its total income from excise duty and value-added tax on drinks (Thurman, 1981; 9–14). Clearly, 'the drinks industry is an integral part of UK Manufacturing Industry' (ibid). It is against this economic background that the state's policies bearing on the production of the alcohol — as distinct from its policies bearing upon the consumer, and his or her health and orderliness — are drawn up.

In 1978 the then Labour Government commissioned its Central Policy Review Staff to review state alcohol policy. This body acts as a 'Think Tank', supposedly independent of Government departments and of particular professions and interest groups, and is supposed to transcend all partial interests and to analyse social and economic problems in terms of the interests of the State as a whole. The Report was prepared on the basis of soundings conducted with the 'large number of different public interests involved' including no less than sixteen central departments of the state, regional and local, law enforcement and health agencies and commercial interests. These soundings were done 'without indications that it is a review' (i.e. a review by the Central Policy Review Staff). In other words, the review was compiled covertly; it was never intended to become public property; and it remains unpublished. The unique value of the review is the evidence it gives of the difference between an alcohol policy that is concerned solely with alcohol, and an alcohol policy that places the question of alcohol into the broader context of the balance of social and economic forces as these are manifested at the level of the state. As the review states:

We do not think that it is realistic to propose a policy that takes no notice of these influences. For this reason we cannot advocate the early adoption of the proposal of the Royal College of Psychiatrists. But we are convinced that, *from the point of view of alcohol policies alone*, it is a proper objective. (C.P.R.S., 1979; 17, emphasis added)

The Royal College of Psychiatrists had recommended that 'steps should be taken so as to ensure that per capita alcohol consumption does not increase beyond the present level, and is by stages brought back to an agreed lower level' (1979; 139). The Royal College made this recommendation on the basis of evidence that the amount of alcohol-related harm in a society is related to the total consumption of alcohol in that society. This is generally referred to as the 'distribution of consumption' model of alcohol problems: it predicts that, in a social system, alcohol-related harm is causally related to the number of heavy drinkers, and the number of heavy drinkers is causally related to the total (and hence average) consumption. The Central Policy Review Staff themselves adhered to this model of 'the issue':

The fundamental issue is whether there is an association between increasing consumption of alcohol and increasing numbers of alcohol-related disabilities; and, if so, what aspects of Government policy should be reviewed . . . the evidence we have gathered in the course of the year shows, in our view quite conclusively, that there is a correlation between increasing per capita consumption and increases in the number of disabilities. (C.P.R.S., 1979; 5)

Basing itself in this view, the C.P.R.S. went on to consider two alternative policy options: to hold consumption at its present level, *or* to reduce the rate of increase of consumption (p.6). They did not put forward the objective favoured by the Royal College — reduction in consumption — as a serious policy option. Of the two options which they did consider, they favoured the first:

level consumption . . . This provides a benchmark against which the various policies can be assessed, and is a clear and comprehensive objective. It should be associated with a secondary objective of also holding at their present level the indicators of alcohol-relating disability. (C.P.R.S., 1979; 6)

Viewed 'from the point of alcohol policies alone' and compared with the more radical Royal College recommendations of actual reductions in consumption, the

objective of the C.P.R.S. may appear timid. But central government policy-making is made in a broader context than 'alcohol policies alone', as the Review illustrates. The state's interests are quite diverse:

The government is directly or indirectly involved in nearly every aspect of the production and consumption of alcohol. It has an interest in the well-being of the alcohol industry, in the trade in alcohol and in the employment generated; it receives a large amount of tax revenue from the sale of alcohol; it imposes certain restrictions on consumption; and it bears the cost of many of the consequences of alcohol misuse. There are thus a great number of alcohol policies. (C.P.R.S., 1979; 4)

Any alcohol policy has to be concerned not simply with drinking and its consequences but also 'with Britain's economic interests in terms of wealth creation, employment and exports'. There are several aspects to this. First, there is the obvious sectional interest of the alcohol industry, which is not too shy to draw attention to its importance to the economy. The Review refers to a report of the Distilling Sector Working Party of the National Economic and Development Organisation: 'Any reduction in consumption or change in the future growth rate (or alcohol production) may affect the prosperity of the industry and so its ability to employ and generate wealth. Moreover, as the Distilling Working Party has pointed out, sudden large changes in duty may be particularly disruptive' (C.P.R.S., 1979; 14). Secondly, there is the Government's own interest in maintaining or increasing tax revenue from the duty imposed on alcohol. Were the duty to be raised to a considerable extent in an attempt to reduce consumption, then sales might fall to such an extent that total revenue would be decreased: this would be 'counter-productive from a taxation point of view', as would any measure 'which in the long term weakens the attraction to drink in such a way which might inhibit its ability to be a source of future revenue' (ibid; 13). Thirdly, 'the ethic associated with drinking is an important influence. It is arguable that a given increase in alcohol duty is more unpopular than a similar change in other taxes and expenditure — perhaps because its effect is particularly apparent on many wage-earners' personal spending power' (p. 14). Finally, each of these considerations was posed within the framework of acceptance of the state's role in facilitating the operation of the economy as a whole:

We have considered how far an approach on the lines

indicated above would be compatible with Britain's economic interests in terms of wealth creation, exports and employment. This is not easy to qualify. In particular, different elements of our proposals are likely to lead to different results. And it is not possible to balance precisely, say, the advantages to industry generally from reducing the costs of misuse with the possible results of restricted growth in the alcohol industry. (C.P.R.S., 1979; 8)

It would therefore be much too simplistic to suggest a conspiracy theory of alcohol policies in which the policy makers are said to be in the pockets of one section of private capital. The state also has fiscal and electoral considerations, and fields these considerations within the general framework of commitment to 'industry generally' — capitalism as a system — as distinct from any particular section of capital.

What is left out of this supposedly comprehensive approach to policy-making is any consideration of the collective interests of working class men, women or children as separate from that of capital. One major consequence of the adoption of any analytic framework within which working class men, women and children cannot be clearly conceptualised is that the review can make no clear suggestions relating to those major population groups. The review is broadly in favour of public debate and health education, and makes a reference to existing health education activities and trends:

There is a good deal of activity in health education in schools. A number of themes emerge as far as alcohol is concerned. There is a growing and convincing belief in the need not to teach about alcohol(ism) problems but about the attitudes and pressures associated with drinking in contemporary society, and the nature of the decisions associated with its consumption. (ibid; 67)

This is however a gloss upon existing opinion in the field of health education, rather than an interrogation and evaluation of that opinion. The review is in fact sceptical of the value of health education, in spite of its advocacy of it; 'a clearer assessment is required than at the moment seems to exist of the potential contribution of health education on alcohol to a strategy on alcohol-related problems' (p. 63). One of the factors obstructing such assessment is, however, the class perspective adopted in the review, and in state policy-making more generally.

REFERENCES

Brewers Society (1980) *UK Statistical Handbook for 1979*. London: Brewing Publications.
Central Policy Review Staff (1979) Alcohol Policies, London, Cabinet Office (unpublished) (reprinted 1982 as Alcohol Policies in United Kingdom Sociologiska Institutionen, Stockholms Universitet).
Cohen, P. (1972) 'Subcultural Conflict and Working-Class Community': *Working Papers in Cultural Studies No. 2*, 9–27.
Glyn, A. and Harrison, J. (1980) *The British Economic Disaster*. London: Pluto Press.
Hawkins, K. and Pass, C. (1979) *The Brewing Industry*. London: Heinemann.
Protz, R. (1978) *Pulling a Fast One*. London: Pluto Press.
Royal College of Psychiatrists (1979) Alcohol and Alcoholism: Report of a Special Committee of the Royal College of Psychiatrists. London: Tavistock.
Sebestyen, A. (1980) 'Women against the Demon Drink'. *Spare Rib*, **100**, November 1980, 22–7.
Stewart, M. (1970) *Keynes and After*. Harmondsworth: Penguin.
Thurman, C. (1981) 'The Structure and Role of the Alcoholic Drinks Industry' (unpublished). London: Brewers' Society.

Section V

Treatment and change

Duncan Raistrick* and Robin J. Davidson†

Consultant Psychiatrist, Leeds Addiction Unit;
† Area Clinical Psychologist, Holywell Hospital, County Antrim

This review of treatment issues in the management of drug and alcohol misuse considers evidence from recent research. From this work it discusses the stages and process of change and the types and place of intervention that have been found to be most effective in the treatment of people with problems of drug and alcohol misuse. Based on this evidence it arrives at some 'general statements' about the management of these problems.

Treatment is not an isolated curative insertion into the lives of drug misusers but rather is part of their whole matrix of experience. This interacts with past developmental events and its effect is filtered through those of the future. This in a way contradicts the more traditional view of treatment as a bridge from illness to cure and administered by external therapists to passive patients. Longitudinal studies show that drug misusers can improve without recourse to formal treatment intervention and evidence suggests that treatment processes are not qualitatively distinct from naturally occurring processes of change. Futhermore it is equally arbitrary to differentiate between aspects of the treatment process itself as the individual is a potential changer from the moment he presents: initial interview, assessment, therapy, relapse prevention and rehabilitation can all be instrumental in the initiation and maintenance of behaviour change.

A LONGITUDINAL VIEW

A distinction has been drawn between the constructs of *career* and *natural history* for drinkers (Edwards 1984) and other drug users (Thorley 1981). It is argued that a career is a psychosocial construct which

indicates sequential role behaviour which in this case is the role of *drug user*. The various environmental influences from birth onwards which shape the drug users career must be understood in the context of the culture and society in which the individual lives. In this context treatment should be seen as an interaction between the therapeutic input and the developing unfolding career (Edwards 1980, Finney et al 1980, Yates & Norris 1981). Treatment has been described as giving the career a 'little nudge in a more hopeful direction' (Edwards 1984). Natural history on the other hand has a more biological emphasis and in medicine is applied primarily to intrapersonal pathological processes although external events may have some bearing on these. Neuroadaptive changes such as withdrawal effects or tolerance are particular examples of phenomena which can be described in terms of natural history. These develop over time and as the sequencing and mechanisms involved are still far from understood (Littleton 1984) there is clearly a need for further natural history studies of the individual's reactivity to drugs. In the future more longitudinally based studies may take into account the interaction between the career and natural history dimensions with the resultant integration of different levels of explanation. To date however virtually all longitudinal studies have focussed on drug taking careers. Edwards (1984) argues that it is essential for treatment to be matched 'to processes and phases of an unfolding career rather than to a static description of the patient'.

Modified from *Alcoholism and Drug Addiction* by D. Raistrick and R. Davidson, 1985. Reproduced by permission of Churchill Livingstone.

THE STAGES AND PROCESSES OF CHANGE

The treatment episode is normally only a short interval in a patient's life and its effect should be seen against the backdrop of the individual's past and future circumstances, as well as his preparedness for change. In line with the current search for general principles of change across various psychotherapeutic and behavioural interventions (Ryle 1984, Goldfried 1982) some workers have attempted a similar exercise for treatment in addictions (Prochaska & Di Clemente 1982, 1983). Not only have they looked at precipitants of change which are common to various therapeutic systems but those which also occur in so called *self changers*. It is argued that individuals whose addictive behaviour improves without undergoing treatment, experience similar precipitants, or what are termed, *processes of change* as those who improve with treatment. To call such change therefore, spontaneous remission is slightly misleading as it is not an instantaneous mysterious recovery but occurs over time and is similar in nature to therapeutically induced change. Prochaska & Di Clemente in their *transtheoretical model* have, as well as looking at process of change, isolated *stages of change* which unfold over time as the successful individual alters his drug-using behaviour. The model has been generated from data on about 900 ex-smokers but the authors point out that it is appropriate for conceptualising change among substance misusers generally.

It is suggested that individuals are at various stages in their willingness or preparedness to change. First there is the *precontemplation stage* in which the person is not aware of having a particular problem perhaps as a result of denial, ambivalence or selective exposure to information. As long as the individual remains here even the most intensive intervention is unlikely to produce a favourable outcome. In this stage he actively resists self-exposure to curative influences. When the individual becomes aware that his drug use constitutes a problem and begins to think about altering his behaviour he is said to have entered the *comtemplation stage*. Data on smokers suggest that this can last for up to one year although this may well vary across substances. Next the user may move to the *determination stage* when there is a serious commitment to

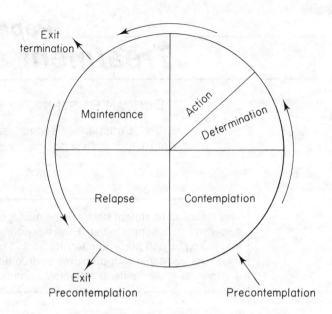

Figure 1   Stages of individual change (adapted from Prochaska & Di Clemente, 1982).

action. Evidence suggests that this is a relatively short time period and is analogous to the age-old idea of reaching a turning point. The commitment and decision to change leads the individual to the *maintenance stage* in which the new habits must be actively maintained through continual vigilance. This maintenance phase can also last for some considerable time until the individual exits the change system to *termination*, i.e. favourable long term outcome. For most people, however, who are attempting to alter addictive behaviour, *relapse* is common, notably in the first six months or so. The individual either exits back to precontemplation or begins to contemplate change once again. After the vigilance of maintaining new behaviour the determinants of relapse could include strength of dependence, negative self evaluation, environment contingencies or inadequate coping styles (Litman 1982). The number of revolutions of change will vary across people and drugs but the data on ex-smokers suggests that they take an average of three revolutions before becoming free of the habit. As long as the individual remains in the maintenance stage the risk of relapse is ever present. The so-called *revolving door* of change is summarised in Figure 1.

LONGITUDINAL STUDIES OF DRUG DEPENDENCE

Perhaps the most intensively studied group of drug users in the United Kingdom were 128 heroin addicts who attended the London drug clinics in 1969 when they were first interviewed, and who were followed up for a period of ten years. The follow-up results have been reported in numerous studies by various authors and summarised by Stimson & Oppenheimer (1982). The sample consisted of 93 men and 35 women whose mean age was 25 years, most of whom had first used heroin in the mid-sixties. It was a representative sample of clinic users constituting about 12% of the total clinic population of England and Wales at the time and was made up of people demonstrating a diversity of backgrounds and drug using behaviour. The authors concluded that there is some cause for optimism about the outcome of addiction, as after 10 years some 38% had become abstinent from opioids, were leading reasonably normal lives and had no major problems with other drugs. Unfortunately 14% of the sample died during the decade with the cause of death being in the main drug related.

A rather different study was reported by Rathod (1977). It was a younger sample (between 16 and 20 years) most of whom lived at home with their parents in a provincial English town. Furthermore, although the predominant drug of use was heroin, virtually all of the young people were polydrug users. Of the sample of 86, about three-quarters were assessed as regular users and after six years follow-up data was collected on 85% of the original group. It was found that approximately one-third had completely stopped using illegal drugs, about one-third were rated as sporadic injectors and the remainder had either died or had a regular continuing habit.

Longitudinal studies of drug dependence have been comprehensively reviewed by Thorley (1981) who concludes that UK data broadly indicate that about one-third of addicts are likely to be abstinent after five years. Vaillant (1970) who reviewed five follow-up studies from elsewhere, three from the USA, and two from Europe, reported a rather smaller rate of abstinence over a corresponding time.

CURRENT ISSUES IN TREATMENT PROVISION

Methodological considerations

The whole issue of treatment effectiveness is a methodological minefield and it is appropriate to consider first the difficulties of evaluative research in this area.

Some of the problems of evaluating the efficacy of treatment have been outlined by Glaser & Ogborne (1982) and Yates & Norris (1981). First, in a study of any intervention multiple outcome measures should be taken into account and each outcome assessed by more than one method. Self and collateral reports in conjunction with record searches or blood and breath tests could for example be used to determine drug use and there should be independent assessment of other psychological, social and economic variables. These authors also suggest that outcome measures should be quantifiable, operationally defined and continuous rather than categorical in nature. The reliability and validity of such measures should be evaluated and it is important to take into account behaviour which may covary with use of a drug, notably substitute drug use. Second, patient characteristics which may add or detract from any particular intervention should be defined and assessed. The clinical importance of matching patients and treatment cannot be overemphasised. Third, there is increasing awareness of the importance of developmental and environmental influences, which prompt help seeking, maintain change, and filter any treatment effect. Indeed one can have a *treatment career* co-existing with a *drug taking career*. Influences which may maximise the effect of treatment for example the support of a significant other or continuous employment should be taken into account. Fourth, there is a need for good research design with appropriate matched or randomly assigned control groups providing comparison data. There is also increasing emphasis on the well designed single case study.

It is, however, a real world in which real people have distressing problems and often methodological considerations must take second place to practical, organisational and clinical constraints. Some authors (Sells & Simpson 1980) have even questioned whether research designs for field studies which examine treatment processes among indigenous communities should be bound by the rules of traditional laboratory-based quality control procedures.

Intensity of treatment

Longitudinal studies have led some people to question whether the rate of spontaneous remission and treatment remission is much the same. The question 'does treatment work?' has been raised on numerous occasions in the alcohol literature (Clare 1977, Smith 1982) and rather less often in the drug literature (Sells & Simpson 1980). Two related issues will be discussed in this section. First, is treatment better than no treatment at all? Second, is minimal intervention as effective as intensive intervention? These questions are really only quantitatively distinct as 'assessment only' groups are often described as having had no treatment in spite of the fact that assessment is part of the treatment process. Furthermore as outlined above, even for genuine no treatment groups the naturally occurring precipitants of change are unlikely to be different in kind from those which are applied to treatment.

Results in the alcohol literature suggest that treatment can be effective although whether intense treatment is better than minimal treatment for most of the alcoholic population is open to doubt. Given the present state of knowledge it is important for workers to steer a line somewhere between therapeutic nihilism on the one hand and uncritical acceptance of the efficacy of all therapeutic intervention on the other. Most commentators would agree with Longabaugh et al (1983) that one of the few generalisations about alcohol treatment which can be made with some confidence is that 'some treatment is better than no treatment'.

Drug studies   A number of years ago Winick (1962) suggested that some drug users mature out of their habit and as time goes by grow into voluntary abstinence. However current evidence suggests that this is something of an oversimplification. Abstinence seems more likely to occur in the three years following first use after which time the rate of remission slows down considerably. Thorley (1981) demonstrates that younger samples whose drug use history is relatively short (d'Orban 1974) will have a higher rate of abstinence after three or four years than older samples with a longer preassessment history (Smart et al 1977). Thorley calls this the 'rush and trickle' with abstinence coming in a rush in the first three or so years and then reducing to a trickle. The implication is that if a user is going to stop he will do so sooner rather than later.

The Advisory Council Report (1982) draws attention to a survey of studies of users who received minimal treatment (Vaillant 1970), which the report calls the closest data we have to a 'spontaneous remission rate depending on naturally occurring processes of change'. Approximately one-quarter of this group were drug free after five years while the rate of abstinence of more intensively treated addicts seems, with some exceptions (Chapple et al 1972), to be higher (Stimson & Oppenheimer 1982, Rathod 1977). The report argues that in general, interstudy comparisons suggest that those who undergo more intensive treatment and rehabilitation programs show superior remission rates and this gives us some indication of treatment efficacy. However comparisons of studies on different populations from diverse geographical locations must be treated with some caution.

Treatment setting

The issue of whether substance misuse is best treated in an inpatient or outpatient setting has profound implications for resources and service provision. It has been demonstrated (Herz et al 1971, Washburn et al 1976) that for some general psychiatric disorders, day patient care as opposed to inpatient treatment is associated with lower relapse and fewer days spent in hospital after discharge. It must be emphasised that discussion of treatment location is complicated by the fact that different patients are admitted to different treatment settings. Skinner (1981) for example compared almost 300 patients assigned to inpatient (IP) and outpatient (OP) treatment for alcohol and drug dependence. Those who had inpatient care tended towards higher consumption and greater impairment. They had also fewer community supports and demonstrated a greater degree of psychopathology.

Treatment settings for drug misusers vary considerably from long term community residential groups to short outpatient clinic withdrawal and there have been no well controlled comparative studies. It has been shown (Sells & Simpson 1976) that regular opioid misusers do benefit from care delivered in a residential or IP setting while non regular opioid users or non opioid users may do just as well as outpatients. Such conclusions are tentative and the question warrants further investigation.

Therapist characteristics

It has been demonstrated that in the treatment of general psychological disorder (Murphy et al 1904) most patients tend to attribute effectiveness of therapy to empathy and understanding on the part of the therapist while most therapists attribute success to their technique. The failure to demonstrate consistent differences between psychotherapeutic treatment methods generally (Shapiro & Shapiro 1982) would support the idea that further investigation of what used to be called *error variance*, much of which was a result of patient and therapist characteristics, would be a fruitful line of research endeavour. There is no reason to suppose that these general observations should not apply to the treatment of addiction in which it is becoming increasingly clear that so called *non specific factors* like therapist characteristics can influence therapeutic outcome. An interesting study quoted by Hodgson (1980) underlines this.

Rapid smoking is a behavioural technique involving, as the name suggests, rapid smoking of a number of cigarettes to the point of nausea. It is argued that continued association of smoking with the aversive experience reduces craving. One group of 18 smokers were given rapid smoking therapy by a mechanical, coldly efficient therapist and received no praise for successfully abstaining between treatment sessions. For a second group rapid smoking was administered by a friendly therapist who recounted his own experience of using the technique and who was enthusiastic about abstinence between sessions. Thus the same treatment technique was administered in two different ways. At three months follow up the abstinence rate was 6% for the cold therapist and 72% for the warm encouraging therapist. Although these differences may be vastly reduced given a longer follow up, the study does make the point rather dramatically that therapist variables, independent of treatment method, can influence the future pattern of substance use. Some professionals could for example learn a lot from Alcoholics and Narcotics Anonymous where first time attenders are made to feel welcome and the warmth and empathy extended to them is very obvious.

As the treatment literature has been technique rather than therapist oriented, little attention has been paid to the outcome effect of particular characteristics which the therapist brings to the treatment situation. Cartwright (1981) could find only two studies which examined the therapist's perspective. There are a number of therapist characteristics which he regarded as important. These are empathy, experience, commitment and a positive attitude towards self, patient and the therapeutic process. He suggests that treatment research in the field of addiction should be guided by the question 'what type of patient improves with what type of treatment given by what type of therapist?' Orford (1980) felt that one of the important limitations of the treatment and advice study (Edwards et al 1977) was that therapist and setting variables could not be taken into account. All of the patients in the study were seen by virtually the same staff in the same setting. He goes on to say that authors of such research should describe therapist characteristics for example in terms of training, orientation and experience as routinely as they describe the characteristics of patients.

Patient characteristics

The third element of the outcome triad after nature of treatment and type of therapist is type of patient. Luborsky et al (1971) looked at the role of patient characteristics in determining outcome in general psychological disorders. As would be expected they were able to make a fairly broad statement on the prognostic significance of age, intelligence, motivation, educational and social achievement. Patient variables which influence outcome of alcohol treatments have been the subject of considerable study.

Individuals who use drugs which incur social disapproval are not necessarily, as is often suggested a more homogeneous group than alcohol users (Blumberg 1981). Nevertheless the predictive significance of pretreatment patient characteristics has been less thoroughly investigated for this group.

With regard to drug misusers the prognostic influence of individual characteristics is not clear. Oppenheimer et al (1979), in the seven year follow up of 128 heroin addicts, attempted to compare abstainers with continuing users on a range of pre-treatment variables including employment, social class, income and degree of criminal activity. The two groups could not be discriminated. What did seem to predict future outcome was age and length of drug taking history before first clinic attendance in that those who were younger with a shorter history of addiction were more likely to be abstinent after seven years. Stimson & Oppenheimer (1982) do however concede that at the onset it would have been 'difficult to choose individual characteristics of prognostic value'. Later differences were more related to withdrawal from opioids than pre-treatment characteristics. Chapple et al (1972) in a follow up study of 108 opioid users confirmed that younger short term addicts were significantly more likely to be drug free after five years than older chronic addicts.

There also appear to be subgroups whose pattern of use on presentation can be differentiated and categorised, and this can have implications for treatment and outcome. Stimson (1973) developed a typology of four distinctive patterns of behaviour among users. *Stables* suffered the fewest psychosocial and physical complications of drug use, were not part of the drug subculture and were in employment. They had homes and were conventional in their attitudes. The *junkies* tended to support their habit by stealing and criminal activity, did not work and were highly involved with the drug subculture. The *loners* had a low rate of criminal activity and little involvement with other addicts. Finally the *two worlders* seemed to straddle the junkie and stable categories in that they mixed with other addicts, had a high rate of criminal activity but yet were employed, residentially stable and had few physical complications. After three years the stables had changed least of all for better or for worse while 50% of the loners and 40% of the two worlders were in the abstinent category (Ogborne & Stimson 1975). Interestingly after 10 years it was the stables who were still most likely to be receiving continued presciptions while the junkies were not represented at all in the continuing user group. It does seem that there are different outcomes for different types of users, which are not immediately obvious. This work may help in the development of treatment strategies which take account of individual differences in behaviour on initial presentation.

MODES OF INTERVENTION

The debate on pharmacological approaches to drug dependence has focused on two broad but nevertheless important issues notably opioid prescribing versus no prescribing and injectable versus oral maintenance medication. With regard to the latter question virtually all of the UK treatment centres have stopped prescribing maintenance injectable heroin to new addicts. This is perhaps as much in spite of, as because of, evidence comparing heroin with methadone maintenance (Hartnoll et al 1980). There is also differing expert opinion on whether total abstinence or long term maintenance prescribing is the most appropriate therapeutic response for a significant group of addicts (Rathod 1977, Blumberg 1976). Those who argue for an increased emphasis in UK clinics on withdrawal and abstinence seemed to be holding sway although a significant number of addicts continue to receive long term maintenance.

Methadone, a synthetic opioid, has several advantages over heroin for longer term treatment of dependence. Its action is longer than that of heroin. Withdrawal effects do not manifest themselves for about 24 hours as opposed to four hours after taking heroin. This leads to a potentially more ordered life style with one daily dose being sufficient and avoids the exaggerated ups and downs associated with intravenous heroin use. It produces less euphoria and larger blockade doses can eliminate the euphoric effect of heroin altogether as a result of cross tolerance, although little use is made of blockade doses as doctors in the main prefer to prescribe the minimum necessary dose. Perhaps the most important advantage is that methadone is effective when taken orally. This reduces the obvious hazards of injection as well as the risk of overdose and methadone is normally dispensed in linctus form which rules out the possibility of injecting in most cases.

Community groups

The therapeutic community plays a major role in the management of drug misuse particularly in the USA although there are a number of such groups or concept houses in the UK. In the main, communities of this type are run by ex-addicts with an emphasis on residents remaining drug free. Alcoholics Anonymous

(A.A.) too is a community group run by ex-alcoholics with total abstinence being a central requirement so it is not surprising that A.A. and drug therapeutic communities have similar historical roots (Glaser 1977, 1981).

Both were significantly influenced by the Oxford group which was a religious organisation in the evangelical protestant tradition and which flourished during the early part of this century in Britain and the USA. The central features of the Oxford group were sharing, open confession of sins, guidance from other group members and change or rebirth. Bill W, the founder of A.A. acknowledged the importance of Oxford group practices in the development of A.A.'s ideas on self examination, acknowledgement of character deficits and restitution (Bill W 1957). Charles Dederick who founded Synanon, the archetypal drug therapeutic community, was an A.A. graduate and incorporated much A.A. practice into its development. Indeed there was close initial rapport between A.A. and Synanon with joint meetings and cross fertilisation of ideas. Glaser (1981) points out that while A.A. have retained their religious emphasis, the drug communities have shifted over the years from theology to ideology although this is a change of content rather than form. He comments that both ideology and theology represent a basic belief system and structure which can give the individual a sense of order and purpose in what may otherwise be perceived as a chaotic and rather random lifestyle. Although the drug communities and A.A. have grown apart over the past two decades the similarities remain more striking than the differences.

Therapeutic communities The drug communities are non-statutory services which as mentioned above are usually run by ex-addicts although some involve trained staff. Synanon which began in 1958 was set up for heroin users and is characterised by an aggressive and directive style of group therapy. New residents are required to cease all drug intake immediately on admission and are *talked through* withdrawal. There is a hierarchical structure within the communities. Progress through the hierarchy and privileges incurred are contingent on the individual's compliance with group norms and values in terms of appropriate behaviour and attitudes. Most of the emergent communities in the USA like Daytop Village, New York can trace their roots

back to the Synanon program. In the UK too such communities, for instance the Ley community, Oxford, and concept houses like Alpha House, have an influential part to play in the national response to drug misuse.

For the use of relevant referral agents the therapeutic community facilities in the UK have been listed and described by Banks & Waller (1983). The Advisory Council Report (1982) recommends that residential therapeutic communities should have a role within the provision of a comprehensive system of managing drug misuse although the report comments that they need not necessarily be provided by the non statutory sector.

The results of the effectiveness of drug free communities are mixed and the attrition rate is high although individuals who do complete the program tend to feel positive about their contribution and do better than drop outs (Romond et al 1975). In a review of outcome studies on community graduates Smart (1976) showed that recovery rate when defined in terms of pattern of drug use was generally quite good although highly variable across studies. He felt that when other outcome indices were used, for instance future employment, the positive contribution of therapeutic communities was less notable. Most of the studies paid little attention to differences in outcome among those who misused drugs other than heroin. Thorley (1981) reviewed some UK follow up studies on ex-community residents (Melotte & Ogborne 1975, Wilson & Kennard 1978) and concluded that the therapeutic community is a powerful experience which can greatly benefit some individuals but actively harm others. He stressed the need to develop more discriminating assessment procedures and a greater understanding of the social learning processes involved in order that potential harm may be minimised. Most commentators would agree that therapeutic communities can be an effective rehabilitation procedure, but as they are relatively few in number and have strict entrance requirements this renders them only genuinely available for, and acceptable to, a small percentage of the addict population.

TREATMENT GOAL

For a significant number of drug users who present for help, total abstinence associated with a return to a drug free life style is the stated objective. For some therapists too withdrawal followed by continued abstinence is the only acceptable treatment goal. However the question of whether abstinence is feasible, or indeed necessary, for everyone has been the subject of some debate over a number of years. A related question concerns the desirability of promoting substitute substance use as a treatment method in itself.

Maintenance

Although the ultimate aim of treating addicts is withdrawal then abstinence accompanied by a return to normal social functioning many still request maintenance therapy. They argue that this would stabilise them enough to function normally in the community by avoiding the problems inherent in the obtaining of illegal drugs.

The pharmacological aspects of methadone maintenance were discussed above and it was suggested that maintenance is now a much less favoured option among clinicians. There has been what Stimson & Oppenheimer (1982) termed a move from 'maintenance to confrontation' and they have traced the development of this change in emphasis since the London drug clinics opened in 1968. It was originally argued that a maintenance rather than an abstinence policy did more to ensure that addicts attended clinics, kept off the streets and were less troublesome to the authorities. It was also in some ways the easiest and cheapest response to addiction. It can, however, neutralise the urgency of employing treatment which could help the individual deal more constructively with his psychosocial problems. Furthermore it conflicts with traditional notions of cure as people are not actively changing but rather maintaining the status quo. Thus many workers now feel that a general policy of maintenance has more to do with social control than treatment and it is argued that social control of addiction is more the role of legislators than clinicians. It also became clear by the mid 1970s that legally available opioids did not prevent illegal drugs from reaching the streets and over the past few years drugs which are legally prescribed represent only a tiny percentage of the weight and number of seizures.

Since the clinics opened therefore there has been a

move from maintenance on injectable heroin to oral methadone then to increased emphasis on withdrawal and abstinence. This is perhaps more likely to stimulate a more active and less rigid view of therapy. It may however be unwise to throw 'the baby out with the linctus' and maintenance should still be considered for some of the addict population who are unable or unwilling to participate in alternative forms of therapeutic intervention.

CONCLUSIONS

A review of treatment issues in the management of drug and alcohol misuse almost invariably raises as many questions as it answers. Based on current evidence however some general statements can be made with a degree of assurance.

(1) Treatment, however defined, is not qualitatively different from the naturally occurring processes of change.
(2) Treatment does seem generally to produce better outcome than no treatment for users of all psychotropic substances although no particular treatment approach has emerged as being consistently superior to others.
(3) Some alcoholics and addicts do however improve irrespective of whether they undergo formal treatment or not.
(4) For most alcohol users, minimal treatment intervention seems to be as effective as long term, intensive multimodal programs. For users of other drugs the effect of treatment intensity would appear to interact with type of drug and pattern of use.
(5) A significant minority of alcoholics can return to a normal drinking pattern.
(6) Improvement in terms of psychosocial functioning and pattern of use if it is to occur is more likely in those with a shorter history of alcohol and other drug use.
(7) For most individuals out-patient care can be as effective as in-patient care.
(8) Thorough assessment is a necessary prelude to the formulation of any treatment program.
(9) Finally and perhaps most important, therapy should be tailored to the individual. What is useful for one person may be singularly inappropriate for another.

REFERENCES

Banks, A., Waller, T.A.N. 1983 *Drug addiction and polydrug abuse: The Role of the general practitioner.* I.S.D.D., London.

Bill, W. 1957 *Alcoholics Anonymous comes of age: A Brief History of A.A. Alcoholics Anonymous*, World Services, New York.

Blumberg, H.H. 1976 British users of opiate-type drugs: a follow-up study. *British Journal of Addiction* 71: 65–77.

Blumberg, H.H. 1981 Characteristics of people coming to treatment. In: Edwards G, Busch C. (eds). *Drug problems in Britain: a review of ten years.* Academic Press, London.

Cartwright, A.K.J. 1981 Are different therapeutic perspectives important in the treatment of alcoholism? *British Journal of Addiction* 76: 347–361.

Chapple, P.A.L., Somekh, D.E., Taylor, M.E. 1972 Follow-up of cases of opiate addiction from time of notification to the Home Office. *British Medical Journal* 2: 680–683.

Clare, A.W. 1977 How good is treatment? In: Edwards, G., Grant, M. (eds) *Alcoholism: new knowledge and new responses.* Croom Helm, London, Ch. 23.

d'Orban, P.T. 1974 A follow-up study of female narcotic addicts: variables related to outcome. *British Journal of Psychiatry* 124: 28–33.

Edwards, G. 1980 Alcoholism treatment: between guesswork and certainty. In: Edwards, G., Grant, M. (eds). *Alcoholism treatment in transition.* Croom Helm, London, Ch 21.

Edwards, G. 1984 Drinking in longitudinal prospective: career and natural history. *British Journal of Addiction* 79: 175–184.

Edwards, G., Orford, J. et al 1977 Alcoholism: a controlled trial of 'treatment' and 'advice'. *Journal of Studies on Alcohol* 38: 1004–1031.

Finney, J.W., Moss, R.H., Mewborn, C.R. 1980 Post treatment experiences and treatment outcome of alcoholic patients six months and two years after hospitalization. *Journal of Consulting and Clinical Psychology* 48: 17–29.

Glaser, F.B. 1977 The first therapeutic community. *The addiction therapist* 2: 8–15.

Glaser, F.B. 1981 The origins of the drug-free therapeutic community. *British Journal of Addiction* 76: 13–25.

Glaser, F.B., Ogbourne, A.C. 1982 Does AA really work? *British Journal of Addiction* 77: 123–130.

Goldfried, M.R. 1982 *Converging themes in psychotherapy.* Spriner, New York.

Hartnoll, R.L., Mitcheson, M.C. et al 1980 Evaluation of heroin maintenance in controlled trial. *Archives of General Psychiatry* 37: 877.

Herz, M.I., Endicott, J. Spitzer, R.L., Mesnikoff, A. 1971 Day versus in-patient hospitalization: a controlled study. *American Journal of Psychology* 127: 107–118.

Hodgson, R.J. 1980 Treatment strategies for the early problem drinker. In: Edwards, G., Grant, M. (eds) *Alcoholism treatment in transition.* Croom Helm, London.

Litman, G. 1982 Factors in the breakdown of abstinence. Paper presented at the Annual Conference of the New Directions in the Study of Alcohol Group. Bollington.

Littleton, J.M. 1984 The future could be bright. In: Edwards, G., Littleton, J. (eds) *Pharmacological treatments for alcoholism.* Croom Helm, London, Methuen, New York, Ch 31.

Longabaugh, R., McCrady, B. et al 1983 Cost effectiveness of alcoholism treatment in partial vs in-patient settings. Six month outcomes. *Journal of Studies on Alcohol* 44: 1049–1071.

Luborsky, L., Chandler, M. Auerbach, A.H., Cohen, L., Bachrach, T. 1971 Factors influencing the outcome of psychotherapy. A review of quantitative research. *Psychological Bulletin* 75: 145–185.

Melotte, C.J., Ogborne, A.C. 1975 Strategies for the successful follow-up of treated drug users. *Journal of Drug Issues* 5: 79–82.

Murphy, P.M., Cramer, D., Lillie, F.J. 1984 The relationship between curative factors perceived by patients in their psychotherapy and treatment outcome: an exploratory study. *British Journal of Medical Psychology* 57: 187–192.

Ogborne, A.C., Stimson, G.V. 1975 Follow-up of a representative sample of heroin addicts. *International Journal of the Addictions* 10: 1061.

Oppenheimer, E., Stimson, G.V., Thorley, A. 1979 Seven-year follow-up of heroin addicts: abstinence and continued use compared. *British Medical Journal* 2: 627.

Orford, J. 1980 Understanding treatment: controlled trials and other strategies. In: Edwards, G., Grant, M. (eds) *Alcoholism treatment in transition.* Croom Helm, London, Ch 9.

Prochaska, J.O., Di Clemente, C.C. 1982 Transtheoretical therapy toward a more integrated model of change. *Psychotherapy: Theory, Research and Practice*: 19: 276–288.

Prochaska, J.O., Di Clemente, C.C. 1983 Stages and processes of self-change of smoking: toward an integrated model of change. *Journal of Consulting Clinical Psychology* 51: 390–395.

Rathod, N.H. 1977 Follow-up study of injectors in a provincial town. *Drug and Alcohol Dependence* 2: 1–21.

Report of the Advisory Council on the Misuse of Drugs 1982 *Treatment and rehabilitation.* HMSO, London.

Romond, A.M., Forrest, C.K., Kleber, H.D. 1975 Follow-up of participants in a drug dependence therapeutic community. *Archives of General Psychiatry* 32: 369–374.

Ryle, A. 1984 How can we compare different psychotherapies? Why are they all effective? *British Journal of Medical Psychology* 57: 261–264.

Sells, S.B., Simpson, D.D. (eds) 1976 *Effectiveness of drug* abuse treatment (Vol 3): further studies of drug users, treatment, typologies and assessment of outcome during treatment in the DARP. Ballinger Publishing Co., Cambridge.

Sells, S.B., Simpson, D.D. 1980 The case for drug abuse treatment effectiveness, Based on the DARP Research Programme. British Journal of Addiction 75: 117–131.

Shapiro, D.A., Shapiro, D. 1982 Meta-analysis of comparative theory outcome studies: a replication and refinement. Psychological Bulletin 92: 581–604.

Skinner, H. 1981 Comparison of clients assigned to in-patient and out-patient treatment for alcoholism and drug addiction. British Journal of Psychiatry 138: 312–320.

Smart, R.G. 1976 Outcome studies of therapeutic community and halfway house treatment for addicts. International Journal of Addictions 11: 143–159.

Smart, R.G., Everson, A., Segal, R., Finley, J., Ballah, B. 1977 A four-year follow-up study of narcotic-dependent persons receiving methadone maintenance substitute therapy. Canadian Journal of Public Health 68: 55–58.

Smith, R. 1982 Alcohol and alcoholism. Leagrave Press, London.

Stimson, G.V. 1973 Heroin and behaviour. Irish University Press, Shannon.

Stimson, G.V., Oppenheimer, A. 1982 Heroin addiction treatment and control in Britain. Tavistock, London.

Thorley, A. 1981 Longitudinal studies of drug dependence. In: Edwards, G., Busch, C. (eds) Drug problems in Britain: a review of ten years. Academic Press, London, Ch 6.

Vaillant, G. 1970 The natural history of narcotic drug addiction. Seminars in Psychiatry 2: 486–498.

Washburn, S., Vannicelli, M., Longabaugh, R., Scheff, B.J. 1976 A controlled comparison of psychiatric day treatment and in-patient hospitalization. Journal of Consulting and Clinical Psychology 44: 665–675.

Wilson, S., Kennard, D. 1978 The extraverting effect of treatment in a therapeutic community for drug abusers. British Journal of Psychiatry 132: 296–299.

Winick, C. 1962 Maturing out of narcotic addiction. Bulletin in Narcotics 14: 1–7.

Yates, F.E., Norris, H. 1981 The use made of treatment: an alternative approach to the evaluation of alcoholism services. New Directions in the Study of Alcohol 2: 32–48.

Community initiatives in drug treatment (making the community therapeutic)

JOHN STRANG

Consultant Psychiatrist in Drug Dependence and Director of the Drug Dependence Clinical Research and Treatment Unit, The Maudsley Hospital

In this paper the recent growth of community-based types of treatment for drug-related problems is described. The different methods of approach used in these various projects are discussed and the possible future developments for this type of work are outlined.

INTRODUCTION

Can the community possibly be therapeutic? At one level it seems foolhardy to view the community setting as potentially positive when it has been in just that setting that the drug taker has come to grief; and yet on the other hand, it is to just such an environment that he or she will eventually return, and with which a more positive relationship must be developed. All too often, peer group pressure is seen as an influence that leads the individual astray; but it is important not to forget that peer group pressure can also be a powerful force for good. The influence of family and friends can help to bring about the resolve to change and the determination to maintain a newly acquired state. (The process of change amongst former cigarette smokers and takers of other types of drug has recently been studied by Prochaska and Di Clemente, 1984.)

The origins of the drive to establish services in the community warrant consideration for they are so varied.At the purest level there is the recognition that it is 'out there' that the problem exists, and that it is 'out there' that the former drug taker has to learn to cope with. If much of the work of drug treatment and rehabilitation involves helping the drug taker to learn new ways of coping with negative aspects of his/her life and teaching new ways of developing positive aspects, then

there is a compelling argument that the services must at least in part exist within the community. However, the motivation for community location is not always so pure. Sometimes it will be born out of despair or frustration. Perhaps no service exists and no facilities are available. As an act of desperation, well-intentioned professionals, former drug takers and their families and other members of the general public will do whatever they can within the limited resources available — and this will often mean an *'ad hoc'* service which is established in the community due to necessity rather than choice. Finally it must be acknowledged that there is also a financial pressure to establish services in the community for there is an increasing recognition of the expensive nature of inpatient/residential treatment. While it is possible that these different motives may coexist, it is important to avoid making a virtue of necessity. Perhaps it is often appropriate for new services to be established in the community, but how wrong it would be for this decision always to be forced by cost considerations with no regard to the needs of the community itself, including the drug-taking population.

Any consideration of drug treatment initiatives in the community must also examine what is wrong with specialist and institutional treatments. At this stage it is important to acknowledge that the argument being made is *not* that such elements are wrong or unnecessary; rather it is being argued that they should form but *part* of an overall network of services. Such specialist/institutional facilities are vital for the treatment of selected more problematic cases; and it is to be hoped that such specialist units also serve the community by developing and evaluating new forms of treatment which may subsequently be adopted by the community-based initiatives. As with psychiatry and with medicine as a whole, the service must exist in the community, but it is essential to be clear that the debate should be over the relative proportion of the response that should be sited within hospital or institutional facilities or the community, rather than seeing it as a crude choice between one or the other.

Over the last two decades, the importance of facilities existing within the community has become increasingly important. The numbers of young people and adults who have developed problems with use of drugs has gone up dramatically in recent years. In 1967, it was believed that there were about 1700 heroin users in the London area with about 2000 or 3000 in the whole of the United Kingdom. In 1987, it is likely that there are probably in the order of 17 000 heroin users in the London area with a national figure of 100 000. Perhaps it was possible in the late 1960s to deal with such a relatively small number of people in an exclusively specialist way, relying to a large extent on treatment and rehabilitation delivered by residential or hospital-based facilities. Whatever the pros and cons of this argument in the 1960s, it is clearly now no longer possible. This point is further supported by the increasing recognition that problems may occur with a much wider range of drugs than was previously recognized. Heroin is not the only problem drug. Other opiates such as dipipanone (Diconal), dextromoramide (Palfium), morphine, methadone and dihydrocodeine (DF 118) all have a potential for causing dependence and problems associated with their use. In addition other groups of drugs have been identified as potentially problematic including the barbiturates, amphetamines, cocaine, solvents and benzodiazepines, in addition to the two most widely used drugs (which cause by far the greatest number of deaths) — alcohol and tobacco.

HISTORY

Treating the drug addict in the community is not a new idea. The so-called 'British System' probably has its roots in the Rolleston report of 1926 which endorsed the view that opiate addiction should be seen as medical not criminal; and suggested that it might often be appropriate to prescribe supplies of the drug to the ambulatory opiate addict in the community if there was evidence that he was able to maintain considerable stability and that inpatient treatment and rehabilitation was unlikely to achieve the same degree of success. In 1965 the second Brain Committee recommended the establishment of specialised Drug Treatment Centres. Here again, although these were mainly attached to Teaching Hospitals and were usually located in hospital premises, they were nevertheless predominantly out-patient services with limited access to inpatient facilities. The vast majority of patients presenting to such services received treatment while they remained in the community — only a handful of the new Drug Treatment Centres had special inpatient facilities.

In 1982, the Advisory Council on the Misuse of Drugs published its report on 'Treatment and Rehabilitation' which gave considerable support and some detailed consideration to services in the community. In addition to recognising the important contribution of therapeutic communities and street agencies, they also described a model of service-delivery which could be followed in the future, involving promotion of services at a local level. This has subsequently been implemented in several parts of the country with the establishment of community drug teams (see later). The 1984 'Guidelines of Good Clinical Practice in the Treatment of Drug Misuse' published by the Department of Health & Social Security recognised the important contribution of the general practitioner and general hospital services. No longer was it appropriate for treatment of drug takers to be seen as the exclusive domain of the specialist. This view opened up the possibility of greater development of services in the community. Drug users should no longer be left exclusively dependent on the specialist units themselves.

DIFFERENT TYPES OF COMMUNITY INITIATIVES AND THEIR EVOLUTION

Rehabilitation houses

Residential Rehabilitation Houses fall into three categories — concept-based therapeutic communities, Christian houses and community-based hostels. At the time of the Treatment and Rehabilitation Report of the Advisory Council on the Misuse of Drugs (1982) there were fourteen drug-free residential rehabilitation houses within the United Kingdom containing 229 places. An analysis was undertaken for the Advisory Council on the Misuse of Drugs in 1980 examining referrals and admissions to eight of the rehabilitation houses. During the year, 998 enquiries about admission were made of whom only one in five was successful in gaining admission to the total of 103 placed in these eight houses. Only half of those found suitable for admission were eventually admitted. Principal reasons for non-admission included lack of an available vacancy, imprisonment of the applicant, or problems obtaining necessary funding. Twenty-nine per cent of referrals came from the Courts, prison or probation; 28 per cent were self-referrals; 26 per cent from non-specialist services and non-statutory agencies; and only 17 per cent from Drug Treatment Centres or general practitioners.

Concept-based therapeutic communities are now the largest body of rehabilitation houses. Maxwell Jones himself has drawn attention to the important differences between the programmatic TCs of the drug field as distinct from the democratic TCs with which he was primarily involved (Jones, 1984). The drug-free TCs were all ultimately spawned from Synanon in California which opened in 1958 under the charismatic leadership of Chuck Dietrich who was himself an ex-alcoholic and member of Alcoholics Anonymous. Despite the eventual demise of Synanon in the 1980s following the excesses of its leadership, the therapeutic community movement has established itself as an important component of drug treatment services. Such houses are usually staffed by a mixture of professionally trained staff working alongside former drug addicts who are graduates from such a treatment programme. Mahon (1973) has summarized the characteristics of such concept houses. A rigid hierarchical structure forms an essential part of the therapeutic community which includes a strict work ethic. Initially responsibility for personal progress is taken by the peer group and the house. The individual then begins to assume responsibility for self before assuming responsibility for others later in the programme. This may be extended to include work outside the house as well as working as a quasi-staff member. In recent years there has been increasing emphasis on assisting re-entry back into the community by the addition of after-care support and re-entry houses. In a study of such a concept house

in the early 1970s Ogborne and Melotte (1977) found that 34 per cent left within one month, while only 32 per cent stayed for over six months. Length of stay was positively correlated with subsequent abstinence.

Within Christian houses there are two clear subcategories. In one category is the house in which the staff are Christian but faith is not a prerequisite for entry by a resident. In the other category are a small number of more extreme/Evangelical Christian houses in which a profound Christian faith is seen as the pathway to cure, and hence the Christian commitment of the would-be resident is essential.

Community houses are the smallest of the categories and are probably the least well defined. More emphasis is placed on efforts to integrate the individual back into society as soon as possible, with early encouragement to become involved in training, work and leisure within the outside community. The structure of such community houses is less rigid and there is less reliance on confrontational and group psychotherapeutic techniques.

Virtually all such rehabilitation houses operate programmes which require the resident to remain for a period of about one year.

In the last few years several 'Minnesota model' rehabilitation houses have been established with a much shorter residential period of about two months, following which the former addict is expected to attend regular meetings of Narcotics Anonymous. Such centres embrace the NA philosophy and see addiction as an illness for which abstinence is the only viable means of overcoming the chemical dependency. Some such Minnesota model facilities operate privately while others provide some assisted places. According to Wells (1987) one such centre provided assisted places to 66 per cent of their patients in 1985.

ROMA is in quite a separate category from all other UK residential rehabilitation. Its residents are current drug users who are receiving their drugs on prescription, and for whom the goal is an increasingly stable existence while still taking drugs. An account of the work of ROMA by Glanz (1983) describes the programme in three stages — the first stage being an induction/settling-in period with little psychotherapeutic demand but substantial expectations of physical work;

the second stage involves greater practical involvement (job-seeking, budgeting, etc.) and personal dynamics (relationships, self-confidence, etc.) and more frequent exploratory counselling sessions; the third stage involves the acceptance of responsibilities and the receiving of privileges, including the chairing of house meetings and the supervision of the work and rules within the house. ROMA residents are typically long-term chaotic drug users and Glanz found that 64 per cent of the residents had been treated at hospital for a drug-related problem in the twelve months prior to admission. The at-risk nature of this population is demonstrated by the high death rate of this population (14 per cent) over the three-year follow-up period.

The Day Centres

Day Centres were a popular innovative response to the drug problem in the early 1970s (for a description of one such Day Centre see Chapple *et al.*, 1970). There were frequent problems with breaches of the rules and problems with local residents, especially during the early 1970s when intravenous barbiturate use became prevalent. By 1980 only one drug specialist Day Centre was still in existence — the Lifeline Project in Manchester which interestingly had been one of the few Day Centres to adopt a 'no drugs on the premises' policy and to exclude a fixing room in which addicts could inject drugs. The style of work in the Lifeline Day Centre is described by Rowdy Yates (1981) as 'encouraging the individual to take responsibility for his attitudes and actions in order to understand the possibility of, and need for, personal change'. The staff actively resisted the efforts by addicts to adopt a powerless/victim/inadequate role and thus challenged the stereotype of the drug addict. Much of the practical work of the Lifeline Day Centre revolved around the negotiating of formal and informal contracts relating to the behaviour, goals, and needs of each attender. Thus 'recovery is dependent on fundamental change in the addict himself and the individual can never be seen as the victim of addiction'. The Lifeline Project encouraged progression on to other rehabilitation facilities such as therapeutic communities; and developed a two-week induction programme as a preliminary to referral to such residential rehabilitation options. In a study of the induction programme (Strang and Yates, 1984) it was found that 54 out of 80 referrals had come from the courts, while the remainder attended on a voluntary basis. Interestingly

there was a higher drop-out rate amongst the voluntary attenders (16 out of 26) compared with those attending as a condition of bail (13 out of 54).

In 1986, an experimental day programme was introduced attached to the University College Hospital Drug Treatment Centre in London. This psycho-therapeutically-orientated day programme for individuals who are undergoing supervised withdrawal off drugs or who have recently become drug free is presently in the process of evaluation. Whatever the outcome, it illustrates the way in which Day Centres have moved away from their original role as 'drop-ins' for 'drop-outs'.

Street agencies and detached social work

The closing of most Day Centres — and in particular the closing of their 'fixing-rooms' — was at a time of crisis for such voluntary agencies. As Dorn and South describe (1985) there were clashes between the staff and the clients with regard to 'ownership' of such projects. By the mid-1970s, most of the agencies had closed their Day Centres and had moved to working as street agencies providing contact points for drug users who were still out on the street as well as providing advice, counselling and referral to other agencies for those who chose to drop in or attend on an appointment basis. Dorn and South describe this change as being influenced by four overlapping forces — (i) changing drug systems and cultures (the reduced availability of injectable drugs on prescription; the increasing popularity of intravenous barbiturate use and the chaotic and dangerous outcome, etc.); (ii) housing and employment situations (increasing unemployment; deterioration in provision for disadvantaged, etc.); (iii) social work influences (professionalization of social work; psychoanalytic/psychotherapeutic drift, etc.); (iv) agencies changing financial situation (greater difficulty securing on-going funding; no opportunity to expand in response to new demands).

For agencies such as The Hungerford Project in Central London, detached social work became the main *raison d'être*. Initially this involved providing a service on the street making contact with drug users who would otherwise fail to establish a link with any agency. However, this gradually changed to being a drop-in service in which the drug user would choose to attend the premises to see a member of the staff. Such work did not aim to be 'in depth' and saw as its main purpose the making of contacts which might subsequently lead to change for the good and which might also provide an opportunity for reducing the harm-laden nature of the client's drug-using ways. However, by the 1980s Dorn and South suggest that the changing factors in the four force areas had brought about further changes in these agencies so that they have changed the emphasis of their work yet again. In their new role they concentrate on service 'complementarity' in which much of their time is spent as an avenue towards other agencies, and in which old inter-agency rivalries have disappeared and referral to different (but more appropriate for a particular individual) projects has become a chosen way of working.

Crisis intervention units

City Roads was born in 1978 after a protracted (and sometimes painful) labour of six years. Having been originally conceived as the SCODA short-stay unit, it represents a remarkable example of collaboration between the voluntary and statutory services. It also bridges both health and social services. (Readers interested in the difficulties encountered and solutions found for such joint works should read *Dealing with Drug Misuse — Crisis Intervention in the City* by Jamieson, Glanz and MacGregor, 1984.) Initially established as a three-year experimental project, City Roads has survived funding crisis after funding crisis and remains an important element of service provision to chaotic drug users in the London area. From the start, its three main aims were: (i) to provide for the immediate needs of young multiple drug misusers who frequently overdose; (ii) to operate crisis intervention in a warm sheltered environment with nursing, medical, social and psychiatric support; and (iii) not to attempt to offer complete treatment and rehabilitation but to see itself as a referral agency on to such establishments (Jamieson, Glanz and MacGregor, 1984). Clients are offered a three-week stay which will include the prescribing of drugs as part of a withdrawal regime when this is necessary.

In their study of City Roads, Jamieson *et al.* (1981) found that half the clients left with no on-going plans, while one-third had specific drug-free rehabilitation arranged (usually referral to a therapeutic communi-

ty/rehabilitation house). Of this latter group, 34 per cent were drug-free at the end of the study period — just under half being drug-free in the outside community with the remainder still resident in a rehabilitation project.

Community drug teams

Creation of Community Drug Teams was included in the recommendations of the Treatment and Rehabilitation Report from the ACMD (1982). The most widespread application of this approach is in the NW Region of England where there are now well in excess of a dozen such teams. These teams usually comprise from 2–4 full-time drug workers (typically a community psychiatric nurse, social worker, etc.) whose appointment is intended to have an enabling effect on the pre-existing local services. Their catchment population will be the local town/District Health Authority population and they will endeavour to generate greater involvement from their general colleagues who may lack drug specialist experience or may lack time and resources for complicated problems. In one such typical service, in their first year of operation they were contacted by 187 drug users, of whom 70 per cent had not previously been in contact with any services. These teams are based in a variety of premises — most are in health centres or community centres although a few are in hospitals. An open referral system usually exists in which the drug taker may write, telephone straight through or drop in (although referrals must be through the local psychiatric services for a few of the teams). A three-year research project funded by the DHSS is examining this system of service delivery and is due to report by the end of 1987.

Self-help groups

Numerous self-help groups have been established in the UK in recent years. The biggest expansion has been the growth of the Narcotics Anonymous (NA) movement. (For an up-to-date description see Wells, 1987b.) Although it was originally established in 1953 as a Californian splinter group from Alcoholics Anonymous, it was not until late 1980 that NA started in Britain. Six years later NS has expanded to 70 weekly meetings in the London area which is its main stronghold. As with its sister movement Alcoholics Anonymous, NA follows 'the twelve steps' which include the recognition that the addict is '. . . powerless over our addiction'; and that recovery involves the decision '. . . to turn our will and our lives over to the care of God as we understand Him'. While for many potential NA members, the idea of 'God' is hard to accept it must be recognized that in practice this is usually implemented by blunt but caring feedback from one's peers within NA who participate in the decision as to progression to the next step of recovery. For many recovering addicts, NA provides important structure to their lives with its emphasis on regular attendance ('90 meetings in 90 days') and its embracing of short-term clearly defined goals ('just for today we do not take drugs'). Abstinence from all psychoactive drugs is the goal and this is assisted by a system of sponsorship in which new attenders are taken under the wing of a more experienced NA member. In a roundabout way, NA manages to state loudly to its members that although they are suffering from the illness of chemical dependency and are powerless over their addiction, they are nevertheless 100 per cent responsible for the initiation and maintenance of their own recovery. Despite the inevitability of a clash between NA advocates and other agencies who do not believe in the disease of addiction, the resulting practical approach with emphasis on personal responsibility may prove to be an acceptable common area for work.

Family groups and parent support groups constitute another important area of self-help services in the community, even though they do not directly involve current drug takers themselves. Parents and spouses have a clear need for support and guidance, irrespective of the needs for their drug-taking loved ones. Indeed, it could be argued that the need of the family is greatest at times when the drug-taker has no wish to be in contact with drug services, at which time the family must endeavour to come to terms with the problem while still

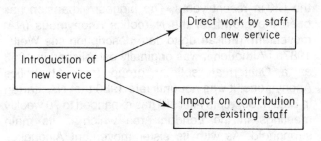

Figure 1   Assessing the impact of a new unit.

attempting to nudge the drug-taker towards treatment and rehabilitation in the future. Plans must be made about the degree of contact, limits and rules within the family and the house, and in a difficult area of the degree of financial and practical support that may be offered or withheld when financial or legal problems become evident.

THE BRITISH SYSTEM TODAY

Dialogue and flow between the different types of drug treatment rehabilitation initiatives is now greater than at any time since the birth of specialist facilities. There is an increasing recognition of the heterogeneity of the drug-taking population. Square pegs should not be forced to conform with the demands of a round hole agency when it would be more appropriate to refer the drug taker on to a different square peg service. Times have changed and so have the drug takers. Consequently it is vital that the services themselves must change as well and this is evident in the ways of working of the Drug Treatment Clinics, the therapeutic communities and other agencies. The encouraging trend today is for the gaps to be filled in the network of services; but it must be recognized that gaps still exist. The drug taker who seems to need more structured support than just a brief withdrawal off drugs over a few weeks in hospital is often forced to choose between premature return to the community from where he/she came or alternatively applying for entry for a year or more at a drug-free therapeutic community/rehabilitation house (see earlier in this paper). Clearly there is a gap here which needs to be filled; and hopefully it will be possible to fill this without challenging the work of either of the previously mentioned options.

EVALUATION

It is a valid criticism to say that most drug services in Britain have been established with very little thought to their evaluation. This is clearly short-sighted, as the drug field is sufficiently new that any of these innovative approaches must be studied carefully so as to evaluate the impact on the extent of service provision and the impact on the target population. In considering the service provided by any new unit, it is necessary to consider not only the contribution made by the new unit, but also the impact on the work provided by pre-existing services (see Figure 1). For example, it is quite possible that the appointment of a worker with special responsibility for drug users might result in a withdrawal of labour from the pre-existing generic colleagues, who breathe a sigh of relief that at last a specialist worker is appointed so they do not need to spend their own time with this patient group. The eventual result could even be that there is less availability of services as a result of the appointment of the new worker.

Another way of looking at this problem might be to look at the service from the point of view of the consumer. Different types of service exist which for the sake of simplicity can be grouped as generic treatments and specialist treatments. If at any one time there is a total population of drug users sized 'N', then a proportion of this population ($n1$) will be receiving treatment from generic services which do not see themselves as drug specialists. If a new specialist service is introduced, then we must look at the benefits which result from the creation of a new population ($n2$) who receive specialist treatments from the new service. What impact does the creation of a population receiving specialist treatment ($n2$) have on the size of the generic treated population ($n1$)? To what extent are $n1$ and $n2$ the same or different populations? At the most basic level we need to look at the total availability of services ($n1$ and $n2$) to see how this has changed as a result of the introduction of the new service. Studying the service over time will involve considering how these two sub-populations (i.e. $n1$ and $n2$) vary compared with changes in the size of the total population N.

Without consideration of the service from the point of view of the potential patient, and without consideration of the impact on the pre-existing service, services might fall into the trap of merely documenting their work and demonstrating that this was greater than the specialist work conducted before their appointment. This would clearly give an incomplete picture.

THE WAY INTO THE FUTURE

Considerable changes have occurred in the last few years in the way services are offered to those with drug problems. This change has occurred at a time of necessary expansion of the services in an attempt to keep pace with the rapid increase in the extent of use of drugs such as heroin. It is not that the traditional elements of service (such as prescribing clinics, specialist inpatient units, drug-free therapeutic communities etc.) have been replaced; rather that we have seen a burgeoning of new initiatives sited in the community. It seems clear that the expansion of services has failed to keep pace with the expansion of the need for such services and continued emphasis must be placed on the importance of improving the provision of varied services for this client group. Inadequate provision or an inadequate range will mean that the uptake is proportionately less. In addition to a resulting increase in the casualty rate, it is also likely that a large proportion of the cohort who might have been captured early in their drug careers will appear at a later stage with a more entrenched habit at which stage the intervention will need to be correspondingly greater. The emphasis for the next few years should be on consolidating the expansions that have occurred and extending them into areas where they do not exist.

A funding crisis may become evident over the next couple of years. The majority of new initiatives have been created utilizing funds available in the Central Funding Initiative. Most of these projects have been given time-limited 'pump-priming' funding for a period of up to three years. It is presumed that during this time the projects will have established whether or not they have been valuable; and if so, the pump will continue to be fed from pre-existing local funds without any identified extra allocation. The reality is that many worthwhile projects are likely to close or to be reduced substantially, and they will need to be seeking new funds from Health and Local Authorities who already believe that there is no slack in the system to fund such new initiatives — however worthwhile they may be. The first of these

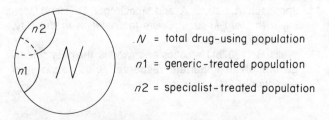

N = total drug-using population

$n1$ = generic-treated population

$n2$ = specialist-treated population

Figure 2 Specialist and generic-treated fractions of the total drug-using population.

are now coming to the end of the pump-priming period, and it remains to be seen whether or not means will be found to continue the worthwhile projects. It is to be hoped that any new initiatives will include greater involvement of Local Authorities and agencies working outside the National Health Service. However, the previous funding arrangements have mainly been via the National Health Service structure, and in many parts of the country there has been an uneasy relationship between Health Authorities and other local agencies such as the Local Authorities. Difficulties such as the lack of co-terminosity, and concerns about the long-term funding arrangements of schemes started today are examples of the problems that interfere with the smooth operation of otherwise worthwhile services in the community.

At the present time public awareness of (and interest in) the drug problem is at a high level and it has been possible to draw on goodwill which may be available within such Authorities when attempting to introduce local schemes for an unpopular client group when viewed from the point of view of the local residents. (A considerable number of projects have been long-delayed in their opening due to such local opposition although the goodwill of the local Authorities has sometimes been sufficient to bring an eventual resolution to local problems; in other areas, such as the proposed hostel site in the Midlands which was the subject of an arson attack, the projects have been abandoned.) The worry is that at a future time when national concern about the drug problem is at a lower level, then the security of such community-based initiatives may become much less certain, and especially if they are seen to be competing for scarce resources with other client groups. Over the next few years the AIDS issue is likely to have a damaging effect on public opinion with regard to services for problem drug takers, with attitudes being driven back to the former situation where drug addicts were seen as diseased individuals who should be dealt with by resorting to leper colony approaches.

Great strides have been made within the last decade or two in improving the general public's understanding of the nature of drug problems and the individuals involved, but it will be important for this progress to be retained if community-based initiatives are to continue in a future time when drug services may receive less popular support.

REFERENCES

1. Prochaska, J.O. and Di Clemente, C.C. (1983) Stages and processes of self-change of smoking: towards an integrated model of change. *Journal of Consulting and Clinical Psychology*, **51**, 390–395.
2. Rolleston Committee (1926) Report on the Departmental Committee on Morphine and Heroin Addiction. HMSO, London.
3. Second Brain Committee (1965) Second Report of the Interdepartmental Committee on Drug Addiction. *Drug Addiction*. HMSO, London.
4. Advisory Council on the Misuse of Drugs (1982) *Treatment and Rehabilitation Report*. HMSO, London.
5. Medical Working Group on Drug Dependence (1984) *Guidelines of Good Clinical Practice in the Treatment of Drug Misuse*. DHSS, London.
6. Jones, M. (1984) Why two Therapeutic Communities? *Journal of Psychoactive Drugs*, 16(1), 23–26.
7. Mahon, T. (1973) Therapy or brainwashing? *Drugs and Society*, 2(5), 7–10.
8. Ogborne, A.C. and Melotte, C. (1977) An evaluation of a Therapeutic Community for Former Drug Users. *British Journal of Addiction*, 72, 75–82.
9. Wells, B. (1987a) NA and the 'Minnesota Method' in Britain. *Druglink*, 2(1), 8–9.
10. Glanz, A. (1983) *ROMA (Talgarth Road): Report of an Information-Gathering Exercise*. DHSS, London.
11. Yates, R. (1981) *Out from the Shadows — Lifeline Project*. NACRO, London.
12. Strang, J. and Yates, R. (1984) Non-voluntary treatment of drug-takers — some preliminary findings. Proceedings of the Pompidou Group, Council of Europe, Strasbourg.
13. Dorn, N. and South, N. (1985) *Helping Drug Users*. Gower, Aldershot, England.
14. Jamieson, A., Glanz, A. and MacGregor, S. (1984) *Dealing with Drug Misuse: Crisis Intervention in the City*. Tavistock, London.
15. Wells, B. (1987b) Narcotics Anonymous: the phenomenal growth of an important resource. *British Journal of Addiction*, 82(1), 1–2.

Paper 26

Some practical approaches to the problem drug taker

ANTHONY THORLEY

Consultant Psychiatrist, Alcohol and Drug Problem Service, Newcastle Health Authority

This paper focusses on individual work with people who have become drug takers. It outlines ways in which assessment and goal setting can be approached, and indicates the skills that it is necessary for health workers to develop in order to be able to help people to modify their drug taking behaviour.

ASSESSMENT AND SETTING GOALS

Problem drug takers are a very heterogeneous group and there is no short-cut to recognition of this kind of client. The long haired 'junkie' of the 1960s is an unhelpful caricature for the worker of the 1980s. Today's drug takers are as likely to come from any class, the employed as much as unemployed, apparently in remarkably good health, as much as being obviously medically and socially deteriorated.

The aim of treatment and case work is to help the individual sort out the problems related to his/her drug taking. This will require working closely with the client to encourage motivation to eventually modify patterns of drug taking, with a view to probably eventually giving up drugs and changing essential lifestyle. Long-term recovery is dependent on a basic change in personal attitudes as much as it is on the short-term amelioration of symptoms, and factors of crisis. Treatment, as identified with crude medical prescribing, places insufficient emphasis on the need for the client to take responsibility for his own life and problems and work them out in collaboration with his doctor and other support agencies. It is in this role of counsellor or case worker that the non-prescribing worker plays a major part.

© Anthony Thorley

A _problem drug taker_ is any person who experiences psychological (personal), physical (medical), social or legal problems in relation to intoxication and/or regular excessive consumption and/or dependence on any drugs or chemical substances excluding alcohol and tobacco.

The definition of a problem drug taker gives some indication of the scope of assessment of drug problems. Many features causally precede significant drug use, and may need to be attended to in the process of long-term rehabilitation. The majority of the problems — medical, social and legal — will be clearly consequent upon the drug taking behaviour, and these will tend to be the ones complained about by the client or his family.

The purpose of assessment is to examine all the factors involved so as to identify some of the vicious circles, and this may require several interviews in the office, or in the drug taker's own house. Interviews with a spouse, partner, parents, or other family members and friends are often crucial in getting a full picture of the drug taking and the related style of life involved.

Many drug takers will explain their drug use as being caused by 'being bored' or 'needing drugs' but a good assessment will try to get behind these stock answers, however true they may be, and make some sense of

163

cause and effects. Never forget that almost all drug takers at some time, and often after many years of drug taking, still get a tremendous amount of pleasure and reward from their drug habits. This hedonistic element should be recognised and acknowledged from the outset, but a fine line often needs to be drawn between appropriate acknowledgement and tacit encouragement. Remember all the ways that you use drugs (tea, coffee, chocolate, sweets, cigarettes, aspirins and cough medicines from the chemists, and tranquillisers from the doctors) in order to cope with your week at work! The problem drug taker is after all only someone who has got into difficulties with their drug taking. There but for the grace of God go all of us.

Assess the problems presented by the client and take into account the problems that you perceive as the worker. If you are clearly all at sea and confused, and have no system of organising this material, the client will soon pick this up and lose heart. Expertise is not necessary to deal with drug takers, but confidence over handling the material is. The jargon of medicine and social work is just as confusing as the jargon of the drug sub-culture.

Remember that the problem drug taker commonly experiences rejection by professional workers. Therefore acceptance of the client as a person with problems is the essence of the interview. Even a moment of implicit judgement passing across the worker's face can limit the emergence of trust and motivation. Denial, deceit and lying about drug taking and associated behaviours are not inherent traits of 'addiction', but more commonly responses to implicit or explicit pressures from the family, friends, community workers, and maybe even the doctor, to stop using drugs at all costs. Because so much drug taking is illegal, drug takers hide a great deal from themselves and therefore the lying and deceit carries over into their social and commercial lives. Sometimes in the interview with a worker this emerges as straightforward lying, but more often it shows up as a kind of delusion whereby the client hardly knows whether he or she is telling the truth or not. Many clients show clear ambivalence about their drug taking from the start. Part of them clearly wants to stop taking drugs. At the same time another part of them wishes to hold the drug taking option open for as long as possible.

Faced with this situation the worker should perhaps avoid talking about drug-taking as the crucial issue of the interview and explore that wide range of potential problems which will or do in fact occur. Motivation about coming off drugs may be rather nebulous, but a client or patient sitting in the office is motivated about something and it is this 'leading edge' of motivation that the worker should concentrate on responding to. Why is the client sitting there and not leaving the room? Sometimes by taking drugs off the centre of the stage and working with more basic problems, denial rapidly fades, the ambivalence begins to sharpen into recognisable motivation, and the client responds positively such that the drug taking pattern modifies to a more harm-free characteristic. Very often the problem drug taker who has been using for many months or years is almost a kind of stranger to his close family and relatives. Drugs mask and defend against the real person within. What kind of person is that? Has the *drug taker* any concern about the real person within? It is important to emphasise from the outset that it is that person that you the worker wishes to make contact with and work with. The problems of that person which have only been ameliorated by drug use can be helped by you the worker, and other agencies, without the use of drugs. The timescale may be a long one, but it is important to make this positive statement of the aims of your work from the outset. All these strategies will encourage personal trust between client and worker and the emergence of mutual motivation and goal agreement.

DRUG TAKING HISTORY

When trust is gained and motivation identified, at some stage assessment must examine the chronology and relationship between causal factors, varieties of drug taking, and consequent problems. There may be no explicit natural history of drug problems or use, but many patients and clients have a distinct drug taking career which repays close examination.

For instance many opiate drug takers show a clear history of transition from cannabis use, to stimulants such as amphetamines, sedatives such as barbiturates to hallucinogens, such as LSD, to opiate drugs such as heroin, methadone and morphine. Many will have had periods of intermittent use, that is taking once or twice a week, smoking for instance heroin cigarettes, or taking oral opiates before establishing intermittent and then regular injection practice. Some will clearly misuse other drugs such as barbiturates, amphetamines and tranquillisers, and therefore have to be viewed as multiple drug takers. Many, particularly the young, will also drink excessively and have an alcohol problem, but some drug takers show little interest in alcohol throughout their drug taking careers. What emerges most clearly from any kind of drug taking history is that there is little value in distinctions made between specific kinds of substance linked drug use. Thus the heroin addict, the amphetamine addict and the barbiturate addict all share the same kinds of problems.

Over the series of consultations or interviews a systematic approach is essential, and the client will respond to a worker confidently using a framework of explanation. The elements of drug taking behaviour should be very carefully gone into, and histories which stress positive factors (periods of abstinence or relatively harm-free drug taking) will benefit the client more than those which confirm traditional stereotypes (using a needle means you're a junkie).

It is useful to ask about the pattern and types of drugs taken on a typical day. What are the key factors during that day? What begins and ends a run of drug taking? Many clients over the whole of their lives have actually controlled their drug taking for most of the time and consequently should be asked how they have done so in the past. Why cannot they manage now? Answers to these questions give clues to casework and counselling management responses, and will begin to remove that most perplexing statement: 'I don't know what makes me do it. I don't know why I use drugs.'

Part of an assessment in a clinical setting will be a physical examination by a doctor and some routine investigations and blood tests. Whenever you come across a client who seems to be physically ill or you are in doubt about his general medical health, it is advisable to try and put that client in touch with a doctor who will give him a fair examination. Finding such a doctor is not as easy as it seems.

RECOGNISING DEPENDENCE

Dependence is basically psychological and best considered as a state of sadness, loss, anxiety and possibly craving, experienced when an individual has to cease carrying out some valued activity. Some careful thought will soon reveal where your own dependence is in your own life. Most problem drug takers are psychologically dependent and their assessment and understanding must take into account the various dependence elements.

(1) *Primary gain*: The reward of the pleasurable, euphoric and intoxicant effects of the drug.
(2) *Habit*: The repeated habitualised use of the drug leading to a reinforced pattern of drug use.
(3) *Sub-cultural*: The likelihood of social and more broadly based societal pressures to continue drug taking.
(4) *Physiological*: Pharmacological dependence is evidenced by tolerance (the way in which the body needs a larger and larger dose to have the same physiological responses) and a withdrawal syndrome, but these factors merely amplify the basic psychological dependence. Not all drugs cause marked degrees of physical or pharmacological dependence. Some substances seem to be more 'sticky' or addictive, than others.

Sometimes physical dependence may occur within 3 weeks of daily injected use (for instance with opiates) and it is common to find physical dependence within 6 months of more intermittent opiate drug use.

THE WITHDRAWAL SYNDROME

All drug takers experience anxiety, depression and some mood change in anticipation of their drug supplies, and as levels of the drug in their blood stream and body reduce, and in some individuals this can be so predominant as to virtually mask any symptoms of pharmacological or physical withdrawal. Thus in these cases psychological factors predominate over physical factors. Assessing various kinds of withdrawal syndromes is not easy, and the following features only act as general guidelines. Whenever the worker is in doubt they should refer patients to a medical practitioner or accident and emergency department for a fuller medical assessment. This is simply because some forms of withdrawal can be dangerous.

RESPONSES TO PROBLEM DRUG TAKING
Setting goals

Assessment information is used to work out together with the client realistic goals regarding the drug problems that are presented.

Of course the worker will identify problems that the client is unaware of. He should share these with the client and develop a joint list of problem priorities and a realistic order and time scale to tackle them. This approach is implicitly contractual. For instance, the worker can immediately respond to an accommodation or financial problem or put the client in contact with medical services, at the same time as using counselling techniques to support and advise the client in making his or her own decisions. To maintain clarity of management it is best to tackle one problem at a time in a planned way. Priority lists are best written down and shared with the client and reviewed together in subsequent interviews. Reviews should reinforce progress and goal achievement as the time scale may be at least several months, and possibly up to a year. Therefore management strategies worked out with the client should be followed through and not lost sight of. Failure to achieve goals requires their modification by client and worker together and until a pattern of positive achievement is established. Patience is not a virtue, it is a necessary skill when working with problem drug takers.

DRUG EDUCATION AND KNOWLEDGE

All case work strategies should be grounded in a preventive approach. Many drug takers are ignorant of some of the most basic risks about drug use. For instance, it is more correct to advise drug takers about sterile injection techniques (i.e. how to inject using a clean needle, clean skin and so on) rather than seeing this as a tacit encouragement to inject. Similarly, accurate information about the legal aspects of drug taking needs to be given to clients. For instance many

clients hold that 'registration' confers a legal right to opiate prescribing. This is quite wrong, and workers should be clear why this is so.

Thus to be effective the worker must be in command of information and knowledge about drugs and their harms. Much of this is paradoxical and cuts across commonly held clinical and lay supposition. However, the paradoxes provide springboards for appropriate case work responses. Often it has been convenient to both worker and client to believe that drug taking is 'out of control' in a kind of implicit determinism. Such denial of personal accountability is both demeaning and hopeless. It is therefore essential to emphasise personal responsibility and volitional factors. Drugs do *not* control peoples lives. They *choose* to use them. Therefore they can *choose* not to use them.

Decisions to alter life style, personal characteristics or drug taking behaviour are taken in the context knowledge that is available and thus education becomes a major tool in the case work setting. Clients should be encouraged to see the relationship between the problems and the pattern, quantity and frequency of consumption. Counting actual numbers of drugs taken, monitoring patterns of drug use, like counting calories, introduces involvement, understanding and, with it, control and self respect, and therefore should be strongly encouraged.

MODIFYING DRUG TAKING BEHAVIOUR
1) Avoiding regular excessive consumption

Having identified regular excessive consumption, clear explanation of current and all future possible problems should be given. What happens when you take a particular drug at above a particular level over a particular period of time? The client should be encouraged to practise counting the number and types of drugs he or she takes and monitoring his consumption with a daily diary. This can be used to understand the patterns of use better and so to set a personal and more relatively harm-free drug consumption level, and so reinforce self control and with it self respect. Some of the drugs used may be prescribed by a Doctor or Clinic, and other parts of the drug use will be bought illegally (scored). The worker should be concerned with the total amount of drugs used each day, and encourage the drug taker to initially reduce the illegally purchased drug component first in the context of a drug taking diary. Having reduced this part of the drug dose, the client can be encouraged to negotiate with the Doctor for the prescribed components to be also reduced in a contracted setting. Thus advantages of reduced consumption should be clearly spelled out, for instance saving money, avoiding arrest. Handled sensitively, bringing spouses and family members into drug consumption monitoring can be very helpful.

2) Avoiding intoxication

Clients should really recognise what their own intoxication (getting high) represents and the specific problems related to it. In particular antecedent emotional problems (e.g. stress, anxiety, anger) need to be examined, ameliorated and if necessary more appropriate responses explored. There is very little experimental evidence for many drugs causing the kind of 'loss of control' (e.g. barbiturates) but clients often show impaired control or willingly abdicate volition in a specific situation. These situations need to be examined in detail, e.g. place, social contacts, types and rates of drug consumed, consequences. Hedonistic elements of getting stoned or intoxicated are universal but unlikely to provide an adequate explanation for regular problematic intoxication. It is more likely that in these cases people are avoiding or evading painful issues in their lives. As well as these processes of self exploration with regard to intoxication, self monitoring of drug taking behaviour leading to intoxication is often very valuable. Drug taking diaries showing situational consumption and success in limit setting should be kept and discussed in subsequent interviews. All successes should be reinforced by approval and congratulations.

3) Avoiding dependence

Much has already been said about dependence as a concept. It is essential that the client understands the point and value in readjusting his dependence to a more constructive and less damaging type. This work is best done in a counselling relationship. Responses involved: 1) *education* utilises the cooperative element and often enables the client to take control of his life and remove disadvantageous dependence on drug taking; 2) *breaking the habit*: the temporal pattern or regularity of drug taking behaviour can be broken in a planned way, e.g. avoiding certain places for scoring or social company; 3) *finding safer psychological props*: this means not by moving necessarily from barbiturates to the allegedly safer Valium, but encouraging appropriate dependence on people or institutions (e.g. your working office or a community based project); 4) *dealing with the loss*: encouraging the client to work through bereavement, encouraging self confidence, self esteem and assertiveness.

4) Supporting abstinence

In addition to some of the principles described above, abstinence from drugs requires specific management in its own right. Abstinence means just what it says and clients have to be effectively assertive to maintain within their own subculture this relatively deviant role. They need counsel and encouragement to develop a satisfactory explanation with friends so as to avoid situations where drug taking is expected. It is useful for abstinent clients to receive a great deal of support from agencies and workers who specifically and continuously encourage abstinence. For instance the local drug clinic where prescribing may be going on does not appear to encourage abstinence as it tacitly supports peoples' on-going drug habits with 'maintenance' prescriptions.

Therefore talking about drug taking and all the secondary reinforcement implicit in that activity should be discouraged. Some clients want (and need) to manage abstinence but cannot. A minor relapse of drug taking should not be reacted to so as to cause further guilt in the client. The client will feel quite sufficient guilt without any reinforcement from the worker! All clients who resume drug taking or feel like drug taking should be encouraged to follow a contingency plan of contacting a worker or some agency immediately. Telephone counselling services are very useful at this point.

As complete and sustained abstinence is almost impossible except for a small minority of people in their initial rehabilitation, particularly in the community, any abstinence should be congratulated and reinforced, as should successful news of the drug taking contingency plan.

It is worth noting that as clients come off drugs, there

is often a pattern of attitude and drug taking that suggests improvement. For instance, multiple drug takers with a physical dependence on opiates would show improvement by following these steps: i) reducing their illegal component of drug use; ii) abandoning injection and preparing to take only oral opiate medication prescribed by the Clinic; iii) reducing the dose of opiate drugs with a possible stabilisation of other tranquillising drugs such as barbiturates or benzodiazepines; iv) possibly a period of intermittent opiate use but in the absence of physical dependence. Barbiturate and stimulant use may continue on a regular basis for some months after last physical dependence on opiate use, and some patients compensate for their cessation of opiates by a period of several months of excessive drinking or excessive cannabis. Provided the worker stays in contact with a client through this process, research evidence suggests that eventually these compensatory patterns of drug use reduced to normal levels, such that one year after last physical dependence on opiate use, drug taking is no more or less than the normal population in society. Hence absolute abstinence is an elusive concept!

REHABILITATION

Strategies of rehabilitation emerge as the major form of work with the drug taking client. *Rehabilitation is the process of personal change and growth which may take many months or a year or two to really show itself*. This process is to some extent spontaneous but can be generously assisted by able counselling and the proper use of various treatments and agencies.

Where a client is being asked to make a major shift in basic functioning and style of life a useful rule of thumb is as follows: the client will need as many months' contact with various agencies keeping to the basic rehabilitation strategy as there are years in the life of the individual concerned. Thus somebody aged eighteen will require about eighteen months' work, and somebody aged forty-five, arguably more entrenched in their position, will require over three years' contact. The point here is that *all individuals have this capacity for change* until dementia or death intervenes! It is important to keep this potential for change in mind throughout all one's case work.

It will now be very apparent that short-term contact or a Doctor's prescription pad is unlikely to significantly improve drug taking problems in the long term, and from whatever base the worker operates it is essential to have a close coordination with other disciplines and agencies. Rehabilitation is a complex process and requires a skilful measure of coordination and management. It may be initiated in the context of continued drug use, possibly illicit but more probably in the context of a maintenance opiate prescription, or long-term withdrawal contract from a drug clinic. It may be initiated in the context of abstinence. Certainly it will continue for many individuals over several years even in the context of minor relapses and returns to other forms of drug taking. It is important to remember that in fact a majority of problem drug takers eventually cease their problematic drug use and achieve non-deviant or conventional ways of life.

Recognition and treatment of alcohol-related disorders

BRUCE RITSON

Consultant Psychiatrist and Senior Lecturer, Department of Psychiatry, Edinburgh University, Royal Edinburgh Hospital

The concept of alcohol as a health hazard is discussed. All workers in Primary Care are well placed to recognize alcohol-related problems at an early stage and the techniques for recognition, motivation, detoxification and rehabilitation are briefly described.

More than 90% of the adult population drink alcohol. On most occasions drinking is convivial and enjoyable and without harm to the drinker or others. However, as we drink greater quantities more frequently, so the chances of consequent harm increase. In Britain the per capita consumption of alcohol has more than doubled since the 1950s and the level of alcohol-related social and physical harm has risen accordingly (Saunders, 1984). The cost of alcohol misuse in terms of sickness, accidents, time lost from work and crime was conservatively estimated in 1983 as £1700 million per year (McDonnell and Maynard, 1985).

SENSIBLE DRINKING

Individuals who keep their consumption well within the limits illustrated in figure 1 are unlikely to be harmed by alcohol. Although moderation of this kind carries no long term health risks, the levels do need to be interpreted with care and good sense.

Twenty standard units of alcohol consumed on a single occasion could have disastrous consequences and any drinking before driving or other complex and hazardous work is unwise. Drinkers should also take into account their general state of health and concomitant use of any other drugs, particularly hypnotics and tranquillisers.

A given dose of alcohol produces a 25–30% higher concentration in the blood of a woman compared to a man, even allowing for their generally lower weight. The main reason is probably that women have a smaller body water compartment and a higher body fat/water ratio than men.

For pregnant women sensible drinking is either abstinence or at the most one or two units once or twice a week. Foetal damage due to alcohol often occurs in the early stages of pregnancy and therefore this advice should be given as soon as a woman thinks she may become pregnant.

The medical and social consequences of alcohol abuse can be divided into those caused by intoxication and

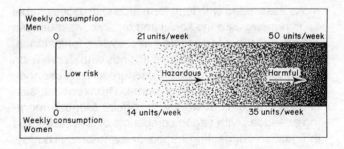

Figure 1   Association between alcohol consumption and risk of harmful consequences (derived from *That's the limit*, published by the Health Education Council, 1983).

Reprinted with permission from *The Practitioner*, May 1986, Vol. 230, pp. 435–441.

Table 1   Health consequences of alcohol misuse

Intoxication/acute effects	Chronic excess
Alcoholic poisoning	Physical and psychological
Acute gastritis	dependence
Diarrhoea	Cognitive impairment
Hangover symptoms	Wernicke's encephalopathy
Amnesia	Korsakow's syndrome
Hypoglycaemia	Peripheral neuropathy
Cerebrovascular accidents	Fatty liver
Cardiac arrhythmia	Hepatitis
('holiday heart	Cirrhosis (30% are
syndrome')	excessive drinkers)
Foetal damage	Carcinoma of liver
Impotence	Pancreatitis (acute and
Accidents	50% chronic)
Head injury	Irritable bowel syndrome
Suicide attempts	Hypertension
	Cardiomyopathy
	Obesity
	Cushing's syndrome
	Diabetes
	Testicular atrophy
	Impotence
	Foetal alcohol syndrome
	Carcinoma of the mouth,
	larynx and oesophagus

Note: 32% of patients attending Accident and Emergency departments have blood alcohol levels above 80 mg%
42% of patients with serious head injuries are intoxicated
49% of drivers killed in RTA are intoxicated

those associated with long-term alcoholic excess (table 1). In primary care the social and family consequences are often the first to become evident when for instance, the problem drinker's spouse attends with depression or the children's behaviour is disturbed because they are upset by arguments at home. Drunkenness also causes problems at work with regular Monday morning absences with vague complaints of headache and indigestion suggesting hangover symptoms (Thorley, 1980). Evidence of a patient's drinking problem may even first come to light through reports of a drunkenness offence or a drink-driving charge in the local paper.

WHO IS AT RISK?

The simple and truthful answer is all of us. The following are particularly at risk: sons of problem drinkers, divorced, separated and single men over 35, individuals living alone or in hostels and those in certain occupations such as publicans, caterers, journalists, members of the armed forces, seamen and medical practitioners, the last of whom have a mortality ratio for cirrhosis which is three times the national average (Hore and Plant, 1981). The ratio of men to women problem drinkers has fallen in recent years and is now approximately 2:1 (Camberwell Council on Alcoholism, 1980).

IDENTIFICATION OF THOSE AT RISK

A primary care team with approximately 2000 adults on the list will have at least 100 patients who are drinking in a harmful way, plus 40 with current problems and 10 who are physically dependent (Paton et al, 1982).

Identification of these patients will be facilitated if the health workers regularly ask themselves whether excessive drinking could be contributing to each patient's problems. Although many patients underestimate the extent of their drinking, straightforward questions about the frequency and quantity of alcohol consumed during a recent typical week will often provide a sufficient guide to consumption which may then be compared with the guidelines in figure 1. The patient should also be asked whether drinking has caused any problems in the past year.

Research suggests that such questions alone often prove as good as measures such as questionnaires or blood tests in identifying problem drinkers. Women appear to under-report the extent of their consumption more than men (Wallace and Haines, 1985).

A clinical hunch may be strengthened by unobtrusive indicators such as a history of head injury or fracture since the age of 18, vague gastro-intestinal symptoms and physical signs such as injected sclerae, excessive capillarisation of the skin and fine tremor of the hands and tongue. Alcohol on the breath is an excellent clue, the best diagnostic aid being your own nose. Raised serum gamma glutamyl transpeptidase (γGT) and an increased red cell mean corpuscular volume (MCV) may provide supportive evidence, occurring in approximately two thirds of excessive drinkers. They are also useful aids to monitoring subsequent progress; γGT declines quite rapidly on stopping drinking, MCV takes several months.

Probably the most straightforward advice on detection of alcohol problems is to remain alert to their possibility. 'In everyday practice there remains no substitute for the alert doctor with a high degree of suspicion and yet sufficient tact to be able to take a good drinking history without alienating the patient' (*Lancet*, 1980).

MOTIVATING THE PATIENT

Persuading patients that their drinking is at the root of their problems is a difficult task. It is, however, an activity which is at the heart of much clinical practice. We are all familiar with trying to motivate patients to make a change in their way of life — 'eat less', 'give up smoking', 'exercise more', 'remember to take the tablets' are well worn phrases concerned with communicating a need to change habits.

Most patients will be ambivalent about changing. A reluctant patient brought by a despairing spouse or coming to avoid dismissal from work needs to be converted into an individual who will take personal responsibility for stopping or reducing his or her drinking. One way of helping the patient to make a judgement about the value of commitment to change is for the drinker to draw up a balance sheet (table 2) listing the advantages and disadvantages of continuing as before or changing (Orford, 1985).

The first interview will have achieved a great deal if the patient is now thinking seriously about his or her drinking and is willing to *contemplate* change. At the end of the interview, show that you regard the pattern of drinking as an important clinical matter and ask the patient to keep a careful diary of all alcohol consumed in the next two weeks (figure 2). This can be reviewed when the patient returns to learn the result of the blood tests (γGT and MCV). Acknowledge that we all find it difficult to change habits but point out that success, if desired, is likely and that help will be available. If possible, try to enlist the help of a friend of the patient or a member of the family.

SETTING GOALS

Regular drinking at levels which are likely to be hazardous needs to be reduced to 'safer' limits. The patient

Table 2 Balance sheet of drinking

	Likely consequences of drinking choices		
	Continuing as before	Reducing	Stopping
PROS of chosen course	Forget my work worries Keep my drinking friends at lunchtime	Be like others Not be a kill-joy with friends	Family want me to Doctor says it is the only way my liver will recover Save a lot of money
CONS of chosen course	My wife may leave Children very upset May lose my job They say I am drunk after lunch Liver failure	Didn't work when I tried before Wife wouldn't believe me Liver damage persists	Could I cope with business lunches? Feel uncomfortable with my friends, particularly at work

Day	Time	Place	People	Other activities	Drink taken in units	Money spent on alcohol	Consequences of drinking (if any)
Tues	12·30	Pub	Work friends	Cards	8	£4	Slowing down, forgetfulness
Wed	12·30	Pub	Work friends	Cards	6	£3	ditto
Wed	8·00	Pub	Friends	Darts, pool	6	£3	Tiredness
Thurs	1·00	Pub	Work friends	Fruit-machine, cards	6	£3	Slowing down, forgetfulness
Fri	12·00	Pub	Work friends	Cards	10	£5·50	No inclination to work
Fri	8·00	Home	Wife	TV	6	£4·40	Relaxing evening
Sun	1·30	Home	Family	None	2	£1·50	None

1 unit = ½ pint beer
1 measure spirits
1 glass wine

Weekly total in units = 44

Figure 2   An example of a drinking diary record.

and the health worker should agree a realistic goal and the patient should keep a diary of the quantity consumed and the occasions on which they overstep this self-imposed limit. These incidents signal the times when the patient is most vulnerable and future sessions should focus on finding new ways of coping with these critical times. Self-help booklets are useful for this task (Chick and Chick, 1984). 'Drinkwatchers' is a self-help group concerned with helping its members attain a less damaging style of drinking.

For some patients abstinence will be the preferred goal. This conclusion may be reached by a painful process of trial and error or it may be mandatory from the start because of serious physical harm such as deranged hepatic function, pancreatitis or cognitive impairment. Patients who have evidence of severe physical dependence on alcohol will require help with detoxification at the beginning of treatment and will be well advised to set a goal of abstinence.

DETOXIFICATION

Detoxification is a necessary prelude to further treatment for any patients who experience withdrawal symptoms when they try to cut down or stop drinking. The withdrawal symptoms are characterised by shakiness, a feeling often described as 'my nerves are bad' or the patient may say he does not feel 'quite normal' until the first drink of the day. Other features are irritability, insomnia, restlessness, anorexia, retching — all relieved by drinking. Provided supportive family or friends are present, detoxification can be achieved in the patient's own home with a health worker visiting regularly.

The patient should be told to remain indoors and abstain from all alcohol; he or she should rest and take plenty of fluids, preferably fruit juices rather than coffee or tea (because of their stimulant effects). Parentrovite injections should be given daily for five days, which requires a nurse to visit. This visit gives the nurse a chance to check that no alcohol has been taken and to monitor the vital signs, being alert to dehydration, pyrexia or confusion. Tremor and agitation can usually be controlled with chlordiazepoxide 20mg three or four times on the first day, reduced gradually over seven days and then stopped.

The development of confusion, increased restlessness, tachycardia and pyrexia may herald the onset of delirium tremens and necessitate transfer to hospital. Specialist help is recommended for patients with a prior history of fits or severe withdrawal symptoms. Fits (one to two days after cessation) and delirium tremens (usually after two to five days) occur in 5–10% of patients during alcohol withdrawal. In most cases detoxification is an uneventful process and the patient feels and looks very much better within one week.

MAINTENANCE

Maintaining abstinence involves learning to cope with life without alcohol and developing a new life style. The necessary changes are often as difficult for the family as they are for the problem drinker. Encouragement and a regular review of blood tests is invaluable throughout this time.

Alcohol-sensitising drugs are often valuable in maintaining resolution. The patients know that if they take it regularly, they cannot drink. Disulfiram (Antabuse) 300mg daily is sufficient to produce a severe reaction to alcohol. This is caused by the accumulation of acetaldehyde in the system and the patient commonly experiences flushing, tachycardia, faintness and nausea. Users of disulfiram should be known to be in reasonably good cardiovascular health and have an intact memory because the reaction carries some risk.

The patient should carry an information sheet about the drug and have a clear understanding of its actions. Disulfiram, supervised by a relative, close friend or even employer, has been found to be particularly effective and has the added benefit of reassuring those most closely involved with the patient. Nonetheless it must be used only with the full agreement and cooperation of the patient.

RELAPSE

'I can resist anything but temptation', OSCAR WILDE.

Most patients will relapse from their stated goals. Although serious, this need not be a catastrophe provided it is dealt with promptly and the patient learns something from the experience. Encourage patients to identify triggers to relapse and find new ways of dealing with these situations (Marlatt and George, 1984).

REFERRAL

Primary care workers will find that the advice they give is sufficient for some patients to make a lasting commitment to changing their drinking pattern. Simple advice given in a general hospital has been shown to produce encouraging results (Chick et al, 1985). There is no reason to suppose that the same procedures cannot work in general practice. Referral to hospital may be necessary for patients who seem likely to have difficulty withdrawing from alcohol at home, have underlying neurotic or depressive symptoms or who have disturbed family and marital relations or where the patient has not responded to the approaches described above.

In addition to specialist services, there are a number of voluntary agencies which can help. Branches of Alcoholics Anonymous and AlAnon (the latter for the relatives and friends of alcoholics) exist throughout Britain. In some areas there is also Alateen for the teenage children of alcoholics. The general practitioner should get to know a few AA members personally and refer via them. A personal introduction makes regular attendance at group meetings much more likely.

Councils on Alcoholism exist throughout Britain and they give free counselling and good advice to problem drinkers and their families. Some areas are fortunate in having other specialist resources such as groups for women problem drinkers, day centres, 'dry' social clubs and hostels. The pattern of available services varies considerably throughout the country and the most sensible plan is for the doctor to get to know the staff of the local alcohol problem clinic, if one exists, or the Council on Alcoholism and ask their advice about resources available locally.

PROGNOSIS

Evidence suggests that 60% of alcohol-dependent patients will improve following treatment although for most of this group transient relapses will continue to occur. Pessimism is therefore misplaced. The remaining 40% who do not change are a challenge for future services. A possible solution for the future is to try to identify hazardous drinking at an early stage when change is less painful and easier to achieve.

REFERENCES

Camberwell Council on Alcoholism. (1980): *Women and alcohol*, Tavistock, London, pp. 207.

Chick, J., Chick, J. (1984): *Drinking problems, information and advice for individuals, family and friends*. Churchill Livingstone, Edinburgh, pp. 85.

Chick, J., Lloyd, G., Crombie, E. (1985): 'Counselling problem drinkers in medical wards: a controlled study'. *Br Med J*, **290**, 965–967.

Hore, B., Plant, M. (1981): *Alcohol problems in employment*, Croom Helm, London, pp. 208.

Lancet. (1980) 'Screening tests for alcoholism' (editorial), *Lancet*, **1**, 1117–1118.

Marlatt, G.A., George, W.H. (1984): 'Relapse prevention', *Br J Addiction*, **79**, 261–274.

McDonnell, R., Maynard, A. (1985): 'The costs of alcohol misuse', *Br J Addiction*, **80**, 27–35.

Orford, J. (1985): *Excessive appetites*, Wiley, Chichester, pp. 367.

Paton, A., Potter, J.F., Lewis, K. (1982): 'Detection in general practice', in *Alcohol problems*, BMJ Publications, London, pp. 14–16.

Saunders, W. (1984): 'Alcohol use in Britain: how much is too much?' *Health Education Journal*, **43**, 66–70.

Thorley, A. (1980): 'Medical responses to problem drinking', *Medicine*, **35**, 1816–1822.

Wallace, P., Haines, A. (1985): 'Use of a questionnaire in general practice to increase the recognition of problem drinkers', *Br Med J*, **290**, 1949–1953.

Paper 28

Tranquillizers: current concerns and treatment practice

MOIRA HAMLIN

Principal Clinical Psychologist, North Birmingham Health Authority

This paper traces the introduction of tranquillizers and the subsequent recognition of the problems that they can cause. It goes on to examine the types of help that people need to withdraw from chronic tranquillizer use, and gives examples of 'good practice' in various settings.

Throughout history we have searched for substances to relieve anxiety and emotional pain: Tranquillizers have now replaced the old remedies of gin and opium. Household names like Valium and Librium were introduced as tranquillizers in the 1960s. They were thought to be safe, effective alternatives to barbiturates which were lethal in overdose and highly addictive.

Tranquillizers were welcomed by both doctors and patients because they gave relief from the immediate pain of a bereavement or a stressful situation which had become overwhelming. There was no danger of over-dosing and no apparent side-effects or dependence problems. Unfortunately the widespread acceptance of pills as a solution to solving problems has had a high price, both in monetary and human terms. In 1980[1] 40 billion doses of tranquillizers per day were consumed worldwide with sales exceeding $1000 million. About 1.5 per cent of the adult population in the United Kingdom take these drugs throughout the year, and 0.7 per cent have taken tranquillizers for over seven years.[2] The high proportion of long-term tranquillizer users is perhaps surprising in view of recommendations for limited short-term use.[3] The Committee on the Review of Medicines in 1980 stated 'that there was little convincing evidence that benzodiazepines [tranquillizers] were efficacious in the treatment of anxiety after 4 months continuous treatment'.

What started out as a short-term solution, a 'breathing-space' to enable people to face problems, turned all too easily into a situation of successive repeat prescriptions and the creation of a hard core of people who were long-term chronic users.

Initial reports of withdrawal symptoms were dismissed because it was thought to be a re-occurrence of the original anxiety.[4] Many symptoms are similar to anxiety, for example: insomnia, tension, headache, fearfulness, panic attacks. Further research revealed that some symptoms such as hypersensitivity to light and sound and perceptual disturbances could not be simply attributed to the original anxiety returning.[5] A true 'withdrawal syndrome' was recognized along with a potential for physical and psychological dependence even at normal therapeutic dose (e.g. 20–40 mg Diazepam per day).[6] In addition it was realized that withdrawal symptoms can be experienced even after brief treatments of 4–6 weeks.[7]

The implications of these findings meant that even people on relatively low doses risked becoming dependent on tranquillizers and after only a short period of treatment. It has been estimated[6] that 5–10 per cent of patients may experience some withdrawal symptoms after six months of treatment. After 6–8 years the proportion likely to develop withdrawal symptoms rises to 75 per cent. Shorter-acting tranquillizers such as Lorazepam and Oxazepam appear to cause more withdrawal problems and patients often find it harder to stop taking them.[8]

Table 1 Benzodiazepines[9] (Ashton)

Generic name	Common brand name	Length of action
Diazepam	Valium	Long, more than 8 hours
Nitrazepam	Mogadon	Long, more than 8 hours
Temazepam	Euhypnos, Normison	medium, 2–8 hours
Triazolam	Halcion	Very short, up to 2 hours
Lorazepam	Ativan	Medium, 2–8 hours
Oxazepam	Serenid	Short, 2–8 hours
Chlordiazepoxide	Librium	Long, more than 8 hours

Tranquillizers have now been with us for 25 years and concern has recently been expressed over their efficacy, dependence potential and possible long-term effects. There are indications that rates of prescribing are down. In the last ten years prescriptions in the UK have dropped from 24.7 million to 14.3 million, and media attention has increased public awareness of the dangers of long-term use. However, there are several key issues which must be addressed before the tranquillizer problem which has been created over the last twenty years can be resolved.

1. How to decrease our general reliance on doctors and medication to provide solutions for personal problems.
2. How to prevent new people becoming tranquillizer users or to limit treatment to short courses only.
3. How to deal with the large number of chronic long-term users who already exist. Conservative estimates suggest 1/4 million people in the UK.

The use of pills for personal problems raises fundamental questions about the type of society we live in, one which predisposes individuals to stress and conversely dodges the issue of personal responsibility for health and expecting medical solutions to problems. It requires us to examine why twice as many women as men take tranquillizers.[11] It is beyond the scope of this paper to examine the social and political issues underlying tran-

quillizer use but interested readers are referred to the publications listed in References 10, 11, 12, 13, 14.

The long-term answer must lie in prevention, to ensure that prescriptions for tranquillizers are carefully considered and monitored. The duration of a prescription should be set in advance and low doses used. It is also questionable whether they should be used in times of crisis such as bereavement or divorce. Undoubtedly they can minimize pain and help someone cope but they can also impede the natural grieving process and prolong it.

The issue of chronic tranquillizer users presents immediate problems for existing services. One and a quarter million people have already been taking tranquillizers for over one year, in excess of the recommended guidelines. The remainder of this paper will look at the type of help needed to withdraw from tranquillizers and what is currently available in the UK.

WITHDRAWAL FROM TRANQUILLIZERS
Primary care

People who wish to withdraw from tranquillizers need information and practical support. Tranquillizers should not be abruptly withdrawn as this can cause severe withdrawal problems if someone has been taking medication for a number of years. It can also create a vicious circle whereby someone is unprepared for the intensity of withdrawal effects, starts to panic and sees this as confirmation of their inability to cope without tranquillizers. A common response is to restart tranquillizers *and* increase the dose. 'I thought I was going mad', or 'I was so frightened I didn't know what was happening to me' are frequent comments.

Gradual withdrawal is generally recommended but there are differing viewpoints about the speed of cutting down and who makes this decision. General practitioners tend to recommend a structured withdrawal programme to their patients spread over several weeks. For an initial daily dose of 30 mg Valium, six weeks is often regarded as the minimum withdrawal period.

There are advantages to a structured withdrawal schedule. It can make the problem seem much more manageable as a clear end is in sight. On the negative side it can set up failure experiences if someone does not meet target reductions or the pace may be too fast or too slow for a particular individual. Most importantly, it takes control away from the patient. Tranquillizers provide an *external* means of coping, and people can quickly learn to rely on the tablet to get through a difficult situation, losing confidence in themselves. Coming off at their own pace helps people to regain control which is vital if they are to remain tranquillizer free in the future. Withdrawal is the first important step but the major issue is how to cope with future stress and stay off.

A recent study in general practice[18] indicated that tranquillizers can be withheld from patients who present with minor emotional problems of stress and anxiety without harmful effects. The non-drug group in the study who received brief counselling (on average 12 min) by the GPs and no medication seemed to recover as quickly as patients who received tranquillizers. Rapid recovery for most patients with or without tranquillizers is encouraging but one-third of the patients were no better at a seven-month follow-up. This group had more severe symptoms when they first saw their doctor, were more likely to smoke, drink and use non-prescribed cough and cold medicines. In order to prevent this group becoming long-term users additional help should be provided: This could include the following:

1. Leaflets on tranquillizers and withdrawal effects.[15] Reading lists or books on self-help.[16-17]
2. Videos of television programmes or specially made films on tranquillizers.
3. Reassurance and support from the doctor throughout the withdrawal period, offering weekly sessions of 10–15 minutes.
4. Referral to counsellor, therapist or psychologist attached to the practice.
5. Contacts for local self-help groups or agencies dealing with tranquillizers.

Good practice example[19]
Leyton Green Neighbourhood Health Service in London places a high priority on help for tranquillizer users. Careful consideration is given before any tranquillizers are used and repeat prescriptions are monitored. Medication is usually given in conjunction with counselling from one of the therapists attached to the practice. Books on tranquillizers and related issues such as postnatal depression are readily available for patients to borrow. They have good liaison with local resources such as mental health teams and self-help groups and weekly meetings are held which include the primary care team plus attached health professionals.

Self-help groups

It has been suggested that our traditional way of seeking help within a medical framework encourages dependence and helplessness.[20] Patients are not equal partners in their relationships with health personnel and attempts at self-reliance may not be sufficiently supported. Some general practitioners have been slow to recognize the problems caused by long-term use of tranquillizers and many people have complained about the lack of professional concern for their difficulties. Television programmes such as the BBC programme 'That's Life' gave a public airing to tranquillizer issues and highlighted the need for sympathetic services. Faced with limited help for tranquillizer withdrawal and a perceived uncaring attitude by doctors, self-help groups began to flourish in the 1980s. Tranquillizer users valued the chance to meet others who could share experiences and self-help groups provided the opportunity to break down feelings of isolation and gave reassurance that symptoms were not unique.

For self-help groups to survive and be effective they must successfully cope with some of the pitfalls inherent in this approach. When everyone has similar problems it is difficult to maintain emotional boundaries and achieve the necessary detachment from another's problems. It can end up with people feeling that they have to cope with all the group's problems as well as their own: too big a burden for anyone to carry. A delicate balance is needed between being sympathetic and caring yet not taking over the person's problems. Having a leader who is slightly removed from the feelings of the group can be a real asset. Many self-help groups do receive psychological support or have a leader with therapeutic experience.

It is also important to have a structure for the group so that it does not stop at simply sharing experiences without any direction to the talk, but moves on to hearing how people dealt with particular problems.

Good practice example[21]
TRANX (Tranquillizer Recovery and New Existence) was founded by Joan Jerome — an ex-tranquillizer user in 1982.

It has an advisory panel which consists of three consultant psychiatrists, four general practitioners and a psychologist. The aims of TRANX are to provide a national advice, information, support and referral service for tranquillizer users and their families. A 24-hour support network has been organized and the TRANX phonelines receive an average of 300 calls per week. Twice weekly evening meetings are held at the group's base in Harrow. These meetings are structured to allow general conversation and introduction of new members but it is followed by reports from each member on their tranquillizer use. Finally, the focus is on particular problems presented by group members. TRANX also produces a quarterly newsletter and advice and information leaflets. It has been instrumental in encouraging a national network of self-help groups. Groups can become affiliated to TRANX and receive advice and support. Joan Jerome recommends that people are tranquillizer free themselves for at least one year before setting up a group. Eighteen months after opening TRANX had received 1500 enquiries. In common with all self-help groups, funding is a perennial problem, the DHSS provided a grant of £53 000 for two years in 1983, but they had to be rescued from closure in 1986 with grants totalling £52 000 from a number of agencies.

In-patient treatment

Some circumstances warrant a hospital admission for withdrawal. If there is a long drug history or if a high dose is taken (e.g. over 100 mg Diazepam or 20 mg Lorazepam), it may be more beneficial to withdraw under medical supervision. Side-effects might cause ill-health or for some people home circumstances make withdrawal too difficult. The potential advantage of in-patient treatment is to speed up the withdrawal process in a supportive environment. While many people prefer to remain in control of gradual and slow withdrawal, there are others whose personalities are best suited to 'getting it all over quickly', even if it is initially harder. Ideally hospitalization should be short (4–6 weeks), provide a supportive and relaxing atmosphere and teach alternative coping skills to taking medication.

Good practice example[22]
Willow Ward, Springfields Hospital, Tooting Bec, London, offers a 4-week in-patient programme. It is an intensive experience with a full weekly timetable. The aims of the programme are three-fold:

(1) to systematically reduce tranquillizer medication to zero during the 4-week stay
(2) to develop alternative coping skills

(3) to achieve an awareness of the reasons for starting tranquillizers

All patients have their tranquillizers switched to an equivalent dose of Diazepam regardless of their original prescription. This is becoming increasingly common practice in view of reported difficulties with shorter-acting tranquillizers such as Lorazepam. During their stay patients can expect to participate in a variety of activities. There is an emphasis on group work and opportunities are provided for (a) educational groups to learn about the chemistry of tranquillizers (b) small groups for examining psychological problems (c) anxiety management groups for learning new methods of coping (d) relaxation training for control of physical tension (e) ward groups for staff and patients to share experiences about the ward (f) relatives group. Fitness training is also an integral part of the programme.

Community drug teams

Since 1983 the DHSS has periodically released funds through the 'Central Funding Initiative' for work with drugs. A large proportion of this money has been used to set up local initiatives for drug users, usually in the form of community drug teams. Often these are joint services run by Social Services and District Health Authorities. A national network of such teams is steadily growing although most are on short-term funding for a few years only. Continuation of these new developments in the future will probably depend on securing mainstream funding from Health or Social Services budgets. The teams tend to be small, with two to three workers operating from a base in the community. It may be a flat, health centre or shop which is accessible to the public. The team is likely to be multi-disciplinary and consist of several of the following: community psychiatric nurse, social worker, field worker with counselling experience, psychologist, health visitor, health education officer, voluntary agency drugs worker. Most teams offer 'drop-in' services for advice and counselling and on-going case work. They tend to have a non-medical orientation and concentrate on prevention and early treatment interventions. Close links for referral are maintained with Regional Drug Dependence Units and specialist rehabilitation services. Although the emphasis of the work is on opiates many drug teams also deal with tranquillizer users.

Good practice example[23]
Bolton Community Drug Team was established in 1985 and consists of a community psychiatric nurse, social worker,

health visitor, plus administrative support. A part-time GP is also attached to the team. Services are provided for three main groups: (1) drug users, (2) relatives and friends, (3) other agencies with drug using clients. Up to 50 per cent of people attending the service are tranquillizer users.

The emphasis of the work is problem-orientated and combines educational techniques and non-directive methods. Clients are encouraged to develop coping strategies and tactics for situations and emotions where they would normally use a drug. At the same time underlying problems connected with taking drugs are explored (e.g. problems of relationships, issues of self-esteem, etc.). Both individual and group sessions are offered within a structured framework which is also contract based. Topics covered include alternatives to drug taking, life planning skills, stress management course and problem solving. Up to 50 per cent of people attending the service are tranquillizer users. An on-going support group with two group leaders is provided for up to eight people. This is an open group which people join and leave when they are ready.

Integration of professional and self-help approaches

In working towards tranquillizer withdrawal it is easy to be sidetracked with the mechanics of withdrawal. Monitoring side-effects, reduction schedules, coping with withdrawal symptoms, etc. can be important but it is not an end in itself. Many people can become tranquillizer free relatively easily and remain so for months or even years. Faced with additional or new stress in their lives they may turn to tranquillizers again and restart a further period of dependency. The main issue which must be addressed is maintenance, 'staying off'. Clearly if someone is habitually anxious and tense or has relationship problems which remain unresolved there is a high probability of restarting tranquillizers. Withdrawal alone may not be sufficient to make a significant change in people's lives. Alternative ways of coping without medication are needed which help people reduce or avoid future stress. Methods can include a variety of psychological approaches: relaxation skills, stress management, assertiveness training, problem solving, social skills training. They offer someone the chance to gain control over their symptoms without using medication and perhaps examine some of the reasons why they started taking tranquillizers in the first place.

Individual therapy or group work led by a professional

therapist is likely to aim for attitude and behaviour change in a systematic and overt way. Professional input to tranquillizer users has several advantages. A group leader is able to remain objective and not be overwhelmed by the group's problems. S/he is trained to provide sympathetic support without undermining a group member's own efforts, or to avoid taking over and give well-meaning advice which does not teach someone how to solve their problems in the future. The disadvantages of professional input may be a lack of time for support. Someone withdrawing from tranquillizers may hit a bad patch and want to talk to someone immediately. Few professionals are willing to provide 24-hour assistance indefinitely. There may be wider issues involved. Many tranquillizer users feel let down by professionals and prefer to seek the help of other users and ex-users. Both professional approaches and self-help groups have valuable contributions to make, but both are limited in what they do. The professionals may not be able to offer the time and commitment for support, and self-help may not be able to give people the chance to learn new and alternative coping skills. An integration of the two, seeing them as complementary rather than separate alternatives, offers a valuable merger. The type of work can take many forms. For example self-help groups may approach professionals and ask for one or two talks, or on-going support for the group leader. Professional workers may initiate contact with tranquillizer users and offer to run groups which would then continue on a self-help basis. Many other combinations are possible. The practical difficulties should not be underestimated. There may be mistrust on both sides, different value systems which must be acknowledged, and lack of experience in working together. However, it does offer the most fruitful potential for work with tranquillizer users.

Good practice example[24]
The WITHDRAW PROJECT within North Birmingham Health Authority offers a clinical psychology service for tranquillizer users. A research study evaluating the effectiveness of the approach is run at the same time. It is staffed by a psychologist, two group workers, a research assistant, volunteers plus administrative support. The emphasis of the approach is on learning alternatives to medication which will enable people to stay off tranquillizers in the future. A variety of group work is offered and all groups are led by a psychologist or counsellor. Short-term groups over ten weeks cover a number of topics such as coping with negative thoughts, relaxation skills, personal development and plan-

ning leisure time. Information and advice is given on withdrawal methods but clients are encouraged to reduce at their own pace whenever possible. In some cases this might take longer as clients learn to make decisions and take responsibility for their reductions. Benefits are likely in the long term with greater future abstinence. Longer-term groups of six months give people with additional problems such as agoraphobia, relationship difficulties, or depression, a chance to resolve those problems as well as withdraw from tranquillizers. Monthly half-day workshops are held for people who have stopped their medication but need additional support. The WITHDRAW PROJECT are also involved in prevention and education. A teaching pack on how to run tranquillizer withdrawal groups has been produced. Regular exhibitions are held in libraries and health fairs for the general public. Lectures and workshops are offered to professional workers and the newsletter of the National Benzodiazepine Interest Group is produced by the team.

REFERENCES

1. Tyrer, P. (1980) Dependence on benzodiazepines. *British Journal of Psychiatry*, **137**, 576–7.
2. Balter, M.B., Levine, J. and Manheimer, D.I. (1974) Cross national study of the extent of anti-anxiety/sedative drug use. *New England Journal of Medicine*, **290**, 769–74.
3. Committee on the Review of Medicines. (1980). Systematic review of the benzodiazepines: Guidelines for data sheets on diazepam, chlordiazepoxide, medazepam, chlorazepate. *British Medical Journal*, March, 910–12.
4. Owen, R.T. and Tyrer, P. (1983) Benzodiazepine dependence: a review of the evidence. *Drugs*, **25**, 385–98.
5. Covi, L., Lipman, R.S., Parrison, J.H., Derogatis, L.R. and Uhlenhuth, E.H. Length of treatment with anxiolytic sedatives and response to their sudden withdrawal. *Acta Psychiatry Scand.*, **49**, 51–64.
6. Petursson, H. and Lader, M.H. (1984) *Dependence on tranquillizers* Institute of Psychiatry. Maudsley Monographs No. 28. Oxford University Press.
7. Murphy, S.M., Owen, R.T. and Tyrer, P.J. (1984) Withdrawal symptoms after 6 weeks treatment with diazepam. *Lancet*, **ii**, 1389.
8. Tyrer, P.J. and Seivewright, N. (1984) Identification and management of benzodiazepine dependence. *Postgraduate Medical Journal*, **60** (Suppl 2), 41–46.
9. Ashton, H. (1983) Drug Newsletter Suppl. *Apr*, 77–80. Newcastle upon Tyne. Wolfson Unit of Clinical Psychology.
10. Lader, M.H. and Higgitt, A.C. (1986) Management of benzodiazepine dependence. *British Journal of Addiction* **81**, 7–10.
11. Cooperstock, R. (1978) Sex differences in psychotropic drug use. *Social Science & Medicine*, **12B**, 179–86.
12. Gabe, J. and Lipshitz-Phillips, S. (1984) Tranquillizers as social control. *Social Review*, **32**(3), 524–46.
13. Melville, J. (1984) *The Tranquillizer Trap*. Glasgow: Fontana Paperbacks.
14. Haddon, C. (1984) *Women & Tranquillisers*. London: Sheldon Press.
15. *Trouble with Tranquillisers*. Release Publications, 1–4 Hatton Gardens, London.
16. Trickett, S. (1986) *Coming off Tranquillisers*. Thorsons Publishing Group.
17. Curran, V. and Golombock, S. (1984) *Bottling It Up*. London: Faber & Faber.
18. Catalan, J., Gath, D., Edmonds, D., Ennis, J., Bond, A. and Martin, P. (1984) The effects of non-prescribing on psychiatric and social outcome. *British Journal of Psychiatry*, **144**, 593–610.
19. Leyton Green Neighbourhood Health Service, 180 Essex Road, Leyton, London E10.
20. Mechanic, D. (1982) The epidemiology of illness behavior and its relationship to physical and psychological distress. In D. Mechanic (ed.) *Symptoms, Illness Behavior and Help-seeking*, pp. 1–24. New York: Prodist.
21. TRANX, 17 Peel Road, Wealdstone, Harrow, Middlesex.
22. Willow Ward, Springfields Hospital, Tooting Bec, London.
23. Bolton Community Drug Team, 27 Maudsley Street, Bolton, BL1 1LN.
24. WITHDRAW PROJECT, North Birmingham Health Authority, Slade Road Centre, Erdington, Birmingham.

Preventing drug problems

LES KAY

Co-ordinator, North West Regional Drug Training Unit, Prestwich Hospital, Manchester

This paper discusses ways in which attempts can be made to prevent drug problems. It discusses education campaigns in schools and more general public education, and goes on to outline some of the more recently debated 'new prevention options'. The paper advocates that greater resources should be devoted to these alternative options.

PROBLEM DRUG TAKING

In recent years there have been major shifts in the basic concepts through which we understand drug use. These conceptual shifts have a particular importance in the consideration of the prevention of drug problems.

A concept of 'problem drug taker' has supplanted an earlier 'disease' concept of drug addiction.

The earlier disease concept assumed a linear set of relationships between the drug, the person and subsequent problems. It therefore produced a linear structure (figure 1) in service responses.

Within this model the presence of the drug available within society will inevitably 'hook' or infect anyone not properly 'innoculated' intellectually against the drug by anti-drug messages. Those who slip through the control and primary prevention nets will inevitably become addicted and clinical treatment of the addiction as disease is appropriate. It was generally understood that like other diseases it could lead to secondary complications if left unchecked. These included consequences such as unemployment, homelessness, poverty, prostitution, etc. Whilst the clinicians went to work on the disease, social workers were deployed to deal with such 'secondary complications'.

The linearization of services naturally flowed in reverse direction to that of the disease process they were designed to combat. The lion's share of resources was diverted to control options designed to remove drugs from the street. The second largest share would go into primary prevention, a slightly lower amount to clinical treatment services and a few bob on the odd social worker.

The experience of a wide range of treatment agencies revealed that the focus on the disease of addiction was too narrow and subordinated many of the important issues to the disease process.

The 'problem drug taker' model takes a much broader view. It was defined as:

any person who experiences social, psychological, physical or legal problems related to intoxication and/or regular excessive consumption and/or dependence, as a consequence of his own use of drugs or other chemical substances (excluding alcohol and tobacco).[1]

It can be seen as an 'interactive' (figure 2) as opposed to 'linear' model of drug use and its problems.

Within this model it is the interactions between

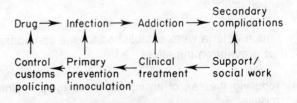

Figure 1   Disease process — a linear model.

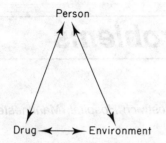

Figure 2   Problem drug taker — an interactive model.

elements that are seen as of greatest importance. These interactions have most lyrically been described by Spencer Madden[2] who explores drug problems using an analogy of the seed, the soil and the environment. This essentially ecological concept is most concerned with achieving the right balance of understanding when weighing the relative importance of each element.

It follows from this new model that there ought to be a new range of services based on the needs of the problem drug taker as opposed to the narrowly conceived needs of the 'addict'. To some extent these new services have already begun to develop and were argued for most cogently in the 'Treatment' report of the Government's Advisory Council on the Misuse of Drugs[1] which coined the 'problem drug taker' concept.

In a later report from the same Advisory Council the subject of prevention was given separate consideration. This report concluded that:

drug misuse is a complex social problem for which no single cause or consistent pattern of multiple causes has been identified; the individual, social groups, economic status and other environmental factors, and the availability of drugs must all be taken into account when developing a comprehensive prevention policy.[3]

Two main criteria were established for the consideration of prevention initiatives.

a)   reducing the risk of an individual engaging in drug misuse
b)   reducing the harm associated with drug misuse[4]

Most attempts at prevention have so far been targeted towards the first of these two criteria. Overwhelmingly, prevention has consisted of school-based education aimed at the secondary school sector. A less important but recent development has been a public advertising campaign through newspaper, television and poster advertisements.

SCHOOL-BASED EDUCATIONAL ACTIVITIES

There have been a series of traditions in school-based education about drugs. The earliest traditions consisted of a didactic method with a major focus on the substances themselves.

Later developments explored experimental methods with a shift in focus away from the substance and onto the person and the ways in which important health decisions are taken.

Materials from agencies concerned with drug education such as TACADE and ISDD[5] explore the minutiae and the techniques of decision making. An example of this would be role-playing the cost/benefit analysis of a particular potential decision to use drugs.

A radical alternative to these foci on the minutiae of decision making was an attempt by ISDD to introduce a more overtly political element into the discussion. This came through exploration of cultural factors which give shape to individual experiences of drug use. Typified in the training pack, 'Health Careers',[6] this 'cultural education' approach encourages young people to explore their collective rather than individual identity. An underlying assumption is that membership of various collectivities will so powerfully influence the range of options within a projected health career that any attempt at skill development will founder if it fails to take account of their impact. Thus at its most extreme the likely health career of a male, black, urban, working-class youngster would be radically different from that of a female, white, suburban, middle-class youngster.

There has been a great deal of discussion about the relative values of each of the above or indeed any combinations of them. It should however be stated clearly at this stage that there is no evidence which can demonstrate *any* behavioural change as a consequence of pursuing *any* educational strategy.

After describing the range of educational approaches ISDD concluded that,

none of these approaches have been shown to reduce either: 1) drug/alcohol experimentation, or 2) any type of harm that may be associated with experimentation, or 3) the chances of experimentation developing into heavy use, in the British situation.[7]

Many of the approaches have stumbled on a very basic and overly simplistic assumption. This is the idea that there is some linear, simple relationship between knowledge, attitudes and behaviour. It has been assumed that if we can provide the right sort of knowledge that this will help restructure attitude which in itself determines behaviour. What we now realize is that behaviour is a much more complicated product of a range of interacting factors than this model would assume.

PUBLIC EDUCATION

What is true for education in schools is also evident in attempts at public education. There have been a variety of strategies used, ranging from the most overt shock/horror presentations through to the more sophisticated current advertising campaign.

Once more the research evidence clearly demonstrates the pointlessness of these approaches based on manipulation of fear. A major problem with this focus on horrific drugs and in particular on the so-called 'killer heroin', is that it serves to manipulate public *mis*understanding. For most people heroin has assumed a demonic status. It is the classic folk-devil and currently the subject of the most enormous moral panic. When we actually look at the harm resulting from heroin use the reality is minuscule compared with 'killer alcohol' and 'killer tobacco'. The mystification of heroin, which is associated with its demonic status is one of the biggest prevention problems we have to confront. We therefore have to take considerable care that we do not ourselves become part of the mystification process.

It is also the case that prevention as a notion, has itself been mystified. We assume, for example, that prevention and education are allied and supporting concepts. This may be completely misconceived. Some forms of prevention and education may indeed be mutually exclusive, antagonistic concepts.

Current approaches to personal and social education (PSE) aim to enhance the power of young people to make free decisions about important life events. The language of PSE is full of phrases like 'autonomy', 'empowerment' and so on. This form of education clearly sees itself having a role to assist young people to make their *own* decisions in the most powerful and autonomous way possible. The notion of *primary* prevention is clearly antagonistic to this powerful decision making.

Primary prevention or prevention of the *incidence* of drug use assumes that we can start with a set of objectives which we can give to young people who will then adopt them as their own. Powerful, autonomous decision making implies they will be able to resist not just peer group pressure, but also our influences, over their decision-making processes. We cannot logically demand of young people that they become more autonomous, and at the same time do what we want them to do! This is a particular problem given our society's hypocrisy about different forms of drug use.

In the light of these insights there is a need for us to establish clear principles to guide the future development of our prevention work.

Firstly we should admit that we do not know how to prevent the use of drugs.

Secondly there is therefore no justification for repeating past mistakes. Future primary prevention attempts should be innovative controlled experiments only.

Thirdly we should unshackle personal and social education from unrealistic primary prevention objectives.

These measures will allow us to develop new approaches to secondary prevention. They should be based on an energetic attempt to demystify drug use. Our orientation should be on the community and our first task is to understand what needs actually exist.

NEW PREVENTION OPTIONS

As we shift emphasis from drugs to problems and from individuals to communities we need to return to basics in our information gathering. We know a little about those problem drug-takers who present to specialist treatment agencies. We know almost nothing about those who do not.

We need to break out of the arrogant belief that we know what education the community needs. In truth we have not much idea what drug problems are being faced within the community.

This is clearly an important area for us to resolve if we are to work out what we should be saying to whom about drug problems. We have a great deal to learn from our colleagues in youth and community work about the issues and methods of community consultation.

We also need to identify and key into local information systems. This will entail a much more systematic approach to work with organizations as diverse as community pharmacists, local libraries, tenants groups, advice centres, trade unions and service organizations such as the Rotary Clubs, Lions, etc.

Working through these mechanisms we can build up a broader picture of the needs of the community for information, assistance, services, reassurance and where appropriate, education.

We should also think about ways to allow the community to become more involved in decisions about services. There is a useful body of experience of neighbourhood consultations in programmes of local crime prevention conducted by NACRO.[8] We should make use of this and look around for other sources of expertise in community work. It is also the case that our interests in local prevention activities dovetail with those of local authorities currently shifting the emphasis towards neighbourhood services.

Social action

The Government's Advisory Council noted that,

although the precise mechanisms are not properly understood, there is a relationship between the prevention of drug misuse and the effects of broad social and economic policies.[9]

This relationship is clearly in evidence in the North West where a survey of new clients seen by doctors and drug agencies showed that some 80.7 per cent were unemployed.[10] Other studies[11] support this finding. Anecdotal evidence from specialist agencies also supports these findings and indicates that their clients can also have housing problems and are often virtually permanently in debt.

Given this picture it is clear that housing, employment creation, welfare rights and a number of other 'social action' options could have a great deal to contribute. Within Rochdale an employment scheme has been created to specifically cater for unemployed drug users. There are also plans to develop much closer links between Community Drug Teams and the Manpower Services Commission.

One of the questions raised by these developments is the advisability of offering these sorts of services exclusively to drug users. By creating specialist employment, housing and similar services do we not run the risk both of further increasing the isolation of drug users from generic services and also perhaps of pathologizing unemployment, housing and similar problems as 'treatable' conditions? The Rochdale scheme (above) was promoted as a pilot with a view to testing out these and other similar questions.

Casualty reduction

The clearest example of this approach was a pamphlet produced by ISDD.[12] This offered advice which would aim to reduce the harm from solvent sniffing. Because it suggested harm reduction strategies it was attacked by some as tantamount to encouraging 'safe sniffing'.

It is also argued by some workers in the drug field that maintenance prescription is the single most important contribution to casualty reduction and should be seen as a valid prevention tool. The debates on maintenance are covered elsewhere in this Reader.

Whilst there is as yet no consensus on these debates it is clear that these are crucial areas in the consideration of future prevention developments.

Campaigning

So far the only drug campaigns have been anti illicit drugs. Given the carnage from licit drugs it might well be appropriate to launch district-based campaigns on, e.g. prescribing patterns of minor tranquillizers.

Drug advertising is another controversial area. There seems little point in putting anti-heroin posters alongside pro-alcohol or pro-tobacco adverts. In one location the 'Heroin Screws You Up' poster was plastered on the gable end of a 'fun pub'.

Local authorities could be encouraged to explore their powers under planning permission to control poster sites.

Another under-explored area is that of first aid for drug users.

There are still many user myths surrounding overdose, how to treat a coma, AIDS and other infectious diseases, etc. A package of first-aid advice could be given to every drug user.

Early intervention in problem drug taking

In order to facilitate early intervention at a point before serious problems develop there is a need for increased awareness and improved deployment of skills, both by professionals and the community itself.

The major obstacle for greater community involvement in self-help services is the mystification of certain forms of drug use.

Most people have been led to switch off their common sense and understanding of life and its difficulties when confronted by drug problems. Parents who would take in their stride a teenager coming home drunk on cider, recoil in horror when the same teenager comes home intoxicated on glue or heroin. A major objective of our community education/awareness activities around drugs should be dispelling some of this mystique. We should help people to recognize and value the key understandings and skills they have from their own use of licit drugs.

Changing the climate

If we are going to turn round the debate from hysteria to rational discussion we will need to address the workings of the media and also those key local opinion leaders who tend to give some shape to the content of local media coverage. If we want to change the climate we are going to have to take a more pro-active approach towards the media within every area of our influence. We should identify and cultivate key journalists to whom we can feed a series of positive messages about drug use. A series of stories about successes and progress made both by people and organizations is the best antidote to the negativism that currently permeates media coverage.

Drugs in the workplace

Alcohol and drug problems are both very costly to employers. There are a range of factors which may cause problem drinking/drug taking. They include long hours, lack of job security, increasing workloads, frustrated ambitions, boredom, routine nature of work, access to alcohol/drugs at work, the culture of the job, etc.

These are all bread and butter industrial relations issues. They ought to lead to a consideration of prevention strategies designed to alleviate boredom, anxiety, stress, etc. in the workplace. Unfortunately once again the mystification of drugs has clouded the matter.

Trade unionists and managers have been led into the blind alley of blaming the drugs themselves. This excessive focus on substances is directly associated with the disease concepts of alcoholism and addiction. Once more acceptance of the problem drinker, drug taker concept is the key to embracing the wide range of issues which should be tackled in a comprehensive workplace policy.

CONCLUSION

These ideas on community access to information, advertising, casualty reduction, workplace policies, and so on are very tentative. None of them are very original, having been employed for some time in the alcohol field.[13] They do, however, represent a series of pathways out of the cul-de-sac within which prevention of drug problems has been locked. It remains to be seen whether policy makers and would be preventers of drug problems are prepared to risk leaving the safe but ineffectual classrooms of primary prevention and open up these new and important areas of work.

REFERENCES

1. Advisory Council on the Misuse of Drugs 'Treatment and Rehabilitation'. Home Office, 1982.
2. Spencer Madden, *A Guide to Alcohol and Drug Dependence*, 2nd edition. John Wright, Bristol, 1984, p. 11.
3. Advisory Council on the Misuse of Drugs 'Prevention'. Home Office, 1983, page 61, para. 7.2.
4. Ibid. p. 4.
5. TACADE is The Teachers Advisory Council on Alcohol and Drugs Education. ISDD is the Institute for the Study of Drug Dependence.
6. Nick Dorn and Bente Nortoft, *Health Careers — Teachers Manual* ISDD, 1982.
7. ISDD, *Drugs in Health Education — Trends and Issues*. Research and Development Unit, June 1982, p. 2.
8. *Neighbourhood Consultations — A Practical Guide* by NACRO Crime Prevention Unit. Available from Nacro, 169 Clapham Road, London SW9 0PU.
9. Advisory Council on the Misuse of Drugs 'Prevention'. Home Office, 1983, page 30, para 4.7.
10. Figures from the NW Regional Database as at 13 July 1986.
11. See for example Paper 11 in this Reader.
12. *Teaching About a Volatile Situation*, ISDD 1981.
13. Philip Tether and David Robinson, *Preventing Alcohol Problems. A Guide to Local Action*. Tavistock, 1986.

Approaches to prevention from grass-roots to campaigns

BARBARA HOWE

Research Fellow, HEC Addictions Project, Durham

In this paper a variety of possible approaches to prevention are described and the implications for all those involved in health education work are discussed. The recent Tyne Tees Alcohol Education Campaign is described, and the possible lessons that can be learnt from this are detailed.

If society's response to problem drug use is seen as a continuum (see Figure 1), prohibition and punishment would lie at one end with education and prevention, often seen as a soft option, at the other. In the storm of media manipulated panic and moral outrage it is often forgotten that, just as drug misuse throws up a wide range of problems in society, it also necessitates a wide range of responses. No single response will be equally effective at all levels and even a selection of responses operating at community, environmental and political levels may do little more than contain the problem without ever tackling the issue of prevention. Before adopting the preventive response, we must be clear about what we are trying to prevent and whether the strategies we have chosen are appropriate in view of our stated aims.

The term prevention means different things to different people. For some it may mean:

- preventing people using illegal drugs.

Alternatively, a broader view might encompass the following:

- stopping the rising incidence of people (especially young people) experimenting with illegal drugs (risk reduction)

Or again:

- minimizing the potential harm individuals may experience in using both legal and illegal drugs (casualty reduction)

Health educators must decide from the outset what they are trying to achieve and why. Continued use of prevention as an umbrella term to embrace all educational initiatives could lead to many being criticized for failing. Prevention with regard to drug use would, in its purest sense, mean stopping people ever using drugs. To work only toward this end, however, would mean attempting to achieve an ideal which cannot hope to exist in reality. Educating about drugs is a broader concept altogether which accepts that:

- drug use is part of an overall continuum of human behaviour (whether legal or not).
- education can help to promote responsibility in drug use.
- education can help to minimize harm arising from drug use.
- many people can and should be involved in drug education.

Whichever viewpoint you accept, both prevention and

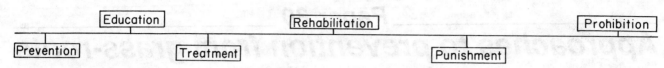

Figure 1   Continuum of possible responses to drug use.

education hold a series of implications for health educators. The successful outcome, however defined, of any educational initiative rests in part on the calibre and skills of the people carrying out the work whether on a one to one basis, in groups, in the community or even as part of a regional or national campaign.

Les Kay, in the previous paper in this Reader, points out that there is no evidence to prove that any known educational approach is capable of changing behaviour and others have noted that education does not reduce experimentation with drugs, harm associated with experimentation, or experimentation developing into heavier use.[1] In view of this, some might argue that there is little point in continuing to fund educational initiatives and to train professionals to carry out preventive work. Following a ten-year Health Education Council campaign on alcohol education in the north-east of England, one HEC member commented:

'the North East (Council on Alcoholism) spent our money — we could have directed it elsewhere'[2]

The campaign was criticized for failing to change drinking behaviour and the comment sums up the attitudes prevailing in some quarters (often those which provide financial backing) that:

- there is a direct correlation between education and behaviour change.
- there is a finite timescale during which these changes can be expected to occur.
- there is a direct correlation between the amount of money spent on education and the degree of behaviour change expected as a result.

If we adopt the Prevention Charter highlighted in Kay's paper and admit that we do not know how to prevent the use of certain substances, should we forget about preventive education altogether as none of it appears to work according to the (narrow) criteria for success often laid down by funding bodies? Alternatively, does drug education have a significant part to play when considering the broader spectrum of drug use including both legal and illegal substances? The Report from the Advisory Council on the Misuse of Drugs clearly supports the latter statement in announcing its decision to concentrate on preventive measures which satisfy the following criteria:

- reducing the risk of an individual engaging in drug misuse.
- reducing the harm associated with drug misuse.[3]

EDUCATIONAL APPROACHES TO PREVENTION: IMPLICATIONS FOR HEALTH EDUCATORS

In view of previous comments about the successes or failures of any educational approach, health educators should be aware of the range of possible approaches and should develop an appreciation of their individual strengths and weaknesses. The following summary of approaches, their content and effectiveness may be helpful.

SUMMARY OF APPROACHES TO DRUG EDUCATION[4]

1. Didactic approach

This can be subdivided into:

(i) *Shock/horror*
Content
- uses fear tactics.
- based on deterrence by horrible example.
Effectiveness
- not effective, may have reverse effect.
- rejection likely if 'fear' message contradicts reality.

(ii) *Scientific information*
Content
- gives factual information.

- assumes that increased knowledge will lead to attitude change which will lead to behaviour change.

Effectiveness
- increases knowledge base.
- does not necessarily lead to behaviour change.

2. Affective approach

Content
- person centred
- examines feelings, attitudes and values.

Effectiveness
- clarifies, modifies attitudes and values.
- marginal effect on behaviour and knowledge.

3. Behavioural approach

Content
- looks at life skills and social competence.
- increases self-esteem and ability to cope with social pressure.

Effectiveness
- seen some limited success with smoking education.
- can be seen as manipulative.

4. Situational approach

Content
- decision-making skills in 'choice' or 'offer' situations.
- facts and feelings become relevant to social situations.

Effectiveness
- knowledge and decision-making skills are improved.
- students may use skills to decide to *use* substances rather than *not use* them.
- slight shift towards less harmful use.

5. Cultural approach

Content
- looks at an individual's position in society.
- considers culture, class, personal income and economic power.

Effectiveness
- no evaluation available.

GOALS FOR DRUG EDUCATION

Once familiar with the range of approaches, health educators should appreciate that, as few of them have any direct effect on behaviour, drug education runs the risk of being condemned as ineffective. At this point, it would be worthwhile considering what outcomes drug education has other than changing behaviour and assessing whether these are helpful and valid in tackling drug problems in society from the educational standpoint.

Some valid goals for drug education might include:

- increasing knowledge about legal/illegal drugs, their effects and potential for causing problems to the individual, the family, the community and society.
- improving self-awareness and clarifying personal attitudes.
- examining society's prejudices and stereotyping.
- enabling attitude change.
- improving decision-making abilities by increasing knowledge and practising decision-making skills.
- promoting social change through the above.

Although none of these will be accompanied necessarily by sustained behaviour change, health educators should decide for themselves whether some or all of these goals are appropriate for those whom they intend to educate.

RESOURCES

Those involved in educating about drugs will need resources and should be able to recognize resources within individuals, organizations and the community. Somehow the term resources always seems to conjure up material things such as films, videos and leaflets and yet it can encompass a much wider range of considerations. These might include:

- Time — a precious resource for everyone but adequate time should be given to planning education, implementation, evaluation and follow-up events (See below Planning and Evaluation.)
- Co-operation — between individuals, organizations and agencies, management and workers. It does not

always occur naturally but can be worked at and used as a powerful resource.

- Skills — an educator's greatest resource lies within himself and the skills he has developed. Skills vary from one person to another and health educators should recognize this and be prepared to use what is available.
- Money — not always needed in vast quantities but a little helps!

For health educators working on a one to one basis or in group situations, the following recommendations should prove helpful.

PUBLIC EDUCATION: SUMMARY OF RECOMMENDATIONS FOR HEALTH EDUCATORS

1. Prevention or education?
   — be clear about the terms you use and what you want to achieve.

2. Approaches to drug education
   — appreciate the range of approaches available.
   — recognize their individual strengths and weaknesses.
   — select an approach which will help you meet your specified goals.

3. Planning and evaluation
   — specify your goals for drug education.
   — build in evaluation.
   — assess what resources are available and know how to activate them.

4. Experimentation
   — be innovative.
   — try things on a small scale or in a pilot before attempting major initiatives.

5. Professionalism
   — investigate information and support networks to increase professionalism and share examples of good practice.

6. Limitations
   — recognize that education can only be seen as part of the total response to drug problems.

— recognize that education alone will not necessarily prevent individuals using drugs or lead to significant, long-term behaviour changes.

The implications listed above relate particularly to work carried out on a one to one basis or in a group situation. It is possible, however, that some health educators will be expected to become part of a local, regional or national campaign and work at this level requires a further set of considerations to be taken into account.

EDUCATION CAMPAIGNS: IMPLICATIONS FOR FUTURE WORK

As with any educational programme, whether on a large or small scale, the effectiveness of drug education will be increased if its limitations are properly appreciated at the outset and if they are taken into consideration during subsequent planning and evaluation.

Three major limitations of education campaigns are coverage, cost effectiveness and co-operation. Health educators must decide in advance whether their campaign will aim for blanket coverage of a target population or whether messages will be directed towards specific groups within that population. In terms of cost, media campaigns are highly visible, extremely expensive and able to reach a wide range of individuals with various messages. Media campaigns can not truly be called educational, as they merely present a message which recipients can (and do) interpret and accept in hundreds of different ways. At the other end of the scale, grass-roots work in the community, although more effective in stimulating awareness, increasing knowledge and raising confidence is, of necessity, low key and labour intensive.

CAMPAIGN SPIN-OFFS

Education campaigns tend to raise community awareness of problems which, although existing previously, went largely unacknowledged. Campaigns to raise awareness of drug problems can lead to victim-blaming and stigmatizing if individuals are not shown a way in which to channel their understandable concerns and anxieties. If the emphasis is on illegal drugs only, there is a risk of putting drug use into a poor perspective and glossing over the harm caused by legal drugs such as nicotine and alcohol.

Increased awareness of possible drug problems in a community will lead to increased demands on services. This can range from demands for clearer information through to demands for treatment services. As demand increases, professional workers themselves may need further information and training and, if local services aro not prepared and are unable to meet increased demands, campaigns may be judged as ineffective or even damaging.[5]

THE MEDIA

Co-operation from local, regional or national media can be immensely beneficial to the perceived public profile of a drug education campaign but such benefits are often accompanied by problems and pitfalls.

Generally, the media can not be relied on for any degree of consistency in its approach to or coverage of aspects of alcohol/drug misuse in society. For every instance of responsible reporting, there is another of sensationalism leading to facts being misunderstood and myths perpetuated. Used positively, the media can inform, heighten awareness and increase concern and commitment. Inversely, the media can spread information which was not previously common knowledge, e.g. how to inhale solvents, resulting in panic and moral outrage. This type of publicity causes concern and leads to action based on emotional, subjective responses rather than a rational plan.[6]

TYNE TEES ALCOHOL EDUCATION CAMPAIGN: STRENGTHS AND WEAKNESSES

Begun as a pilot study in 1974, the alcohol education campaign sponsored by the Health Education Council in the north-east of England comprised both mass media inputs and local initiatives. The media work, designed by a national agency, took the form of a five-week advertising spread and stressed the health damage related to heavy drinking. Viewers were encouraged to seek help with their alcohol problems

and, within three months, the local Council on Alcoholism had received over 900 requests for help. The services had not been adequately prepared for such a response and found it a struggle to cope. Following the pilot campaign, two major problems emerged. Firstly, people began to expect that there was a simple, direct link between media advertising and sustained attitude and behaviour change. Secondly, as the damage message about heavy drinking had been highlighted, people not wishing to identify themselves as alcoholics, were missing the wider implications and risks involved in their long-term heavy drinking.

During 1977—9, the whole approach to the campaign was reconsidered. Media advertising was modified and the new phase attempted to define primary prevention more clearly. The concept of 'sensible drinking' was promoted and target groups included women and young people, as well as men over 25. Media work was supported by a comprehensive programme of conferences and seminars aimed at adult professionals who were likely to encounter people with alcohol problems in the course of their day to day work. Industry also became a target group for alcohol education due to the increasing concern both locally and nationally, over alcohol-related accidents, absenteeism and reduced productivity in the workplace.

The conferences and seminars stimulated professional interest and led to further demands for information and in-service training. In response to this demand *Drinking Choices: A Training Manual for Alcohol Educators* was written in 1980—81 and disseminated throughout England and Wales by the HEC Addictions Project. The campaign also had implications for treatment services as more people requested advice, information and counselling in relation to their alcohol problems. A two-year Voluntary Alcohol Counsellor Training Scheme was established to augment the developing network of treatment services. Excellent relationships were also established with local media, as campaign workers became involved in a series of local radio and television programmes on alcohol. One programme with Tyne Tees Television gave rise to the alcohol information booklet *That's the Limit!* which was later expanded and published for use at national level.

During 1979—80, media advertising was temporarily suspended, while local alcohol educators intensified

WEAKNESSES

- Media advertising was expected to affect behaviour change in the short term.

- Poor communication between national and local workers.

- Media work designed at national level (Saatchi and Saatchi,1974 and 1977)

- Lack of baseline data before Campaign launch. Insufficient evaluation points during/after Campaign.

- The Campaign seen as media work only.

- Pilot media campaign→pressure on services→people asking for but not receiving help.

STRENGTHS

- Media advertising raised the public profile of the Campaign and achieved high penetration with specific messages. (David Bellamy advertising 1981.'2 or 3 pints, 2 or 3 times a week."Why spoil a good thing?')

- High degree of co-ordination and co-operation among local workers.

- Media work designed at local level (Redheads Advertising 1981 and 1982)

- New regional campaigns to have evaluation points before, during and after.

- The Campaign seen as activities and initiatives at grass-roots level including the media work, education, counselling and other treatment responses.

- New services set up at local level.

Figure 2 Tyne Tees Alcohol Education Campaign 1974–86.

campaign activities. Exhibition and display work was developed to provide information on alcohol and health, drinking and driving and alcohol and pregnancy. The education work with both the public and professional workers continued and a local advertising agency was appointed to handle the media component of the campaign. The appointment was beneficial in that the agency was well acquainted with the area, its people and their drinking culture and it also provided campaign workers with direct access and input to media initiatives. After consultation with local expertise, the agency commissioned Dr David Bellamy to front a media campaign which moved away from proscription towards hedonism. The new media work had limited objectives and attempted to put across specific pieces of information related to alcohol. It also gave general guidelines on what constituted safe, harm-free drinking. The positive, beneficial aspects of alcohol were emphasized and 'Why spoil a good thing?' became the media slogan.

A retrospective evaluation of all campaign work to date was commissioned and carried out by the Centre for Mass Communications Research, University of

Leicester. It found that the campaign was increasingly meeting its objectives, particularly as regards the promotion and development of a unique local network of treatment and education services, co-ordinated between a large number of health districts. The evaluation report states:

In a sense, the north east alcohol education campaign is an example of a developing realism of what might legitimately be expected from health education projects. Few people involved in this project would now claim that the campaign is likely to change the pattern of drinking in the north east overnight, or even in the foreseeable future. What it has done is to provide a context in which people now seem to be willing to talk and think about alcohol use in new and constructive ways. This is surely not an inconsiderable achievement.

A summary of the perceived weaknesses and strengths of the campaign may prove useful to those intending to set off along similar roads.

Finally, a list of recommendations is offered to help health educators who may be, or may wish to be involved in public campaign work at this level.

PUBLIC CAMPAIGNS: RECOMMENDATIONS FOR HEALTH EDUCATORS

1. Planning
   — clearly define achievable aims and objectives.
   — decide on blanket coverage or specific target groups.
   — choose appropriate content and method.
   — build in evaluation at various points.
   — check resources (including time).
   — check finances.

2. Management structure
   — clarify areas of responsibility.
   — clarify levels of accountability.
   — set up agreed channels of communication.
   — work towards agreed networks of support.

3. Monitoring, evaluation and research
   — carry out research before, during and after programme implementation.

4. Services
   — consider the possible effect on all local services.
   — prepare services in advance to deal with increased demands.

5. Experimental approach
   — use it on a small scale, in pilot situations to test out new approaches.

6. Professionalism
   — use in planning, implementation and evaluation.
   — develop information and support networks to increase professionalism and share examples of good practice.

7. Limitations
   — appreciate the limitations of education campaigns and do not expect to change the world (or an individual) overnight.

REFERENCES

1. *Drugs in Health Education — Trends and Issues*, ISDD Research and Development Unit, June 1982, p. 2.
2. Budd, Gray and McCron, *The Tyne Tees Alcohol Education Campaign. An Evaluation*, Centre for Mass Communication Research, 1982.
3. *Prevention*, Advisory Council on the Misuse of Drugs. Home Office, 1983.
4. Howe and Wright, *Dealing with Drugs*, Health Education Council Addictions Project, 1987.
5. Budd, Gray and McCron, *The Tyne Tees Alcohol Education Campaign. An Evaluation*, Chapter 3, p. 27, Chapter 8, pp. 80—88.
6. Howe, *Alcohol Services Information Pack, Good Practices in Mental Health and Alcohol Concern*, Chapter 3.

Index

Terms in inverted commas indicate 'street' terms in drug abuse.